Order My Steps

The Life of
Missionary
Paul A. Dennis

As Told to
Barbara Westberg

Order My Steps

The Life of Missionary Paul A. Dennis

Order My Steps
The Life of Missionary Paul A. Dennis

As Told to Barbara Westberg

Cover design by Laura Jurek
All photos used by permission

Copyright © 2011 Paul A. Dennis

All rights reserved. No portion of this publication may be reproduced, stored in an electronic system, or transmitted in any form or by any means, electronic, mechanical, photocopy, recording, or otherwise, without the prior permission of Word Aflame Press. Brief quotations may be used in literary reviews.

Printed in United States of America

WORD AFLAME PRESS
8855 Dunn Road, Hazelwood, MO 63042
www.pentecostalpublishing.com

Library of Congress Cataloging-in-Publication Data

Dennis, Paul A., 1935-
  Order my steps: the life of missionary Paul A. Dennis as told to Barbara Westberg.
    p. cm.
  Includes bibliographical references and index.
  ISBN 978-1-56722-746-8 (alk. paper)
  1. Dennis, Paul A., 1935- 2. Missionaries--Biography. 3. Missionaries--United States--Biography. I. Westberg, Barbara. II. Title.
  BV3705.D45A3 2011
  266.0092--dc22
  [B]
                           2011001505

DEDICATION

To my wife and best friend, Shirley Ann "Charlie Brown,"
my faithful supporter in good and bitter times.

To my daughter, Paula Ann, and her husband, Keith,
my children, co-laborers, and best friends.

To my grandson, Barak,
in whose hands I place the family birthright and blessing.

ACKNOWLEDGEMENTS

To Keith and Paula Ann: Thank you for working hand-in-hand with us in Okinawa and allowing us to work hand-in-hand with you in Tulsa. We are so glad you are ours.

To the Foreign Missions Division of the United Pentecostal Church International: Thank you for believing in Shirley and me and supporting us for thirty-one years. We appreciate the executives, the foreign missions board members, and the staff for your dedication to detail. Many times your efforts smoothed the way for us so we could fulfill God's will in our lives.

To my friends who wrote letters: I apologize because space would not allow us to print your letters, word for word. In seven decades of living we have compiled a multitude of friends, and we value each one. Your names may not be in the book, but they are written in our memory albums with permanent markers.

To a host of colleagues and friends: You have helped me build the heritage I will leave behind. I couldn't have done it without you.

To the Lord: Thanks for giving my mother an unending prayer for me; her prayers were the anchor that held me to You.

To my family: You knew the "old Paul" and you know the "new Paul." Thank you for loving both.

To my author/editor: Thanks for doing a splendid job.

From the author Barbara Westberg:

To the subjects of this book, Paul and Shirley Dennis: Thank you for being so gracious as I pried into your lives, asked hundreds of questions, stirred up emotions that invoked laughter and tears, and uncovered memories long buried under the busyness of everyday life. Thanks for trusting me with your life's story and your reputation. Working with you has been a pleasure.

To everyone who wrote a letter: Your memories filled in gaps and gave me a picture of Paul and Shirley that their modesty prevented them from revealing. Although your letters are not in this book, and your name may not be mentioned, you will find your memories, words, and thoughts woven into the fabric of Paul's story. Thank you for sharing.

To my husband, Francis: Thank you for listening, encouraging, and instructing.

TABLE OF CONTENTS

FOREWORD..13
PREFACE 15

Section I—The Old Paul **18**

    Run, Paul, Run 20
    Deprogrammed..26
    The Flying Thirty 31
    Basic Training..34
    Under Arrest 39
    Crash Landing 41
    The End of the World...48
    Another Crash 55
    Running from Guilt 59
    Back to #8 Hollow 62

Section II—The New Paul **66**

    A New Road 68
    Romance..75
    Honeymoon 82
    Homes Sweet Homes (Mostly) 86
    Sorrow Strikes 92
    Home Missions...97
    Insurance Claims 102
    A Visit with Rub 108
    The Announcement 114
    The Vision 120
    From Tragedy to Triumph..125

Order My Steps

Section III—Missionary Paul 131

A Conference Call...134
A New Home for Cricket 139
Roads, Rubber, and Rewards 143
The Land of the Rising Sun 149
Laugh and Learn 154
Fitting In 164
Back to the Future 170
The Family Grows 174
Reaching Out 179
A Giant Step...186
A Bottle of Oil and a Hammer 193
Adding to the Church 197
Saying Goodbye 201
Open Windows 204
Coming and Going 209
Family Matters 215
From Missions to Missions with Love 220
Here Comes the Bride (and Groom) 224
From Hot to Cold...231
Cockroaches and Customs 235
Homeless 239
Needed TLC 244
Preachers' Wives 248
Peace! Be Still!..253
ASAP 256
Ditched! 259

Paul A. Dennis

Section IV—Regional Field Supervisor Paul A. Dennis 263

    Fitting into New Shoes 266
    Asia Region FMD Map 270
    In Their Steps 272
    Follow the Leader 275
    India—Rags to Riches 279
    Cambodia—Step by Step 289
    Sri Lanka—Checkpoints and Coconut Water............293
    Bangladesh—The Right Door 299
    Pakistan—Signs and Wonders 302
    Vietnam—White Shirts and Orange Soda..................305
    Tulsa—A New Home 311
    Epilogue 315

FOREWORD
by T. F. Tenney

I thought I knew Paul Dennis. The Paul I knew was Paul A. J. (after Jesus). I now feel I know him B. J. (before Jesus) as well. To have come from a place called Hollow and a very hollow life to a man of God is quite a journey. He is truly a trophy of grace.

Having been his director of foreign missions and friend for many years, it is a privilege to recommend his book to you. Most assuredly, this is a faith-building biography. From admittedly a crude and rude rank sinner to the high echelons of responsibility in Kingdom enterprise, every line reeks with faith. Read it, ingest it, and watch your faith-ometer rise. If God can do this for Paul and Shirley, He can surely do it for you.

I introduce you to Paul A. Dennis, redeemed by grace, preacher, pastor, missionary, executive, and now, not in retirement but in refirement. Paul and Shirley are like Goliath's sword—there's none like them.

PREFACE
by Fred Kinzie

Paul and Shirley Dennis and daughter Paula began attending First Apostolic Church in Toledo, Ohio, in 1964 after moving to Bowling Green from Lima. Later they moved to Toledo, and he worked at the Newcomb Baker Shoe Store in Miracle Mile Shopping Center. They were a talented couple who added a new dimension to our worship and ability to evangelize. They blessed the church and the church, in turn, blessed them.

They fit into First Apostolic Church like a hand in a glove ready to work anywhere and at anything. We were getting ready to build a new sanctuary, and Paul joined the building crew in the evenings after work. Shirley became my secretary, filing and paying bills, and kept everything current. She was exceptionally efficient; always checking to be sure every bill was valid. They worked as though they'd been here for years. They were aggressive, enthusiastic Christians eager to do everything they could to help things progress. They were deeply appreciated by everyone.

Later, after the sanctuary was built, they took charge of maintenance, keeping the church clean and everything in good repair. In the winter time Paul was on the job, keeping our parking lot clear of snow.

They were involved in the ministry of the church with Shirley teaching Sunday school and Paul serving as the youth leader. Later he taught the youth class. At one time Shirley taught a twelve-week course on doctrine to the youth.

While Paul and Shirley were youth leaders, they organized a Christmas drama that later developed into a three-night production. The dramas continued in the schedule of the church, each year drawing large crowds. Many folks came to the Lord through them.

Shirley Dennis, Click Hunt, and Dennis and Sue Condon put on a children's program that was so interesting. Shirley was a fine musician and played the piano for song services and often the choir. My wife, Vera, the musical director of the church, kept her involved

Order My Steps

in about every musical presentation performed. Both Paul and Shirley were remarkably competent in everything they attempted. No wonder the Lord called them to the mission field.

Paul drove our church bus and van whenever people needed transportation. Later they moved into the house the church owned next door so they could be close when needed for anything. They were persuasive Christians with positive testimonies for Christ. They brought others to the Lord Jesus.

In 1970 they returned to Lima to help the church there. Three years later they returned to Toledo to become pastor of the Antioch Apostolic Church in the area. They did a lot of alterations on the older part of the building and built a new sanctuary. While they pastored they assembled a large congregation with a thriving Sunday school. They pastored this church before it was a UPCI church; under Paul's leadership it was brought into the UPC. The church was running around twenty-six at the beginning and about six months later, thirteen people left. By the time they entered foreign missions work the church was running between 155-160.

They were tremendous assets to our church, benefited the area churches and also the Ohio District while pastoring at Antioch.

After three years the Dennises accepted the call to foreign missions work in Japan. After appointment they held their first deputation service at First Apostolic Church. We were thrilled to send them off with a generous offering to get them started raising their budget.

Several years later while they were in Kyoto, Japan, we visited them on a trip back to the United States from Australia. They were great hosts to the Newstrands and us, helping us onto the bullet train headed for Tokyo. They called ahead to our missionary in Tokyo to meet us at the station. It's a good thing they did, for I think we would still be trying to find our way out of that train station to this day.

If every church had an assembly full of people like Paul, Shirley, and Paula Dennis, it would be a progressive assembly. Not only were they good church workers, they are genuine, Holy Spirit filled people with unique abilities.

Paul A. Dennis

This letter was written when Brother Kinzie was ninety-four years old. Brother Kinzie's personal note to the Dennises:

Paul and Shirley:

I hope this is what you want from me. If there are any inaccuracies straighten them out. If you think of something that I've missed go ahead and add it. I trust you that much. If it's something derogatory to me put it in anyhow. I make mistakes like any human being . . . and forget so easily at my age. It is not possible that I could cram everything I know about you folks onto one page.

My memory fails me. So much water has slipped under the dam since those days that I can only remember a trickle.

If Vera were here, she'd have a lot of things to add to this. Sandy remembers some things. She reminded me of the twelve-week class on doctrine that Shirley taught.

I am so glad you're writing this book, Paul. It'll help you remember; and as you scrutinize your past, you will see many things to pat yourself on the back and many more to kick yourself for. One thing about life it never goes too smooth . . . there are always a lot of bumps and potholes in the road to keep one alert.

It's a little like a group of women at a quilting party. As they were discussing everybody in the neighborhood, a young man went walking by the house whistling. As each woman read his pedigree (which wasn't good), they finally came to a lady who always seemed to have something good to say about people. All the women held their breath when they finally reached her and not a word was spoken. In the quietness of the moment his whistling could be heard really loud and clear. Finally she spoke. "There's a good thing that can be said about him. He's a good whistler."

'Nuff said. God bless you both. Keep going . . . but slow down a little. When you get old you can't drive like you did when you were dashing young folks.

God bless you,
Brother/Pastor Fred Kinzie

Section I
The Old Paul

Pauly on tricycle

Paul's parents, Dorsey and Mary Dennis

Paul, Brother Donald, Sister Jean

Rub, Donald, Jean, and Paul

Paul at graduation 1954

Paul's mom and his stepdad, Rub

Paul at Sampson after basic training

Paul at his barracks door December 1956

Run, Paul, Run

Mary was pregnant with Paul when Dorsey, diagnosed with cancer and tuberculosis, was admitted to the veterans' hospital in Dayton. When the doctors had done all they could for Dorsey, they sent him home to #8 Hollow to spend the rest of his days surrounded by family. Baby Paul was three months old when his dad died. It was December 1935.

Two years later Mary Elizabeth Dennis became Mrs. Jessie "Rub" Preston Shirkey, and Paul acquired a stepdad.

When Paul was six, Audrey Louise was added to the family; and big brother Paul appointed himself her protector.

Rub picked up his battered lunch bucket. Turning to Mary, he threatened, "Tell Paul that if those weeds in that backyard ain't cut when I get home tonight, he'll answer to me. He's not gonna lay around here doin' nothin'. Time for that boy to get to work."

"But, Rub, you know there aren't any jobs . . . " The slam of the screen door cut short her protest.

Mary sighed. She reminded herself, *Rub is a hard worker. He works from daylight until dark every day in the mine, has for years.*

With the back of her wrist, she shoved a strand of damp hair out of her eyes. The sun was barely peeking over the eastern horizon into #8 Hollow and already sweat tickled her upper lip. She dumped Rub's dirty plate and coffee mug into the dishpan.

As she poured hot water from the teakettle over the dirty dishes, she cocked her head toward the stairs. "Paul, get up! You can't sleep all day. There's work to be done."

Paul A. Dennis

Silence.

"Paul! Get up!"

A faint grunt from the second floor told her that her words had hit their mark.

"Pauly, get up! Dad said for you to cut the weeds in the backyard today."

Silence.

Mary grimaced. It was going to be another long, hot day.

Around noon Paul jerked the lawnmower, a long-handled scythe, from the shed where it was half hidden among the junk. He glared at the backyard, a pond of knee-high weeds shimmering in the heat.

With half-hearted swings of the scythe, he started to work. As the sweat poured, Paul steamed. *Rub's always bossing me around. It's not my fault that construction job only lasted three months, and there's no more jobs around here. If my dad had'a lived, I'm sure he would'a understood. He wouldn't have threatened me and beat me. I've had about all of Rub Shirkey I can take.*

Paul's dad was his hero. Dorsey Virgil Dennis, a World War I veteran, had fought in France, where he was exposed to chemical gases. When he was discharged, he returned home to McLuney, Ohio. His beloved wife, Mary, and children, Emojean and Donald, welcomed him back to peaceful #8 Hollow.

Those were good days for the Dennis family, but they hadn't lasted long. So Mary said.

All Paul knew about his dad—his real dad—was what his mother told him, and that wasn't much. He did know that on the day he was born Dorsey had planted the maple tree that now stood guard over their front yard.

Paul stood in the overgrown backyard engaged in a glaring contest with the sun, and the sun was winning. Sweat dampened his dingy T-shirt, forming circles under his armpits. Paul seethed. *I'm not a kid anymore. I'm a grown man—eighteen years old. I don't have to do what I'm told! I'll just go to the recruiting office and join the military. I don't have to take being cussed out and ordered around. I'm gonna be my own man.*

He threw down the scythe. *Let Rub put it up.* That was the last decision Paul made of his own accord for a long, long time.

In the kitchen he stopped by the washbasin and splashed cool water on his face.

"Through already?" his mother asked.

"Yep, I'm done!" Paul snapped. He stomped up the stairs and pushed aside the curtain hanging over the doorway to his bedroom. Asserting his independence called for a change of clothes.

A few minutes later he entered the kitchen and announced, "I'm going to join the military, Mom."

Mary didn't look up. "OK."

Paul winced. *Isn't she even going to argue?* Without another word, he walked out the front door, past the magnificent maple tree, across the yard to the gravel road, and headed for a world far away from #8 Hollow. Run, Paul, run.

A few hours and twenty miles later, Paul knocked on the door of his brother's house in Zanesville.

When Donald opened the door, he grinned. "Hey, Paul, come in. What brings you to town?"

"I'm joining up, Donald. I'm . . ." He gulped; then his words tumbled out. "I'm not taking any more cussing and beating and stupid orders. I'm sick of Rub and his threats."

Donald didn't blink. A few years earlier he had joined the army for the same reason.

After supper the brothers lounged on the front porch and talked. "What's your plan, Paul?" Donald asked.

"I'm going to join the air force. Ray said I'd have a better chance of getting a college education there." Their brother-in-law, Ray Hill, was a former B-17 pilot.

Donald, a Korean War veteran who had been awarded the bronze star for service above and beyond the call of duty, eyed his little brother. "Military life isn't easy."

Paul bristled. "Neither is living with Rub."

"I know that." Donald paused, twisted his mouth, and continued, "Military life is based on discipline. You know a lot about punishment, Paul, but not much about discipline."

"Then I'll learn." Paul stood and stretched. "How about we hit the hay? Tomorrow's my big day."

The next morning Donald dropped Paul off at the recruiter's office. After Paul answered a myriad of questions and filled out multiple forms, the recruiter asked, "When do you want to leave?"

Thinking only about getting away, not about where he was headed, Paul replied, "It doesn't matter."

"Good. Be back here tomorrow by noon. We have a bus going to Cleveland where you'll get a physical. If you pass, you'll be sworn into the United States Air Force on Saturday."

Paul walked out in a daze. It was almost too easy.

After supper Donald drove his little brother home. Their mother met them at the door, wringing her hands in her apron. "Where have you been, son?"

Paul plopped down on the tattered sofa. "I told you I was going to enlist. I joined the air force today." Donald sat down beside him, reinforcing Paul's decision.

The color drained from Mary's face. "Oh, Pauly, you didn't! I thought you were just talking through your hat because you were mad about cutting the weeds."

She stood studying her boys. Paul knew what she was thinking. He'd heard it often enough.

Order My Steps

Wasn't it only last month that my boys were little tykes? Dorsey was so proud of his sons, even though he knew he would not live to see them grow up. Their dad was an army man; guess it was only natural that they would be too.

But Mary knew that more than love for the military had propelled Donald into the army and now Paul into the air force.

She didn't ask Paul why he had enlisted. She knew. She only asked, "How long did you sign up for?"

Paul stared at the ceiling. He croaked, "Eight years."

Mary grabbed her stomach and gasped, "Eight years!" She buried her face in her apron, blotting her tears.

At least I know she cares, Paul thought, feeling like a jerk. He had never understood how his soft-spoken, kind mother had hooked up with a hot-tempered, foul-mouthed guy like Rub.

Paul jumped up and put his arms around his mother. Her shoulders shook as she nestled her head under his chin. "Awww, Mom, don't cry. I go to Cleveland tomorrow for a physical. I might not pass."

But he did. Saturday he was sworn in and immediately received his first orders as a member of the United States Air Force. "Report back to Zanesville on Tuesday. Wednesday you will be bused to Sampson Air Force Base training center in Geneva, New York."

New York? For a country boy who had never been outside of Ohio, New York was the epitome of wild life—crime, gangsters, violence. Paul was both horrified and energized.

Tuesday morning he sat on the well-worn sofa watching the clock, waiting for Donald, his ride to the bus.

At the sound of heavy footsteps, Paul glanced toward the kitchen. Rub walked in and over to Paul. He tossed a carton of

Lucky Strikes into Paul's lap. "Now you won't have to hide and smoke," he smirked.

Paul's mouth dropped open as Rub walked out of the room. *How did Rub know he smoked?*

The crunch of car tires on the gravel road brought Paul back to reality. Ready or not, it was time to say goodbye.

Clinging to her baby boy, Mary rubbed his face and head, praying in Jesus' name. "Pauly, oh, Pauly, you be good and write to me. I will pray for you every day."

Although Paul was not interested in church or prayer, his mother's promise comforted him. *Maybe someday I will look into this God-thing and whatever it is that makes my mother such a good, strong person in spite of everything around here,* Paul thought. *But not now. I've got too much on my mind to think about religion.*

As Paul opened the car door, Rub came around the corner of the house. He stuck out his hand. Paul hesitated, and then accepted his stepdads handshake.

Rub looked over Paul's shoulder. "Good luck." He cleared his throat, turned, and walked away.

Donald glanced at his watch. "Time to go, Paul."

Mary stood in the yard and waved until the car disappeared. Paul did not look back.

Deprogrammed

Hurry up. Line up. Sit down. Slow down. Halt. Shut up. Wait. These orders summarize life in the USAF.

Before Paul boarded the bus for New York, he was given a brief orientation. "Here's a white card with your name and serial number and a green card. Before you debark, you must memorize this number and the Eleven General Orders on the green card." The officer continued, punctuating his speech with a few words even Rub had never used. "This is not a request. It is an order—because from this hour until you are discharged you belong to Uncle Sam and the United States Air Force."

So much for getting away from having to take orders. So much for getting away from being cussed out. The discipline had begun. Paul memorized the number and the orders.

Late that evening the Greyhound bus filled with anxious boys on the edge of manhood arrived at Sampson Air Force Base, far away from the wild New York that Paul had envisioned.

A low-grade officer with a high-grade ego boomed, "Get out and line up in two columns."

He hustled the recruits into a large building where military cots were lined up like opossums clinging to their mother's tail. For the first and last time during Paul's military career, his cot was made for him.

"Take your pick. Put your stuff on it."

Thirty minutes later the tired and hungry guys lined up and marched (civilian style) to the mess hall for a late supper. Paul soon learned that he hadn't lost all his rights. He still had the right to choose. *Chicken or beef?* Not fried or baked, not white or dark, not rare or well done—just chicken or beef. For drinks: *milk, coffee, or water.* That was it. Take it or leave it.

Paul A. Dennis

Forty-five minutes later, another loudmouth barked, "Time's up. Line up. Go to the clipper window. Empty your tray in the garbage can. Place your tray on the tray-stacking space. Put your spoon in the spoon pan, fork in the fork pan, knife in the knife pan. Put your cup upside down in the cup basket. Form a double line at the door."

Paul muttered, "Check brains at the door. Zip lips. Open ears."

Back at the quarters, another guy with a cavernous mouth shouted orders peppered with profanity. "Go to your sack. Stand at the foot. Lights out at 2200. Be in your sack before then. You are to be showered, shaved, and ready for duty by 0600."

Again they had a choice—shower in the morning or evening. Not being an early riser, Paul chose to shower that evening. When he walked into the shower room, he gulped as the reality of military life hit him. *Modesty out the door.*

He stared at the communal area with showerheads sticking out like paralyzed goose necks. On the other side was the latrine area (he was already picking up some military terms). He watched for a few minutes and then nodded. Standard military process. Hurry up and get in line for the shower, for the toilet, and for the sink. Then wait.

Home was never looking better—Rub and all.

The next morning Paul awoke to organized confusion. At 0600 sharp, profanity polluted the air—which wasn't exactly sweet to begin with—as another loudmouth shouted orders.

"Does everyone around here think we're deaf?" Paul muttered to anyone listening. But no one was. Everyone was trying to absorb the high-decibel orders.

Breakfast was eaten in double-time; not a problem to Paul because the food wasn't worth chewing. Just stuff it in the mouth and swallow while Old Loudmouth marched from table to table bellowing, "OK, ladies, let's get that stuff down."

Order My Steps

Paul grimaced as he choked down his watery eggs and burnt toast. *I'm beginning to not like this man; this is not the lifestyle for me.* His heart dropped to the region of his knees as he realized this *was* his lifestyle; he had signed on the dotted line.

After breakfast they were led to another building into a room filled with school desks, chairs with armrests that flared out like paddles. "Take your seats alphabetically, last name first, first name second, and middle name last."

"What?" "How do you do that?" "I don't get it." Confusion reigned as the bully behind the desk heaped ridicule on the befuddled guys.

"Hurry up, you dummies! Don't you know how to spell? Don't you know your name or the alphabet?" Of course, all this was mixed with words that would have sent Paul's mother running for a bar of soap.

Eventually, the mob unscrambled to form rows of browbeaten boys. The mental dust settled and Paul looked around. He, Dennis Paul A., was seated near the front.

Next, the commanding officer taught them how to come to attention and stand there *until*. They practiced the rigid stance until fatigue set in, and then the bully ordered, "Sit." It felt good to sink into the chair until . . .

"Attention!"

Heads bobbed up and froze. Paul concentrated on his position: arms at his side, heels together, toes spread about ten inches apart, back stiff as a board, eyes straight ahead. He assumed that those around him were doing the same thing.

Through a front door strode a man in a beige uniform, spit-polished shoes, wrinkle-free shirt, and knife-creased trousers, carrying a hat under his arm. One sharp-looking man.

"At ease!"

Paul relaxed, putting his hands behind his back and spreading his feet about eighteen inches apart.

Paul A. Dennis

"This is your Technical Instructor (TI), Airman Second Class *Joe Blow.*" Not his name but an appropriate alias. "From this time on you will answer him 'yes, sir' or 'no, sir.' He will be with you until the last minute of your training. You will do exactly as he says. You will not add to or diminish from any order. Do you understand?"

"Yes, sir!"

Next, they ran the recruits through the barbershop like sheep to the shearing. Paul had always worn a flat-top haircut, but he came out of the barber chair, rubbing his head, staring at a sea of upside-down smiles topped by bald heads. He could feel his identity being peeled off layer by layer.

Next stop: Barracks for Flight 3516, their new home, where Paul and his buddies were each handed a footlocker. "Line up!" shouted TI Joe Blow. "Fill each floor alphabetically. Set your footlocker at the foot of your bed and stand at ease beside the locker."

This was followed by a twenty-five minute lunch break. *Gulp! Gulp! Belch!*

The next lesson was bed making. "How hard can that be?" Paul groused to John Lapp, his new friend from Ohio. "My mom taught me that years ago."

Ahhh, but Paul had never made a 45-degree corner with a sheet, or measured the overhang, or pulled out all the wrinkles, or . . .

I could show them how to make these beds faster, Paul thought. But no one asked him. After two hours he could make a bed military style, even in the dark, just as the TI ordered.

"All you airmen fall outside and form four ranks facing the barracks. On the double!" the TI barked.

They were going to learn to march, but first the instructor had to make sure they knew their left from their right. He stood facing them, lifted his right hand, and ordered, "Raise your right hand." Paul did a quick mental calculation and realized the TI's right was on his left. But not everyone reached that conclusion fast enough.

A spicy speech on the airmen's intelligence followed. Each one who had raised his left hand was ordered to pick up a rock and carry it in his right hand until they finished marching. They drilled and marched, marched and drilled until Paul felt his personality oozing out the holes the TI's sharp orders were poking in him.

Identity gone. Personality zapped.

Eyes and ears open. Mouth shut.

It was called *deprogramming*. Less and less Paul was feeling and thinking like a civilian. More and more he was becoming the property of the United States Air Force.

The Flying Thirty

"Strip to your shorts!" roared the TI standing in the drill hall. "Start with your shoes and socks. Put them in the bottom of your bag."

No one protested. Off came shoes, socks, trousers, shirts. Everything was shoved into the blue cloth bags. Paul placed his wallet on top of his clothes, tied the bag, placed it on his right, and took five steps forward, per orders.

In single file they marched into a building where each man received a large white duffle bag and then the uniforms: seven pairs of shorts and undershirts, seven pairs of work socks, seven pairs of dress socks, two pairs of work shoes, one pair of dress shoes, four khaki-colored uniforms (trousers and shirts), two blue dress uniforms with two jackets (one blazer style and one "Ike" style), four light-blue dress shirts, three pairs of one-piece fatigues (which they would live in most of the time), one field jacket and liner, and to top it off, two neckties. Not a bad wardrobe for a country boy.

The uniforms were "tailor made," three sizes fit all: small, medium, and large. The shoes came in whole sizes.

The TI shouted, "Put on one pair of your fatigues, work socks, and shoes. Roll up the legs and sleeves of your fatigues eight to ten inches." Nothing was left to chance.

Paul looked around and grinned. He felt as if he were standing in the middle of a field of beanstalks in burlap bags. No room for individuality here. Before he burst out laughing, he bent over and packed the remaining items neatly in his duffle bag.

Carrying their packed bags, the men marched back to where they had left their civvies in the blue bags. Then, bags in tow, they marched to the barracks where they were taught how to hang up their clothes and stow their underwear and linens in their foot-

Order My Steps

lockers. Paul's mother had spent years trying to teach him this same lesson. Strange how quickly he learned this time.

As he hung up his uniforms, spacing them two fingers apart on the length of pipe behind his bunk, he shrugged. Apparently, brains were not required for basic training, just reflexes. Don't think, just obey. Move, stand still, go to bed, get up, eat, shower, shave, put *this* on like *this*. No questions accepted; all decisions had been made long before Paul and his buddies arrived.

He had been in basic training only two and one-half days, each day a week long; but he was ready to awaken from this nightmare and go home. *Dream on, Paul. Your new life is just beginning.*

Then came the good news: they were going to receive a pay advance. For some strange reason it was called "the flying thirty." *Oh, well, no matter what it is called, bring it on.*

The TI quashed the enthusiasm. "Not so fast. You have to learn how to get paid."

Why does the military complicate everything from making a bed to getting a check? A big question mark floated in Paul's head, but he did not bat an eyelash.

"We are going to do a role play," the TI announced. "I will be the paymaster, and here's what you do if you want to get paid."

Paul wanted to get paid, so he listened carefully. When it was his turn to practice, he marched up to the paymaster, snapped to attention, and raised the volume on his voice box. "Sir! Airman Dennis, Paul A., AF 5837 reporting for pay, sir!"

The next morning at breakfast, chatter vibrated the mess hall as the men planned what they were going to do with a few extra dollars in their pockets. Some planned to make deposits in the heretofore-off-limits Coke and candy machines. Others planned to play a little poker or a crap game. Anticipation ran high.

After gulping down their watery eggs and burnt toast, they reported to the real paymaster in correct procedure. The paymaster handed each man thirty dollars and another blue bag, this one smaller than the first one. As Paul stuffed the money into his pocket, a sense of pride enveloped him. At the back of his mind was the AF rule that they were not to give or borrow money from anyone. He wondered how long it would be before a buddy hit him up for a loan.

Back in formation, they marched to the parking lot of the base exchange (BX).

"Halt!"

Column by column they proceeded into the store where, behind an exceedingly long counter, men and women wearing sheepish smiles waited for them.

"Open your bag and move down the line," TI Joe Blow ordered.

Soon Paul's bag was stuffed with necessities—towels, washcloths, razor, blades, shaving cream, comb, toothbrush, toothpaste, soap, deodorant, laundry soap, bleach, foot powder, even a package of sewing needles and spools of black and white thread.

Sewing classes too? Paul wondered. *Mom would love this.*

"OK, ladies, move on to the checkout."

Checkout? Do we have to pay for this stuff?

Paul watched as the government's cash register gobbled up his thirty dollars. He had four dollars left, in case he ran out of something before the real payday.

"So much for Cokes and candy," Paul said to John.

His new friend snorted. "Don't matter. I just heard that the vending machines are still off limits."

Back at the barracks they learned exactly how to arrange their toiletries on the top shelf of their footlockers. When his little blue bag was empty, Paul placed his personal from-home items in it, sealed it with a special tag, and addressed it to his mother.

His Adam's apple bobbed and his eyes misted as someone tossed his bag onto a cart with all the others. His last physical link to home was pushed down the aisle and out the door.

Civilian items were no longer needed. As an official airman in the United States Air Force, Dennis, Paul A. would use only issued items.

Basic Training

For the first couple of weeks of basic training, Paul lived on the edge of his nerves. Although he was accustomed to being threatened, cursed, and ordered around, the officers took bullying to a new level. Even the non-commissioned officers took advantage of their surrogate authority.

Everything was done in double time. Run, don't walk. Hurry, hurry, hurry. One class or drill after another.

One class classified Paul to enter the medical field, which was his preference. He hoped someday to become a doctor. After basic training he would be processed to that school. Meanwhile, he had classes on how to assemble and disassemble his M-1 rifle, pitch a tent, dig a foxhole. Every day, every minute of the day, he worked, learned, exercised—pushups, jumping jacks, sit-ups, chin-ups, weight lifting.

He learned to spit shine shoes, wash clothes, and iron uniforms (no wrinkles allowed).

The first few weeks as Paul's flight practiced marching dressed in oversized olive drab one-piece fatigues, they were easily targeted as newbies. Often they heard, "Jeeps! Jeeps! Jeeps!" Eyes forward, Paul cooled his temper by reminding himself that one day he would be the one chanting, "Jeeps! Jeeps! Jeeps!"

Orders. Orders. Orders. Kitchen duty, latrine duty, guard duty, charge-of-quarters duty. And, oh yes, police duty; that was the shocker.

When Paul was assigned to police duty, they gave him a garbage bag and instructed him to walk around the base and pick up trash. He had to "field strip" all cigarette butts—tear the paper off the tobacco, fling the tobacco to the wind, roll the paper into a pinhead size, and put it in the trash bag.

Paul A. Dennis

White-glove inspection hung over their heads like a starving eagle ready to swoop down on its prey. Faucets, nozzles, and floors had to reflect the sweating faces of the *housekeepers*. Racks had to be kept in white-collar order. Bedding had to be stretched so tightly that a quarter dropped on the blanket would bounce at least three inches.

Little did Paul realize what was happening to him. He was too busy and too tired even to think about it. But by the end of his first month of training, he had a different bearing than the country boy who had enlisted. His shoulders were straight, his eyes clear, and his mind sharp. He automatically responded to commands, sights, and sounds without questioning or even processing the steps he needed to take. He was being programmed to make quick wartime decisions, and he was enjoying the discipline.

The second month of training, Paul and his buddies moved to the field, a simulated war area. They lived in tents and used garbage cans for latrines.

Paul's most frightening experience was his trip through the tear gas chamber (TGC), one of the few buildings in the field. This elongated building had a door at each end. A long trail led up to the TGC. The airmen walked along the trail, carrying their gas masks, on alert for a gas wave.

"Gas!"

A tide of arms raised masks to faces. They arrived at the TGC looking like aliens emerging from a space ship.

The ever-present TI yelled, "Inside this building are instructors who will tell you what to do."

About halfway through the building, Paul was feeling pretty cocky. *There's nothing to this.*

"Stop! Take off your masks."

OK. I can do that. No problem. W-w-what?

Paul's eyes caught fire. His eyelids crashed. His nostrils bloated and closed. He gasped for breath.

Order My Steps

"Stop!"

Stop? Is this guy crazy? I've gotta get outta here! But Paul stopped, his feet stapled to the floor.

"Turn around and face the man behind you. Eyes wide open."

Paul squinted and turned around. With mental energy he pried his eyes wide open.

"Now turn around and face forward."

Paul turned. Scalding tears flooded his burning eyes. He squinted them open just enough to get his bearing. He sprinted for the door.

Outside he heaved and struggled to breathe life back into his searing lungs. As his hand went to his face, an instructor roared, "Do not rub your eyes! Do not rub your eyes!"

The next day the obstacle course was fun and games compared to the TGC. It reminded Paul of his boyhood, swinging on wild grapevines pretending he was a Kamikaze pilot; crossing the creek on a foot log and crawling from tree to tree while playing cowboys and Indians; jumping over fences and running from outlaws.

Paul was amazed to discover his mental and physical strength. With each maneuver every fiber in him was stretched.

After the obstacle course, they broke up camp and marched the two or three miles back to their barracks where they washed the grime of the war zone down the shower drain. They cleaned and checked their rifles, returned issued equipment to the supply squadron, and did laundry. Paul's head barely hit the pillow that night until his snores joined those vibrating the walls. And he had once thought this bunk was hard.

The next morning, normal life resumed, although everyone knew this was The Day. Wake-up call. Check-in. All accounted for. Off to breakfast and back to the barracks to await orders.

"Attention!"

Everyone jumped to his feet.

Paul A. Dennis

"Get dressed in your class B uniform. Then you are on your own to report to the drill hall."

Paul pulled his khaki shirt and trousers from their hangers. He had to lift his feet high to put on the trousers because they were starched so stiffly they could stand alone. He put on his shirt with the U.S. insignias on the collar. Before he put on his dress socks and shoes, he ran his hand over the shoes, making sure not one speck of dirt marred their glassy surface. Last, the necktie.

"On their own," John and Paul strolled to the drill hall. Groups of chairs were set in sections of seventy to eighty chairs. When they saw the flag "Flight 3516" in front of a section, they quickly found their seats, alphabetically.

After the formalities, the base commander congratulated them for completing their training and reminded them the sky was their goal—no limits.

"Attention!"

Everyone snapped to and saluted the base commander as he exited.

Their TI came to the podium with good news and bad news. "As I read your name, stand." When he finished his list, most of the men, including Paul, were standing. "Move to my right. You have been promoted to Airman Third Class (A/3C)."

Those seated were told to report to the training center the next day for transfer to another flight. They had to retake the course.

They gave Paul his pay and a week's pass and told him that when he returned he would receive his orders for on-the-job training (OJT) as a medic. He boarded the first train to Zanesville. Every time he settled in to catch a few winks, the train pulled into a station. The trip took twenty-four hours.

Paul couldn't wait to get back to #8 Hollow. The surly boy who had left returned a self-assured young man. He had undergone a major attitude adjustment and gained ten pounds.

Order My Steps

Mary was thrilled to see him. Although Paul and Rub were in the same house, their paths did not cross. They easily avoided one another as Rub worked dawn to dark. In the three days Paul was home, Mary sewed stripes on his uniforms and asked a thousand questions. He evaded his mother's invitations to church, but he stayed as long as he could; so long that his mother and brother paid for his ticket to fly back to the base. It was his first plane ride.

As Donald's car pulled out of the drive, Paul leaned out the window and waved until he could no longer see his mother standing in the front yard.

Under Arrest

Hurry up and wait.

Back on base as Paul waited for orders from the top (wherever that was), he played a mental guessing game. Where? When? Who? How? Where would they send him for his OJT as a medic? When would his orders come? Who else from his flight would be going there? How would they travel?

The assistant TI approached the men in Flight 3516. "Guys, TI Joe Blow just received some really bad news. His mother is dying, and he needs to get to her as soon as possible. Problem is he's got to have new tires for his car before he can make the trip. I'm wondering if we can help him."

Paul thought, *If my mother were dying, I'd sure want someone to help me.* Each man's heart melted as he thought of his mother.

"If each one could give just a couple of dollars, it sure would help," the assistant TI suggested.

Every man reached for his wallet and pulled out two dollars.

As the assistant TI collected the money, he said, "This is great. You guys won't regret this. I'll see that Joe gets this money."

Another day passed. And another. Then the third day of waiting. No classes. No maneuvers. No orders. The men were getting restless. The fourth day the guys were lying around the barracks, some smoking, some reading. All waiting.

"Attention!"

Everyone, whatever his state of dress, snapped to attention. An officer carrying an attaché case accompanied by two sergeants walked in. Paul was sure they were about to get their orders.

"At ease."

The officer stepped forward. "Men, I am an attorney with the USAF. I am here to tell you that you are under arrest. Some or all of you have broken AFR (Air Force Regulation) 36-29. You were not to give or borrow money from anyone. I am here to find out who gave money to your assistant TI four days ago."

The airmen were stunned. Paul gasped. His eyes smarted. It was the tear gas chamber all over again.

The officer continued, "Your TI and assistant TI went AWOL. They have been picked up and are now in the stockade awaiting their trials. Now tell me. Who gave money to your assistant TI?"

Everyone was guilty.

Before the day was over, the men were informed they had been "red lined." They would not receive their orders until after their instructors had their day in court. Date uncertain. Days or weeks in the future.

Paul spent the next week wiping mental sweat and kicking himself. *If only* . . . but it was too late. All he could do was stick it out. He thought he was good at waiting. But not so. He had flashbacks of Rub threatening, "When I get home, I'll take care of that boy!" Fear twisted his mind. On the positive side he realized that he could have received an Article 15 (nonjudicial punishment) and/or be sitting in the stockade with Joe Blow and his assistant.

They were told, "You have been put on hold. When the Command receives word from another base of needed personnel, you will be sent *wherever* to fill *whatever* job openings are available."

The openings came in two and three at a time. The men were sent out in alphabetical order. How else? Many times Paul silently thanked his dad for his last name.

Finally, Paul's orders came through. He had to report to Bolling Air Force Base, Washington, D.C., to the Fire Fighting and Crash Rescue Squadron for OJT. His dream of going into the medical field went out the window.

A $2 mistake had cost him his right to choose. Two dollars had changed his destiny. It was years before he looked back and realized God was ordering his steps that day.

Crash Landing

New York and now Washington, D.C. Paul A. Dennis, country boy from McLuney, Ohio, was getting around. Although his travel involved more work than sightseeing, Paul's world was expanding. So was his knowledge of the other side of life.

Along with Paul's assignment to Bolling Field Air Force Base came a two-week leave. He turned around, repacked, and headed back to Ohio.

Again, his schedule and Rub's did not jive, but that did not bother Paul one bit. The less he saw of his stepdad, the better he liked it. He spent his days being babied by his mother and bumming around with whatever friends he could find. Paul, the experienced traveler, fueled his high school pals' imaginations with tales of life beyond McLuney.

At the end of his leave, he again boarded a plane; this time he flew to Washington, D.C. At Bolling Field Air Force Base, he reported to the USAF 311th Fighter-Bomber Squadron, Crash Rescue Fire Department.

What a change from boot camp to OJT; it was almost as drastic as going from kindergarten to college in one giant leap. Loudmouthed officers did not belt out orders every ten minutes, which made Paul and the others responsible for keeping up with what was going on.

He was assigned a room in the crash crew barracks. He had to keep his room presentable for inspection, which was pulled every other day. He worked twenty-four hours on, twenty-four hours off. OJT was just that—a job and training.

The training was both academic and physical. Paul learned to read pressure gauges, figure pounds of water pressure lost with each foot of fire hose, and memorize the layout of the airport.

Order My Steps

And that was just the start. He acquired a detailed knowledge of each type of aircraft that he might come in contact with, its use, and what kind of cargo or ammunition it carried. Then he learned the layout of the base—the location of each building and water hydrant, along with the blueprint of the barracks area. Plus he memorized every place of business and what materials were in the buildings. Knowledge was crammed into every brain cell.

But Uncle Sam was only beginning. Each type of emergency had a different alarm. As a firefighter he had to recognize each alarm; know how to approach each type of fire or aircraft crash; instantly decide what line, hose, nozzle, turret, and extinguishing agent to use. Then, of course, he had to know the operation of every fire truck the USAF had in service.

For weeks every day and often into the night, Paul studied or did live training.

Live training really turned on the heat. Into a drill pit lined with a ten-inch-wide concrete wall, they lowered the fuselage of an aircraft with dummies strapped inside. They dumped old oil, gas, and aircraft fuel into the pit and set it on fire.

On training days Paul and the men lived on the edge, waiting for the alarm to sound at any time. Sometimes the fuselage was a passenger plane; other times it was a fighter jet.

The firefighters' first and foremost task was to save the passengers or pilots. The people were dummies, but the fire was real, very real. Paul and his buddies had to fight their way through the flames to rescue the people, then go back and completely extinguish the fire. Going into the fire energized the country boy from Ohio.

No one told him where to be and when. It was his responsibility to check the bulletin boards and show up at the right place at the right time. During his months of training, he was on call 24/7.

The days he was on duty, he ate, slept, and bathed at the station where the bunk room was on the second floor. He kept

Paul A. Dennis

his uniform and equipment beside his bed. When the alarm sounded, he leaped out of bed, instantly wide awake. In three to four seconds, he dressed, pulled on his gear, and slid down the 40-foot brass pole to his appointed truck and station.

His first real aircraft emergency came one sweltering summer afternoon. The guys were working around the station cleaning, polishing brass, keeping things spic and span, when the alarm sounded. Automatically, no questions asked, they rushed to their stations. The crew chief filled in the details as they sped to the scene.

The base commander's plane, a C-47 converted to his personal use, had a stuck landing gear. The pilot had circled the field several times and touched down a couple of times, trying to loosen the gear while using up most of the fuel to prevent a large fire in case of a crash landing. The touchdowns did not loosen the gear.

The pilot circled a couple more times to lower the fuel. Then the announcement came that they were coming in for a crash landing. The trucks spewed foam over forty yards of the runway.

Paul's truck was in place and ready for action. He and Eddie, the other guy assigned to his truck, were the linemen and rescue men. They were in full gear, hot and heavy. Sweat collected in Paul's boots. His muscles contracted. Adrenalin kicked in. His heart pumped double time. Fear threatened to paralyze his memory. He forced his mind to rewind.

First, fight your way through the fire to the plane. Remove all personnel. You must not fail because people in that plane are depending on you to save them.

The firefighters' eyes were glued on the sky. As the plane came in for a landing, everything looked normal; the rear wheel and the left landing gear were visible. The aircraft touched the runway a few feet from the foam, then plowed right into it. The right wing dug into the concrete. Sparks and metal flew.

Order My Steps

At that moment all sense of fear vanished. Paul's mind and body kicked into motion. He knew exactly what to do. The turrets on the truck would aim at the base of the fire and shoot foam and water. As linemen, Paul and Eddie would be the first into the fire. Scooting their feet, they would make a path for the crew chief, who would follow them. He would then lead the way to rescue the people.

The plane spun in two full circles while skidding down the runway. Then it stopped, pouring smoke and vapors. The crew chief, who had stayed in radio contact with the pilot, told the men, "Hold fast! Do not make entry! Stand on alert for a possible fire or explosion."

Eddie and Paul held their ground, waiting for further instructions . . . then the cargo door bulged, moving up and down. They knew that at any second it would blow. Paul looked at Eddie. Eddie looked at Paul. Their eyes sent a message. "Are you ready?"

POW! The door crashed back against the side of the plane.

Paul froze. Ready for anything.

Then through the smoke they saw their crew chief standing in the doorway. He had entered through the cockpit window and kicked open the door that had jammed on landing.

Paul took a breath and looked around to give Eddie a thumbs-up sign. But Eddie was gone.

Paul spun around. Had Eddie changed positions? Yep! Sure enough, he had. He was on the ground, passed out cold. Paul knelt and removed Eddie's hood. He was pale green. They took him back to the station via ambulance, the only casualty of the crash.

After the equipment was cleaned and stored and the trucks were in the stalls, a sense of euphoria swept over Paul. *I did it! And I did it right! I was the right man at the right place at the right time.* And it felt so good.

Paul A. Dennis

That night, lying on his bunk, he kept replaying the whole scenario. As he drifted off to sleep, he remembered another crash scene.

He saw a four-year-old boy sitting on his transformer tricycle. Handlebar grips and pedal pads were missing, but that tricycle was magical. Sometimes it was the big yellow school bus; other times it was Rub's Model-A.

"Never, never leave the yard on your trike, Pauly," his mother repeated daily. Large coal trucks often roared past their house in and out of #8 Hollow, stirring up huge, choking clouds of dust.

That day as Paul sat on his *it-can-be-anything* trike, a brilliant idea fueled his imagination. Across the road a steep dirt path ran up a hill to his uncle's house. What a race track.

He wheeled to the edge of the yard and looked up and down the road, twice. No dust clouds. No trucks. Quickly, he pedaled across the road. Then climbing off his trike, he pushed it up the hill until he decided it was high enough. He stopped and turned his race car around. He climbed onto the seat and looked down the hill across the road to the finish line, his front yard. He pushed on the pedal rods, pulled his feet up onto the seat, and started his motor. *Varoom!* He was off!

Soon the pedal rods were spinning faster than the eye could see. Paul lowered his feet and attempted to intercept the spinning rods but could not tame these flying monsters with his bare feet. *Varoom!* No brakes. *Varoom varoom!*

His white knuckles clutched the metal handlebars. His eyes bugged. He chortled with terrified glee as his race car zoomed down the hill.

Oh, no, the coal-truck road! He had to cross it! He jerked his head both ways. No dust clouds. No trucks.

Order My Steps

Zip! He flew across the finish line! Bang! He crashed into the front door, which gave up the ghost and caved inward. Little Pauly crash landed on his mother's living room floor.

Never again did he leave the front yard on his tricycle.

Airman Paul A. Dennis was grinning as he drifted off to sleep.

The next day he realized that his whole outlook had changed. He was a crash rescue fireman, and he was a good one. He stopped kicking himself for that stupid $2 mistake. He started looking forward to live drill pits and structural fires, synchronizing his movements and operating the truck and equipment.

Eddie survived the ribbing and made it through his training. Paul advanced to a permanent position on one of the main crash trucks. His self-confidence sprouted wings, but the added responsibility kept him rooted to reality.

Living on the edge, constantly alert for the alarm, waiting for the next crash, awakened in Paul a craving for adventure that started him on a downhill slide.

"When I work, I work hard; so when I play, I am going to play hard," he reasoned. Every month he was issued a three-day pass. It was a world away from #8 Hollow, yet seemingly very close. A bottle of beer from Rub's stash and a seven-seven drink from a Washington nightclub produced the same results. Drunkenness. Immorality. Insanity.

On some of his passes, Paul visited the capital's landmarks. When Dwight D. Eisenhower was inaugurated, Paul's unit stood guard on the side of the street as the parade marched down Pennsylvania Avenue.

He and his buddies fished in the Potomac River. To prove his manhood he ate raw clams in the half shell, which was much harder than entering the fire-drill pit. But he did it. He was young. He was crazy.

The days, weeks, and months of OJT rocketed by until it was time for a permanent assignment at a base in the United States or overseas.

More forms to fill out. More questions to answer. "Do you want an overseas appointment?" Paul checked "yes," thinking he could never be so lucky.

More days to wait. He was in the barracks when a sergeant called, "Eddie Coshane and Paul Dennis report to the orderly room."

They quickly changed into their uniforms and reported as ordered.

"Personnel is needed for crash rescue operations in Japan. Coshane, you are in line for these orders. If you don't want them, they go to Dennis. The assignment is for two years."

Japan? Two years? Eddie couldn't decide.

"Well, yes or no, Coshane?" the sergeant demanded.

Eddie hesitated.

The sergeant pulled a half-dollar from his pocket and flipped it. "You call it, Dennis."

A $2 mistake and a flip of a coin. Was chance determining Paul's destiny or was something deeper happening? He didn't even think about it. "Heads," he said.

The sergeant looked at the coin in his hand. "Get packed, Dennis. You're going to Japan."

A few years later Paul's spiritual Commander in Chief gave him those same orders.

The End of the World

Hurry up. Two weeks to process out of his assignment at Bolling, pack his bags, fly to San Francisco, and board the troop ship *General Hugh J. Gaffey* with two thousand other guys. Destination Yokohama, Japan—*the end of the world*, Paul thought.

Wait. Eleven days of gambling, smoking, fighting, ocean-viewing, hanging over the side of the ship, and swinging in his hammock. No alcohol was brought or bought on board the ship.

"Hey, guys, tomorrow we will cross the International Date Line. Be watching for it. It's the chance of a lifetime," one of Paul's buddies announced.

Another guy cocked his head and replied, "Really? What's it look like?"

The International Date Line? Paul dug around in his mind, and came up with a fact from Mrs. Cleo Brown's sixth-grade geography class. That was the year he had not missed one day of school, and he had learned a lot.

The teaser explained, "It's a big black line that extends from north to south."

Ahhh, yes, Paul grinned. The International Date Line, the imaginary line where the day changed.

Paul joined the laughter and slapped the gullible guy on the back. Teasing relieved the monotony of blue sky, blue sea, blue moods.

The ship's PA crackled. The static brought everyone to a halt. "Prepare for docking in the Yokohama Bay. Docking will be within two to three hours."

This rang bells in the guys' ears. They were ready to put their feet on terra firma.

Paul A. Dennis

After docking they loaded onto buses. Paul dropped into a window seat. The cracked yellow plastic seat felt so familiar. As he gazed out the dirty window at a new world, he was consumed by memories of home. The big yellow school bus that had carried him on his first venture into the exciting, frightening world. But this time no big brother or sister sat beside him, softening his entry into the unknown. The gruff laughter of his air force buddies faded into the voices of children headed into the first day of school. The landscape whirred and blurred until Paul saw only a gravel road and the hills of #8 Hollow.

He blinked and shook his head. Here he was in a new world, and he could only think of the old one. Home. Paul hated to admit it, but he was homesick. He wondered how long it would take his mother's letters to catch up with him.

Before they got off the bus at the Yokohama Base Port Command, the orders Paul had come to expect and rely upon were given: "Check the bulletin board in the orderly room every day. Your orders will be posted. Do not go into the city alone. Stay in groups of three or more. There are still a lot of postwar feelings here. These folks remember the atomic bombs we invested in them."

They got off the bus and were led into the billeting quarters, where they were assigned to motel-style rooms, three to four men to a room.

In the next few days before Paul's orders came through, he spent his waking hours in town, and he wasn't sightseeing. In the daytime the town was quiet and quaint. That's when the airmen caught up on their sleep.

At night the town lit up, and so did Paul and his buddies. At the door of every bar (which were plentiful), four or five girls lured the men into their enticing clutches. Music. Liquor. Sex.

The polite Japanese girls taught crash courses in immorality. The American boys paid in dollars, drinks, and drags. Paul was quickly pulled into the whirlpool. Not one hint of remorse

Order My Steps

plagued him. He was young. He was invincible. He was uninhibited.

Then came his orders. Transfer to Misawa Air Force Base, Honshu, the northern tip of the island. Paul was out of smokes and cash, hung over, and ready for a change. A paycheck awaited him at Misawa.

At Misawa while Paul waited for his barrack assignment, he strolled around the base. *Here I am at the end of the world.* A heavy emptiness sat on his belly, pushing against his lungs. *What am I doing here? What do I do next? Someone tell me.* The guy who had run from orders now depended upon them.

Misawa was a culture shock—total country. Little open street markets and muddy dirt roads. Horses pulling carts driven by elderly farmers. The base was the only spot of civilization. However, Paul's exploration of Misawa was short lived.

They called him into the orderly room and said, "You're not staying here. You have been assigned to the 4th Fighter Bomber Wing, 1100th Installation Squadron Crash Rescue Fire Department at Chitose Air Force Base on the island of Hokkaido."

Time for another geography lesson. *Mrs. Brown, where are you when I need you?*

Looking out the window of the plane, Paul muttered, "This really is the end of the world."

He soon learned that Chitose was on the southern tip of Hokkaido. The northern tip was neighbor to Russia. Winter lasted from September until April or May. Snow was measured in feet, not inches.

He processed in with his squadron and discovered that his barracks was one of the open-bay Quonset huts that squatted all over the base. In winter they were totally blanketed by snow. The older ones were heated with fuel-oil space heaters. The newer ones were heated with steam. Paul was assigned to an older hut.

He spent several months in training, learning the layout of the base and buildings. In addition, he studied Japanese signs, as the firefighters responded to off-base fires for military personnel, as well as the city of Chitose.

After training he was transferred to the crash rescue barracks where he was assigned a private room. Again as at Bolling, he worked twenty-four hours on, twenty-four hours off. Every ninety days he received a three-day pass. Paul was hooked. Fire fighting and crash rescue became his forté. He took every course possible. He was promoted to crew chief and then station captain on A shift. He also became the instructor for training Japanese firefighters.

One day Paul was told to report to his commander's office. The Red Cross had a message for him. That was not good news. His stomach churned. His lungs tightened.

At the center his commanding officer handed him an envelope. Paul's nicotine-stained fingers shook as he opened it. He read it once; then twice.

"Bad news, Paul?" the officer asked.

Paul nodded; then shook his head. "My mother is getting a divorce." Was it bad news or good news? He couldn't decide. As he stared at the yellow paper in his hand, he saw another scene.

A little boy was glued to the doorframe, eyes wide, peeking around the corner. Rub pointed a double-barrel shotgun at his mother's stomach. "I'm gonna blow you in half," he bellowed.

The little boy covered his ears; but he could not shut out Rub's voice as in his liquor-crazed rage, he called Mary every ugly word he could think of. And Rub had a vast vocabulary of ugly words.

Order My Steps

The little boy's heart stopped as his godly mother grabbed the gun. It broke in half! Not at the breakover, but right in the middle of the wooden stock.

Rub let out a string of profanity and threw the gun aside. With ugly, grasping claws, he grabbed Mary's neck.

She gasped, "Jesus!"

Rub's hands flew up and he stumbled backward, as if a bolt of electricity had shot through his body.

The little boy drew a long breath. Wow! "Jesus" must be a magic word.

Airman Paul A. Dennis stared at the paper in his hand. *I ought to kill him!*

"Paul," his CO's voice brought him back to the present. "Do you need to go home to be with your mother? I can get you an emergency leave."

I can do it. I can go home and kill him. That scum doesn't deserve to live. I can....

"Paul, are you OK?"

Paul blinked and nodded. He took a deep breath as he remembered the one time he had been under arrest in the barracks at Sampson Air Force Base. Even the satisfaction of wiping that smirk off Rub's face was not worth a lifetime in prison.

"Do you need to go home? Does your mother need you?" the officer repeated.

Paul shook his head. "No, sir. She's fine . . . but thank you, sir." The boy-turned-airman saluted and walked out of the room.

Paul remained in Chitose for the next two and one-half years and enjoyed every day of it . . . well, almost every day.

One day Paul and Red, both two sheets to the wind, were touring the town in a rickshaw operated by a man on a bicycle when Paul had a brilliant idea. "Why should we pay this guy to pull us around? Let's bail."

Red agreed. "Yeah, why should we pay him a hundred yen? How much money is that anyway?"

Paul shrugged. "'Bout thirty-six cents, but it's not the money. It's the principle. Why should we pay him when we've got two good legs?"

As they lifted the side flaps to make their escape, the driver looked over his shoulder.

They jumped. He yelled and braked. Off they raced, down the street, around a corner, then up another street with the screaming driver in pursuit. *Would that guy never give up?*

On his right Paul spotted a small building. "Let's hide in there," he puffed.

Red waved and kept running. Paul jerked open the door and stepped waist deep into the most foul-smelling liquid of all time. He had stumbled into a *benjo,* an outdoor toilet. The driver lost all interest in Paul. He ran right past him, hot on Red's trail. Later when Paul went through the main gate to the base, the MP waved him right through, not even asking to see his ID.

The culture of the Japanese in Chitose captivated Paul. Many were hunters and fishermen of Ainu decent. He called them "the Indians of Japan." Often he went to their villages for a good time.

Most of the buildings in Chitose, dubbed the VD hole of Japan, were small, dark, and dirty bars, designed to snare the Americans and their dollars. Paul was happy to accommodate the Japanese. The rate of exchange was about 360 yen per U.S. dollar. A quart of beer cost 100 yen. When off duty he and his buddies ate, drank, and lived for the day. They cared not for anything or anyone but themselves. Men of the

Order My Steps

cloth, officers, married men, all enjoyed the bar activity and the red light district.

One guy, Charlie Cherry, was very religious—no smoking, no drinking, no bar hopping, no movies. Charlie became the butt of constant jeers and jokes. Paul often joined in the prodding. "Awww, come on, Charlie, loosen up. Live a little. We're gonna have fun. Don't be such a holy Joe."

One night as Paul and his buddies were doing the bar scene, some drunks staggered down the sidewalk toward them. The custom when meeting drunks was to go straight forward (well, as straight as drunks can go) and see who left the sidewalk first—a walking game of Chicken.

As the drunks came closer, Paul's heart sank. There was Charlie as drunk as a skunk, and there was Paul feeling lower than a skunk's belly. Soon after that Charlie shipped out, but Paul never forgot him. Bringing a good man down didn't feel as good as he thought it would.

The only time Paul ever had a religious thought was when he received a letter from his mother. She always ended with, "Paul, I am praying for you every day." And Paul always ended his letters, "Keep praying, Mom." He wrote that to make his mother happy, not because he felt a need for prayer. He was happy living at the end of the world.

He was young. He was uninhibited. He was invincible.

Another Crash

November 6, 1958, a day Paul will never forget.

"Mom, I'm taking the car into town to meet some of the guys," Paul lounged against the kitchen doorframe; a cigarette dangled from his mouth. He had served his four-year stretch in the air force and opted for four years in the reserves to complete his obligation. He had been home for a year. It had not been a good year for his family. His mother did housework, took in ironing, and sold Watkins products to earn a few dollars.

When Paul was discharged, he was given twenty-eight weeks of unemployment, but not much of it went to help at home. What was Paul's was Paul's. He spent most of his money on smokes, drinks, and partying. He was the big shot returned from an exciting life on the other side of the world, and certainly everyone felt honored to have him home.

Mary looked up from the dough she was kneading. "Son, I wish you wouldn't. I don't have insurance on the car."

Paul shrugged. What could happen? He was only going into town.

Seventeen-year-old Audrey came down the stairs and put her arm around her big brother's shoulders. "Let me go too, Pauly." She gave him her you-can't-say-no-to-me grin.

Mary frowned. "Paul, I wish you wouldn't."

"Awww, Mom, you're a worry wart," Paul said. He picked up the keys and grinned at Audrey. "If you're ready, Deuce, you can go, but I'm not waiting for you to go through your glamour routine."

Soon after they arrived at the gathering place, one of Audrey's girlfriends called and asked for someone to come and get her.

"I'll go," Dean Bateson volunteered.

Order My Steps

Never one to be left behind when the wheels were rolling, Audrey left with Dean. Paul hardly noticed. He and his buddies were planning the night's activities.

The wail of sirens interrupted their planning session. "Fire truck and ambulance," someone sitting by the window announced.

The guys jumped up and ran to the door. "Police too."

Paul reached for his jacket. "Must have been a wreck up the road. Come on, let's go."

They jumped into the nearest car and raced after the emergency vehicles. About a mile out of town they came upon the scene of the accident. A car had hit the back of a coal truck that was parked with its left wheels on the road.

"Hey, that looks like Dean's car," someone yelled.

Paul's heart did a double flip. Before the car came to a full stop, he was out and running down the bank to where the EMTs were lifting a body from the ditch.

One of the EMTs yelled, "Hey, you, get back!"

Paul ignored him. As they turned the body over, he groaned. He was looking into the face of his little sister, the sister that a six-year-old Paul had vowed to protect.

"Get out of the way, Buddy," the EMT ordered.

"That's my sister and I'm staying." Paul had responded to crash scenes. He was tough. He was trained for tragedy, but nothing had prepared him for this.

He stared at Audrey's twisted face and broken body. Blood was everywhere. A bone was sticking out of her right leg. Her mouth was deformed, and her chin was out of place. She was unconscious. Her body was jerking and jumping. Three men wrestled to hold her still.

"She's choking! She's choking!" Paul yelled.

One of the EMTs reached into his kit and brought out a long silver S-curved object. He forced it down her throat. Blood gushed out. She had been drowning in her own blood.

Paul A. Dennis

As they loaded Audrey into the ambulance, Paul climbed in behind her. *Oh God, it's all my fault. If I'd listened to Mom, Audrey would be safe at home. It's all my fault.* Guilt crushed him to his knees beside the gurney as the ambulance sped to the hospital.

Paul stayed with Audrey as she was rolled into ER. White-coated nurses and doctors buzzed in and out of the cubicle. Buzzzzz . . . Paul's escape mechanism clicked in. He was a little boy again.

Anticipation tickled Paul's ribs as he followed his stepdad and uncle into the woods. Every possible inch of skin was covered. The little boy's nose was clogged by the smell of old car oil from the rags wrapped around the stick that Rub carried. The hunters were armed with an ax, a two-man crosscut saw, steel wedges, and Mary's washtub. It was honey-harvesting time.

Rub stopped and pointed, "Here's the tree."

As Rub and Uncle John cut down the tree, Paul geared up to run.

Wham! The tree hit the ground. Quickly, Rub struck a match and set the rags ablaze. No one had to tell Paul to get back. He knew it was time to move.

Rub beat out the fire and stuck the smoking rags into a hole in the tree. Angry bees swarmed from the hive. The men and little boy froze, waiting for the bees to leave or die. After a time the air cleared. Rub and Uncle John hacked away part of the tree and notched out a big hole. They reached in and pulled out their treasure, a beehive dripping with honey.

Buzzzz . . .

Paul shook his head to clear the buzzing sound. He was back in the cubicle surrounded by white-clad professionals swarming around his beautiful sister's broken body. There was no escape,

Order My Steps

no place to run. Paul sat with his head in his hands, tears seeping through his fingers. *It's my fault. Oh God, it's my fault.*

"Young man, we need you to step out," a gentle voice said. Paul stood and hesitated. The nurse turned him toward the opening.

As Paul stepped into the hall, his mother came running to meet him. She was wailing, "Oh God, don't let my baby die." Guilt strangled Paul. He could only hold his mother and cry as she travailed, "Oh God, don't let my baby die."

Minutes crawled by. Paul worried. His mother prayed. After several hours one of the doctors came into the waiting room. "Mrs. Shirkey, we have done all we can do for your daughter. It's up to a higher power whether she lives or not."

When they were finally allowed into the room, an anguished cry escaped Paul's lips. His mother, strengthened by a power Paul did not possess, put her hand on his arm and shook her head. Her look said, "No crying in here."

Day and night Audrey moaned and groaned while Mary talked to God as if He were sitting beside her. Paul, big brother, little sister's protector, shut down. Nothing could lift the rock crushing his soul.

In the following weeks, surgery followed surgery. Audrey's jaws were wired shut, bones were set, metal pins were put in and taken out.

"It will be months before she is up and around," the doctor told them. "She may never completely recover. She may be permanently disfigured and crippled."

Paul's mother listened to the doctors and talked to the Great Physician. Audrey paid the price for Paul's rebellion, and the coal company's insurance paid the medical bills. But no one could settle Paul's account with guilt. Finally, he couldn't take any more. He had to get out, away from doctors and hospitals and therapists. Away from fear and guilt and memories.

Once more he left #8 Hollow.

Running from Guilt

Next stop: Orlando, Florida.

A friend got Paul a job tending the bar at a nightclub. He also got a second job working for a building contractor as a set-up and mortar man, laying blocks and bricks.

During the next twenty months, life was one drunken weekend after another. Occasional letters from his mother told of Audrey's constant rounds of therapy. Although his mother wrote of her faith in God to heal Audrey completely, Paul lacked that faith. He determined to drown his guilt in liquor, but it kept resurfacing.

The guilt fueled anger, until one weekend somebody said something Paul didn't like. He exploded. When the fight was over, he was taken to the hospital. Again insurance paid most of the bill, but Paul did not have any spiritual insurance to cover his guilt.

When he was dismissed from the hospital, the contractor told him, "Sorry, Paul, I've got to let you go." Just like that, his best job was gone; all he had left was a weekend bartending job. He had way too much time on his hands and not enough money in his pockets.

While lounging on a borrowed bed in a friend's trailer, Paul decided to talk to his mother's God. Her relationship with God often puzzled and astounded him. Often when he acted like a jerk because he didn't have money to buy a drink or cigarettes, his mother simply whispered a prayer and sang. "Honey, do you want a cup of coffee and a piece of pie?" Her gentle spirit had calmed Paul's agitated nerves many times.

Another scene filled his memory.

Order My Steps

Pauly was again trying to make himself invisible while Rub ranted and raved. "What do you do with all the money, woman? I work hard at the mine from dawn to dark to support this family, and then you tell me there's no food in the house. What'd you do with the money?" He kicked a chair and let loose a string of profanity.

The little boy put his hand on his growling tummy and willed it to hush. He knew where the money went. Rub knew too, but he would never admit it.

Pauly leaned closer to hear his mother's quiet voice. "Rub, everything will be all right. God will take care of us."

This only infuriated Pauly's stepdad. He kicked another chair and screamed, "You think your blankety-blank God cares about us? You think you'll just walk out to the mailbox and pick up a check God has sent us? You know what I think? I think you're crazy." He stomped out to the well where he stored his stash of courage. They might not have food in the kitchen, but there was always beer in the well.

Little Pauly watched as his mother walked out the door and across the yard to the mailbox. As she came back in the front door, Rub came in the side door. They met at the kitchen table. Without a word Mary handed Rub an envelope. He opened it and pulled out a piece of paper. A strange look crossed his face.

The little boy forgot about staying invisible. He walked over to Rub and looked at the paper. It was a check for $20 from Aunt Audrey, Rub's sister, who was a Christian.

Rub pulled a note out of the envelope. He read silently. "Mary, I was praying, and God told me to send this to you. Love, Audrey." Rub dropped the note and check on the table and stumbled out the door. He needed another drink.

Paul knew his mother and God had a thing going. Something the grown-up Paul both feared and desired. So from a

Paul A. Dennis

friend's trailer in Orlando, Florida, he decided to talk to his mother's Friend. Perhaps it would calm his stretched nerves.

"God, I'm tired of living like this. I want to go home. If You'll get me home, I'll go to church with Mom and serve You."

Paul listened. No booming voice from Heaven. Not even a whisper. He growled, jumped up, and jerked on his clothes. If Mom's way wouldn't work for him, he'd try Rub's. Out the door he went; he needed a drink.

Sitting at the bar sipping his drink, Paul overheard a man at a nearby table. "I've got a long drive ahead of me. Gotta get to Columbus, Ohio."

Columbus, Ohio? Without a second thought, Paul got off the barstool and went over to the man. "Mister, I'd like to get to Ohio myself. I'd be happy to help with the gas, what little I can. Think I could ride along?"

The stranger looked Paul up and down, and asked a few questions. When Paul's answers satisfied him, he nodded. "The gas isn't a problem. You help drive and that'll pay your bill."

That night Paul left the bar, leaving behind everything—his black-and-white dinner jackets, his bow ties, work clothes, and tools. It was time to return to #8 Hollow.

Back to #8 Hollow

When Paul walked in, sans luggage, his mother smiled and hugged him. No questions asked. It was as if she knew he was coming.

He got a job working for the county, repairing roads. With his first paycheck in his pocket, he promptly forgot his promise to God and headed to his favorite bar. *Okay, I'm back on my own turf. I know my way around. Now I can handle things.*

Audrey was back to normal so Paul could look at her without feeling guilty.

One shock awaited him, though. Donald and his wife had been transformed. His big brother, his partying buddy, his emergency banker, was a changed man.

"Sorry, Paul, but no smoking in our house. Not on the porch either," Donald laid down the new rules. "And watch your mouth. I don't want my children exposed to that kind of talk. Sit down here and have a cup of coffee. I want to tell you what God has done for me. You won't believe it."

Paul sat down and sipped his coffee as Donald tried to convert him. Don's voice faded as Paul's mind slipped into reverse and his memory film rolled.

A young teenage boy was standing in the kitchen doorway watching, listening, and learning things he had no business knowing. His big brother hero Don had recently come home from Korea, where he had won some acclaim as an ambidextrous Golden Gloves boxer.

As the beer flowed down their gullets, the discussion between Don, Rub, and Rub's brother John caught fire. Soon Rub and Don were going at it with their fists. John, a peace-loving man, grabbed Don to break up the fight, and at the same time Rub punched Don in the face. Don, fueled by anger, pushed John off and pushed Rub to the floor. He climbed on top of his stepdad and began hitting him in the face with his fist. With each blow, he yelled, "This one is for Mom. This one is for Paul. This one is for me."

The teenager watched in awe. This was his protector, his big brother.

Don's voice jerked Paul back to the present. He stared at his Golden Glove boxer brother who was talking about love, the love of God. What had happened to his brother? Were his mother's prayers this powerful?

With determination Paul tuned out Don's words, but it was impossible for him to ignore Don's actions. Don had even taken back the tools he had stolen from his employer years ago. *That's crazy,* Paul thought. *Why in the world would he give up those tools? He's had them for years. His boss didn't even know they were missing.*

Donald's wife, Mary, was different too.

Paul's family ganged up on him. Every time he turned around, someone invited him to church. Didn't they know he was trying to forget that silly promise he had made to God in Florida?

One day his mother said, "Paul, the church is having an auction over at Chant Dunlap's farm. It'll be lots of fun. Come and go with me."

Paul hesitated. He was all for a day of fun, but he wasn't sure he could stomach a day with "the saints."

"Please?" Then his mother threw out the bait. "One of the girls wants to meet you. She wants to touch your hair. She said it has always looked like a brush to her."

Order My Steps

What? A girl wanted to touch his hair? That was ridiculous, just ridiculous enough to catch Paul's interest. He had been to church with his mother a few times, but none of the girls had caught his eye, mainly because he knew they would not have anything to do with a guy like him.

"Who?" Paul asked.

"Shirley Ann. She's the piano player. Remember the Mellingers?"

Paul nodded. "Kinda."

"You probably didn't see them many times. They lived about thirty miles from the church and only came on Sunday mornings, and you weren't there many Sundays."

"I think I remember Shirley being prissy, too prissy for me."

Mary smiled, "Shirley is a beautiful young lady, and she wants to meet you."

So Paul was hooked. He played horseshoes with Donald and baseball with the guys. The ladies served hot dogs, soft drinks, and other goodies. Laughter rang out. Appetizing aromas swirled. Children ran wild.

Mary called, "Son, come over here, please. I want you to meet someone."

Paul approached his mother and the smiling young lady beside her. "Shirley, this is my son Paul," Mary said proudly. "Paul, this is Shirley Mellinger."

At that point Paul lost his voice and his manners and placed his heart in jeopardy. Did she touch his hair? No one remembers. But Paul did agree with his mother. Shirley Ann was one pretty gal.

When everyone gathered for the auction, Paul was intrigued by the evangelist George Christoff. "Where's that guy from?" Paul asked Donald. "He's got the jolliest laugh, and he talks like a foreigner."

"Bulgaria," Donald replied. "You should hear him preach. Man, he sets the place on fire."

Paul A. Dennis

Paul's interest in the evangelist cooled somewhat . . . until the bidding started. The evangelist bid on a jar of peaches, then some guy offered a counter bid. The preacher bid again. Another counter offer. This went on for some time.

Crazy, Paul thought. *Doesn't that preacher know that jar of peaches is not worth that much money? He's being taken for a ride.*

Then suddenly George stopped bidding, and the teaser was left with a high-priced jar of peaches. Paul was impressed. *Not so dumb after all. That other guy got just what he deserved.*

It was an enlightening experience for Paul as he watched the church folks play, laugh, and joke. Not one person got mad. Not one fight broke out. Amazing.

Section II
The New Paul

Pastor and Mrs. Ernest Howell

Shirley's graduation

Shirley with her dad and mom

Shirley the bride

Howell, Don, Paul, Shirley, and Sharon

Almajean and Clifford Bryan

Paul's mentors, Fred and Vera Kinzie

Paul, Shirley, and Paula— new pastors at Antioch Apostolic Church

"This Is Your Life" birthday party at Antioch Apostolic Church

A New Road

Burley Run Inn Bar and Dance Hall. The paint was peeling on the weather-beaten sign. But Paul didn't need a sign to know where he was. He had spent numerous Friday nights, Saturday nights, and Sunday nights inside the bar's dark belly.

He parked and cut the motor. Looking around the parking lot, he did not see his cousin Tommy's car. *He said he'd meet me here. Maybe he caught a ride with someone else.*

As Paul started toward the building, an image filled his memory: church folks laughing, playing, and joking. He shrugged, trying to rid his shoulders of an invisible weight. *Those church people are OK, but they're not my kind. They make me feel . . .* he searched for the right word . . . *uncomfortable. Yeah, that's the word. Something about them makes me feel twisted and uptight. Burley Run Inn is my kind of place. A night of dancing and drinking and I'll feel like myself again. I fit here.* His mind hit a speed bump. *Do I want to fit here?*

As he walked in the door, a blast of country music assaulted his ears. He plowed through a nicotine haze to the dance floor. Suddenly his ears buzzed and the room whirled. He leaned against the doorframe and shut his eyes.

What's happening to me? He blinked, trying to clear his vision. Peering through the blue smoke, he saw a bunch of rats running in a circle. Rats on the dance floor? He froze. He blinked. He stared. Yes, rats! They were multiplying! Where were all these rats coming from?

Am I losing my mind? I haven't even had a drink yet. What's going on?

Gasping, he rushed past the bar and out the door. He gulped fresh air into his lungs. Once. Twice. His head cleared. His senses sharpened. His pulse slowed. Crickets chirped. A breeze whispered. The moon beamed. *No rats out here,* he thought. *Unless you count me.*

Feeling emotionally twisted, Paul climbed into the car and drove home. When he walked in, Mary looked up. It was Friday night and her son was home. But she asked no questions. She could have answered his, but he didn't ask.

"I think I'll turn in early tonight, Mom," Paul said. "I've been working pretty hard."

As he started for the stairs, his mother said, "Paul, Brother Christoff is going to be preaching Sunday night. I sure would like for you to go with me to hear him."

Paul's hand clenched into a fist. He remembered the accent, the laughter, the teasing. There was something about that preacher. "I'll think about it, Mom," he promised as he dragged his heavy soul up the stairs.

Pushing through the curtain covering the doorway of his room, Paul sat down on the edge of the bed and buried his face in his hands. *Rats? What is happening to me?* He groaned, fell back on the bed, and stared at the ceiling.

A gentle summer breeze ruffled the curtain on the open bedroom window. Paul shivered. He breathed deeply, trying to compose himself. Gradually, the rats on his mind's monitor faded and were replaced by a scene from another summer.

The church windows were open to let the breeze in and the singing out. People were dancing, not on a ballroom floor, but in the church aisles. He was across the street sitting on the ground with his buddies. How old was he? Eight or nine? Probably. It was the year they had moved to town because of Rub's new job. It was the only year he had not attended McLuney School.

Order My Steps

Throughout the congregation funeral-home fans with tongue-depressor handles swished back and forth like fly swatters in the hands of three-year-olds.

Paul and his buddies didn't have money for a movie, but they didn't mind. Who needed a movie? They were having a great time watching the show taking place inside the church. People sang, shouted, and jumped. Women danced as bobby pins flew through the air, releasing strands of long hair. The preacher threatened and promised and wept. Then everyone gathered around the front—more shouting, praying, running, dancing. Paul and his buddies had no idea what it was all about, but it certainly was entertaining.

Then Mary started attending that Holy Roller church and that put a stop to Paul's summertime pastime. His days of sitting outside making fun were over. He didn't understand it all, but he wasn't going to mock his mother. After all, a guy had to have some loyalty.

The first time he went to church with his mother on a Sunday night, he scrunched down as far as he could in the pew. He knew the guys were in their grandstand seats across the street.

Mary never forced him to go to church at night, but on Sunday mornings she applied more pressure. Paul was surprised to discover some of his cousins in his class. But Paul's church attendance was sporadic, even at its best.

The bedsprings screeched as grown-up Paul turned over. He sighed. Now his mother was again, oh so sweetly, pressuring him to go to church. Well, he hadn't said he would go, only that he would think about it.

So he thought about it. In fact, that's all he thought about for the next two days. What was the magnetism that drew him to that preacher and those folks? He didn't understand it when he was a little boy, and he still didn't understand it.

Paul A. Dennis

Sunday evening as they drove into the parking lot, Paul switched his cigarettes from his shirt pocket to his trousers. No sense advertising his sin.

As they walked down the aisle, Mary stopped again and again, proudly introducing him to her friends. Smiles and firm handshakes greeted him. The nicer the people were, the more Paul sweated. *What have I gotten myself into?* He could walk into an inferno without fear, but walking down the aisle of that church was stretching every nerve in his body.

With her son breathing down her neck, Mary moved closer and closer to the front. Paul looked over his shoulder, judging the distance to the exit. Finally she stopped—third row from the front right side. It could be worse. Quickly Paul took a seat on the end, in case he needed to get out of there.

Some people were talking. Others were praying. Pastor Ernest Howell stepped to the pulpit and rang a little bell. A hush filled the sanctuary as everyone found a seat.

The pastor welcomed them and then asked, "Does anyone have a prayer request?"

Paul cringed and sent a silent message to Mary, hoping that ESP from the womb still worked. *Mom, don't you dare request prayer for me!* She didn't. But Paul knew that she had many, many times before when he was in New York, Washington, Japan, Florida, and even the Burly Run Inn. He didn't want to think about what might have happened had she not prayed for him. He shoved that thought back into a crevice of his brain.

A big masculine guy stepped to the pulpit to lead songs. When he opened his mouth, the windows rattled. Paul raised his eyebrows. *Man, that song leader is no wimp!*

Paul knew some of the hymns and some he didn't. The music transported him back to that summer when his mother had done a U-turn. He remembered overhearing her telling Rub that she had received the baptism of the Holy Ghost. Rub

Order My Steps

hadn't been impressed, but Paul had. His mother was a good woman, but after that night she was even "good-er."

The song leader was puffing and wiping sweat, but he kept booming out the songs. Paul twisted and fretted. *That guy needs to shut up before he has a stroke.*

Finally, the song service ended; another man went to the pulpit and *what*? Another chorus? *Boy, these people love to sing.* That song didn't last long, though, because this guy needed money to cover the evangelist's expenses. Paul let loose of a dollar.

Then, lo and behold, the pastor announced a couple of special songs. More music, hand clapping, and shouting.

Finally, the singing stopped, and the pastor introduced the evangelist. Paul leaned forward, intent on hearing that fascinating accent again.

"Before I preach, I want to sing," Brother Christoff said.

Another song?

As the preacher with his Bulgarian twang sang, "I'm in love with Jesus," every word impacted Paul's crusty heart.

Then he preached. Paul listened to the ebb and flow of his accent, but paid little attention to the message. That is, until that gutsy guy came to the edge of the platform and pointed his finger straight at Paul. Their eyes connected. "You cigarette sucker, booze drinker, woman chaser, and fornicator, if you don't change your ways, you're going to end up in the pit of Hell."

Paul's blood pressure rose several points. He glared at the preacher and then at his mother. She had set him up and told that preacher everything he had ever done.

I don't have to sit here and take that! I've got to get out of here; get a smoke to cool down. He started to get up, but something glued him to the seat. Maybe it was the preacher's eyes or his words.

Paul A. Dennis

Finally, when Brother Christoff asked everyone to stand, Paul jumped up. It was time to make his escape. As he turned toward the door, someone or something grabbed his shoulders and twisted him back around, toward the altar.

He protested, *I'm not going to cry and go through that Jesus-Jesus-thing*. But as soon as his knees hit the floor, the shell fell off his heart. Tears of repentance flowed down his cheeks, washing away bitterness and pouring a healing balm over his sin-weary soul.

That experience so rearranged his brain that Paul did not know himself.

Monday morning when he awoke, he had that "something is different" feeling. He ran his tongue over his teeth and lips. What was different? Then he realized that the nasty aftertaste of nicotine was gone and so was the craving for a cigarette. The fog had lifted from his brain. The pollution had been washed from his lungs. He sprang out of bed and pulled on his clothes. He had a job to do.

Down the stairs he plunged and without even saying good morning to his mother, he picked up his long-time friend Zippo and left the house. Standing at the edge of the yard, he drew back his arm. With all the strength he could muster, he sent Zippo flying through the air. It landed somewhere in the brambles and briers.

Paul dusted his hands and walked back into the house. Now to find his cigarettes and burn them. He searched the living room, but no cigarettes. Hmmm, that was strange. He was sure he had left them on the end table.

He was staring at the index and middle fingers on his hands when Mary walked into the room. "Don't worry about your cigarettes, Paul. I took care of them for you."

Order My Steps

The old Paul would have been furious. The new Paul grinned. "Thanks, Mom." Then he held up his hands. "Look."

Mary stared at his hands in bewilderment. "What?"

"My hands! Look at my fingers!"

She looked closer. "What's wrong?"

"Nothing's wrong. Everything's right. Even the nicotine stain on my fingers is gone."

Mary took his hands in hers. Her tears splashed on them. "Oh, Pauly, it's a miracle. Not only has God cleaned you up inside, He has even washed the stain of sin from your fingers. They are as clean as a baby's."

"I'm free, Mom. Can you believe I'm free?" He chortled with glee, as he grabbed his mother and swung her around and around.

The next week the revival continued. Paul was there every night, waiting impatiently for the preaching to end so he could seek the baptism of the Holy Ghost. Repentance had emptied him, now he hungered to be filled.

The next Sunday night, he told Don, "If I could be baptized, I would receive the Holy Ghost."

Don went straight to the pastor. Soon, chairs, music stands, and other items were moved to the sides of the platform. The platform carpet was rolled up toward the pulpit. Paul watched in amazement as a trap door was lifted to reveal a tank of water.

Paul was led into another room and handed a change of clothes. Then he went down in that bone-chilling, teeth-chattering water in the name of the Lord Jesus for the remission of his sins. He came up warm and speaking in a heavenly language as the Spirit of God filled his empty soul.

On June 12, 1960, Paul A. Dennis turned around and started to walk a new road, a road that would lead him to worlds far away from #8 Hollow.

Romance

Paul's conversion was exactly that—a conversion. The girl he had been dating dropped out of the picture. The bars, the dance halls, and the movies no longer attracted him. Cigarettes, beer, and liquor repulsed him. His new life consisted of work and church. He sang. He laughed. He teased. Now he understood the camaraderie that he had felt at the auction. He was smack dab in the middle of it.

In church one evening he managed to sit where he could see the pianist, Shirley Mellinger. She wasn't a bit hard to look at. In fact, she was easy on the eyes. So he fastened his eyes on her, knowing that eventually she would look his way. When she did, he winked. She blushed and smiled and kept playing. Paul grinned as the song leader stumbled, trying to keep up with the increased tempo.

He left the service that night encouraged. He might have a chance with Shirley Ann after all. They certainly had lived different lifestyles, but now that Paul's steps were ordered by the Lord, who knew what would happen? He could dream.

On Pentecost Sunday one of the young men approached Paul. "Do you want to go with us to a special service this afternoon at Brother Rose's church in Jewett?"

"Sure, but I don't have a way," Paul answered.

"Shirley Ann is going and you can ride with her."

Paul had no problem with that. He grinned. "All things work together for good." Even not having a car was good, in this case.

Another Sunday Don and Mary invited some young people to their house for dinner. "You can ride with Shirley," Don teased.

Order My Steps

As they got in the car, Paul could hardly tear his eyes off the driver. She looked every inch a Pentecostal lady—long white gloves, a picture-frame hat, and spike heels.

When they stopped at a traffic light on the edge of town, Don pulled up beside them. He called out the open window. "Wanna drag?"

Paul's mouth fell open as Shirley jerked off the gloves and tossed them into the back seat; then she pulled off the hat and with a flip of her wrist sent it sailing after the gloves. She slammed the clutch to the floorboard, pulled the gearshift into low, gripped the steering wheel, gunned the engine, and sang out, "Let's go!"

Paul braced his hands on the dash and prayed. "Dear Lord, my life is in the hands of a hot rodder!" He was learning a lot about a lady called Shirley Ann Mellinger.

Another Sunday Paul and Shirley were again invited to dinner at Don and Mary's. Since Shirley's mother, Ann, had the car, Shirley needed a ride too. Don said they could ride with him and his family. As they piled into the car, someone said, "Oops! Overload here."

"No problem. Shirley can sit on my lap," Paul volunteered.

Shirley raised her eyebrows and bit her lip; she glanced around to be sure Pastor Howell was not watching. Then grinning she climbed in.

Dating rules at Crooksville Apostolic Gospel Church were strict. Dating couples did not spend time alone. Mainly they saw each other at church. This added a definite flair to the services—winks under the guise of prayer, come-hither glances during the sermons, promising smiles over the heads of weeping seekers at the altar. They could pair off when they were with groups and were allowed to double date. A sterling rule was "no kissing until you are engaged."

Many nights after church Shirley drove Paul home. They sat in the dark car in front of his house and talked and talked, held hands and talked, and shared a kiss or two. Pastor Howell wasn't watching, but God was, so the kisses were short and sweet.

Reviewing the past, Paul realized that not only had the devil drained his soul, he had picked his pockets. As he deepened his walk with the Lord, he paid tithes and gave offerings; and the windows of Heaven opened. His mother got a new job and a car, which she let him drive to work and when they went to church. She even let him borrow the car to go to Zanesville to see Shirley, who lived in an apartment. Now he felt like a young man courting, rather than a young man being courted. Strange what a set of wheels did for his masculine ego.

One day when Paul stepped into Shirley's apartment, a tantalizing aroma greeted him. "Yummm. Smells good in here."

Shirley grinned, "Ready-to-bake chocolate-chip cookies."

Ready-to-bake or made-from-scratch, it smelled like love to Paul. "My favorite," he said. Anything Shirley baked was his favorite.

Shirley was not a cook, but she was a pro at decorating. Her little apartment looked like a *Home and Garden* centerfold.

Love was blossoming. Kisses were increasing, and a proposal was looming. Paul was in love and he was worried. How could he show Shirley the respect she deserved?

One evening he sat down on the tattered living room couch and cleared his throat. His mother's eyebrows raised a question mark.

"Mom, how should I act when I'm with Shirley?"

Mary looked into her son's serious eyes. "She is a lady, Paul. Just treat her like you have the other girls you have dated."

A loud bong resonated in Paul's brain. He flinched. His head hurt, and his heart sank. No way would he treat Shirley like he had treated the other girls he had dated. He hoped his mother never found out some things.

Order My Steps

As the weeks and months flew by, it became general knowledge that Paul Dennis and Shirley Mellinger were "going steady."

In August they went to the church's summer picnic. Late that afternoon, Shirley said, "I've got to go, Paul. I'm going to drive Mom, Sharon, and Becky back to Cumberland so I can keep the car this week."

"But it will be awfully late by the time you get back to Zanesville," Paul protested. Then he snapped his fingers. "I know what. I'll go with you for protection, of course."

"But how will you get home from Zanesville?" Shirley asked.

"I'll just hitchhike," he said.

Shirley flashed her sparkling smile. "It would be nice to have company. You can keep me awake."

So they loaded into the car. Ann drove and Sharon, Shirley's middle sister, rode in the front. Shirley's little sister, Becky, tumbled into the back seat with Paul and Shirley. Exhausted from playing, she pulled her feet under her and put her head in Shirley's lap. She was asleep almost before they left the Crooksville city limits, which was about as far as a hyper flea could jump.

Later that night as they drove back to Zanesville, Paul watched Shirley's profile by the light from the dash.

"It feels so good to be together like this," she cooed.

Paul gathered his courage. Now was as good a time as any. "It could be like this forever." He scooted closer to the driver. "Will you be my wife?"

Shirley gripped the steering wheel and stared straight ahead. "Why would you want to marry me?"

Paul got the hint. He cleared his throat. It took a few minutes for the words to form; then he made a lifetime declaration, "I love you."

Paul A. Dennis

Shirley's grip on the steering wheel relaxed. She smiled and sighed.

Then she bit her lip. "Billie Sue, Linda, and I are planning to go to the UPC general conference next month in Texas," she explained. "I'll give you your answer when I get back."

That was not the answer Paul wanted. "If you go to Texas, I will not be here waiting for you when you get home." He was not playing games.

Shirley got the message. "Yes. I will be your wife, and, Paul, I love you too!"

Her promise was sealed with a kiss. Shirley did not go to Texas.

As soon as possible Paul made a trip to the Mellinger home in Cumberland. Since Shirley's dad, Dutch, had died when she was nineteen, Paul asked Shirley's mother for permission to marry her daughter. Without hesitation Ann gave them her blessing.

Next stop was the church to tell the pastor about their engagement, but he was out of the state. So they told the assistant pastor, Chant Dunlap. Immediately, he placed a call to the pastor.

When Pastor Howell heard the news, he growled, "Does that boy have a job?"

"Yes, that boy has a job at the pottery plant."

Wedding plans went forward. The date was set—October 15, 1960.

"How much do weddings cost?" Paul asked.

Shirley hedged. "Well, that depends."

"Do you want a big wedding?" Paul desperately hoped that she did not.

"It would be nice," she hesitated, "but it would also be foolish when we need so many things."

"Like a car," Paul said.

"And furniture," Shirley added.

Order My Steps

When Shirley's mother heard they were planning to be married at the pastor's house, she suggested her home where Shirley had grown up. Change of plans: the new location, Cumberland.

They traveled to the Muskingum courthouse and applied for their marriage license. "You need to have blood tests," the court clerk told them.

More money that Paul did not have. Shirley opened her purse and handed him a few dollars. "I'll pay you back," Paul promised.

Shirley's brown eyes twinkled. "I know you will."

A friend of a friend volunteered to make Shirley's dress, if she would pay for the material. Things were falling in place. The bride had a wedding gown and stairs to walk down.

Invitations were sent to everyone in the church. Plans were made and revised and tossed out and revised.

As the wheels of activity buzzed, the sound of wedding bells drew nearer. Hurry up. Slow down. The calendar's feet dragged, and the clock's hands flew.

Then it was October 15.

Billie Sue Clark's fingers flew over the piano ivories, and wedding music floated through the Mellinger home. Paul, his best man Don, and Pastor Howell stood at the foot of the stairs. Sharon, Shirley's sister, dressed in a lavender party dress, waltzed down to meet them.

A moment's hush. Then Billie Sue struck B-flat octaves with lots of oomph. Paul's brain was numb, his lungs paralyzed. Looking up, he saw standing at the head of the stairs his beautiful, beaming bride on the arm of her uncle Elmer. With "The Bridal March" vibrating through every fiber of his being, Paul had eyes only for Shirley as she descended step by step until she reached his side.

The next few minutes seemed frozen. He felt as if he and his bride were draped in a cloud of glory. He emerged from the fog when Pastor Howell announced, "Ladies and gentlemen, I give you Mr. and Mrs. Paul A. Dennis."

Congratulations. Hugs and kisses. Laughter. Pictures. Gifts. Punch. Wedding cake.

Eventually Shirley went upstairs to change into her traveling suit. When she came down, she stood on the front porch and threw her bouquet toward a huddle of single girls. Paul tapped his foot. He bit his lips. He took deep breaths. *Will we ever get away from here? Oh, no! I almost forgot Pastor Howell.*

He needed to pay the minister. Where was Brother Howell anyway? He found him deep in conversation with some of the saints.

"Pastor Howell, could I speak to you for a minute, please?" Paul asked.

The pastor looked up. "Sure, Paul. Excuse me, please. I'll be right back." He led the way to a private corner.

"How much do I owe you, Brother Howell?" the nervous groom asked.

The pastor grinned, "Just pay me what she's worth."

Paul gulped as he thought about his priceless bride and the honeymoon dollars in his wallet. "I couldn't—"

Pastor Howell chuckled. "It's taken care of, Paul. God bless you and your lovely bride. See you when you get back from your honeymoon."

A few minutes later the groom and his bride were seated in his mother-in-law's car. Once again Paul was leaving; this time he would not be gone long, and he was not alone. He started the car, and Mr. and Mrs. Paul A. Dennis commenced their journey as best friends and the love of a lifetime—"I do" united an ideal couple.

Honeymoon

Bang-bang! Click-clang. Ann's car rattled down the street. People smiled, cheered, and waved. Tin cans, streamers, and shaving cream adorned the 1960 white Falcon.

Shirley, radiant in her lavender suit and prissy hat, snuggled close to the driver's side. With his free hand Paul grasped hers and beamed at the platinum band with small diamond chips glistening on her finger. As he drove the borrowed car around one curve after another, he clicked his wedding ring against the steering wheel. Click. Click. Click. He loved the sound. He was rich. Shirley Ann Dennis belonged to him.

About a mile out of town, he pulled onto the shoulder of the highway. Still dressed in his wedding suit, he restored the car to normal—ripping streamers, removing tin cans, and wiping off shaving cream. Their lives were anything but normal, but no need to announce that to the whole world. Privacy, please. Thank you.

He climbed back into the car, gazed at himself reflected on a background of stars in his wife's eyes, and gave her a slow, tantalizing kiss. God smiled, and Pastor Howell would have too, had he seen it. Finally, kisses were legal and unlimited.

After a bit the Falcon turned north. Detroit, Michigan, be forewarned, Mr. and Mrs. Paul A. Dennis are headed your way.

Supper time. Columbus city limits. Paul was starving; Shirley wasn't. They choose a new Howard Johnson's restaurant.

"No hamburgers and french fries this time," Paul said magnanimously as he picked up the menu. "Order anything you want."

Paul A. Dennis

Shirley scanned the plastic-covered pages. Her mental calculator whirred. "I think I'll take ham," she said sweetly. It was the cheapest dinner on the menu.

"Are you sure that's what you want?" her husband asked. The wallet he was sitting on wasn't plush, but whatever Shirley wanted, Shirley could have.

She shook her head. "Ham sounds really good. I haven't had a good ham dinner in a long time."

So ham it was for their wedding supper.

Back on the road, Paul watched the billboards, searching for the perfect motel. He was in a hurry to stop. Shirley was and she wasn't. Two hundred miles from home, they entered Upper Sandusky. A huge neon cowboy boot captured their attention: Boots Motel.

"Their vacancy sign is blinking," Paul said.

Shirley surveyed the surroundings. "Looks clean," she said, giving her approval.

The next morning Paul walked into the office to check out. The owner grinned, "You folks newly wed?"

Paul blushed and nodded. "How'd you know?"

She grinned and pointed out the window. Hanging behind the front bumper were white and purple streamers, celebration remnants that Paul had overlooked.

"Congratulations." She shook his hand. No discount for newlyweds, but lots of good wishes.

Mr. and Mrs. Dennis were on the road again. It was their first full day of married life, the beginning of their story together, one that would fill a book with miles and memories.

Motels were a luxury, so they planned to spend the rest of their honeymoon with Aunt Audrey, Rub's sister, his opposite. She was a member of the Apostolic Church pastored by Charles C. Kirby. The young couple whose lives revolved around God and His church were excited about visiting one of the largest United Pentecostal Churches of the day.

Order My Steps

Sunday morning sitting with Aunt Audrey, they were surprised when Pastor Kirby announced, "I want to welcome Brother and Sister Paul Dennis. They are on their honeymoon. We need more dedicated couples like them."

Paul and Shirley blushed as the congregation applauded. Going to church on Sunday on their honeymoon had not seemed unusual to them. Going to church on Sunday, honeymoon or whatever, was what they did. Faithfulness to God's house was as much a part of them as the cells that floated in their bloodstreams.

"Let's go sightseeing tomorrow," Audrey's son Bob said.

"Great idea," his wife, Dolly, agreed. "The president is going to be in town. Maybe we can see him."

"Oh, let's!" Shirley hooked her arm through Paul's.

"Sure. Sounds like fun," Paul said. "I have seen President Eisenhower before."

"Really? When?" Shirley's eyes were glued on her bigger-than-life husband.

"When I was stationed at Bolling Air Force Base in Washington, D.C., my unit did crowd control during the inauguration."

"Maybe the president will recognize you," teased Shirley.

The president did not see them, but they saw him, and that was enough to make a Kodak moment for their life's journal. They had a marvelous time exploring Detroit with veteran Detroiters Bob and Dolly.

The honeymoon was wrapping up. Jobs were waiting. Goodbyes were said, and the young couple headed to the nearest service station to check the oil and tires and fill the gas tank.

The miles flew by as they relived the past week and planned the future. As the last rays of the sun retired, Shirley yawned. "We'd better find a motel," Paul said.

"Hmmm. How much money do we have?" Shirley wondered aloud.

Paul A. Dennis

Paul twisted until he could reach his wallet. He handed it to her. She counted. "Thirteen dollars."

Paul looked at the gas gauge. "We have to have gas."

Shirley put her head on Paul's shoulder. "Then we better forget the motel."

So Shirley's knight in shining armor drove on through the dark night with his bride sleeping soundly at his side.

"Honey, wake up! Shirley? Mrs. Dennis, open your eyes. We're home."

"Huh? What?" Shirley stretched and yawned. The streetlight haloed 521 Woodlawn Avenue.

Paul walked around the car and opened the passenger door. He picked up his bride, all ninety-four pounds of her, and carried her over the threshold of the apartment where Shirley Mellinger had formerly lived alone.

Welcome home, Mr. and Mrs. Paul A. Dennis.

Homes Sweet Homes (Mostly)

Four large, white columns graced the front porch of 521 Woodlawn Avenue, a southern plantation style, two-story red brick building. Stairs bookmarked the house into four furnished apartments. If one listened closely, whispers filled the halls as history haunted this former Underground Railroad station. But the newlyweds were too engrossed in each other to listen to the past.

Monday morning the alarm clock shocked Shirley back to the real work world. Paul turned over and covered his head with a pillow.

"Up and at 'em, Mr. Dennis," Shirley prodded as she rolled out of bed. She had to be at work by 9:00. Paul could sleep in because he worked the second shift—4:00 PM until midnight.

But Shirley vetoed her husband lying in bed while she toiled. "Come on, Paul. Get up. If you're going to get your things from your mother's, you need to get started."

So Paul made a trip to #8 Hollow and brought back his clothes and personal items. The country boy was morphing into a city guy.

The middle of that week the assembly line at the pottery plant broke down. The machinist told the workers, "It will be hours before we can get this problem fixed; it may even be tomorrow."

Paul was not at all dismayed by the news. He thought, *There's nothing to do here. I'll go home and be with my wife. She'll be thrilled to have an evening with me.*

All the way home he envisioned Shirley's surprised and delighted expression when he walked in.

Quietly, he opened the door and stood waiting for her to notice him. She was sitting on the couch reading. When she looked up, she gasped in fright. Then the frightened expression evaporated and her eyebrows formed a question mark. She met his grin with a frown. "What are you doing home?"

Paul A. Dennis

He plopped down on the couch beside her and put his arm around her shoulders, pulling her close. "Assembly line is down. They can't get the products to my area for inspection, so I came home to be with my sweetheart."

Shirley moved away. "Why didn't you stay there anyway so you could get paid? You know we need the money."

Paul wilted, his passion cooled. But he wasn't going to let her know that. He answered smugly, "Well it's too late now. I'm home."

That evening at home did not go exactly as Paul had planned. So much for surprising his bride. Apparently, paying the bills was more important to her than an evening with her lover.

Friday was payday, so Saturday morning the newlyweds with grocery list in hand drove to the Big Bear Supermarket. The man of the house pushed the cart, as the lady of the house filled it.

"Oooh, this looks so good, PD," Shirley held up a box with an eye-grabbing label.

"Looks good to me too," Paul said. "Do you want it?"

"Well, I've never cooked it, but it looks like it would be easy to fix and delicious. But it's not on our list."

"Ahhh, who cares? Go ahead and get it," the big-hearted husband said.

Up and down the aisles they wandered, paying more attention to each other than to the cart or the list.

"Oh, we've got to have this," Shirley said, as she picked up a cake mix. "My mother uses this to make the best cake in the world. You'll love it."

Paul gazed into the eyes of the best girl in the world and nodded. If Shirley wanted it, Shirley should have it.

This went on until they neared the last aisle. "There's just two more things left on my . . . Oh, my," Shirley pointed at the overflowing cart. "Look at all we've bought, PD. We'd better stop."

Suddenly Paul realized how heavy the cart was. He nodded and headed for the checkout counter.

Order My Steps

The checker pulled out item after item, announcing each price as he rang it up. In those pre-computerized days, there was no running total to warn the customer when to yell "stop!"

When the checker announced their total, Shirley gasped and her face turned bright pink. She turned to her provider. "Paul, I need a few more dollars, please."

The color drained from Paul's face. He knew and she knew that he didn't have any extra money. Slowly he pulled out his wallet, trying to appear calm and cool, while sweat rolled down his spine. What in the world was he going to do? They would have to take something back, and that would be so humiliating. Why did this have to happen on their first shopping trip as husband and wife? The clerk and everyone behind them would know that they had overspent.

Stalling for time, he opened his wallet. Then he blinked. Their tithe envelope stared up at him; it was filled out and ready to drop in the offering basket the next day. What an answer to prayer. Or was it? He didn't take time to ponder that question. Without showing the envelope, he opened it and pulled out the needed dollars.

Shirley's eyes asked one question. He whispered for her ears only, "It's all right, honey. We'll put it back next week."

She smiled and took the money. They paid for their needs and their wants, and loaded them into the car.

The next day they felt like bandits as they walked past the bulletin board in the church. There, listed for the whole world to see, was the name of every church member. Those who paid their tithes got a checkmark; the names of those who did not were followed by a blank space. Brother and Sister Paul A. Dennis knew that the first 10 percent belonged to God. Will a man rob God? Sometimes.

It took Paul and Shirley two months to pay back that week's tithes. Never again did they use God's money for their wants or their needs. And from that time on, they were extremely selective about what they put in their shopping cart. One lesson well learned early on.

Paul A. Dennis

Their landlady, Mary Jennings, lived in a first-floor apartment when she was not traveling. When she was out of town, Shirley collected the rent, made bank deposits, and paid the bills for her.

One day Mrs. Jennings approached the young couple. "I am going to sell this building," she said. "I want to give you the first chance to buy it."

They stared at her as she added, "I am only asking $20,000."

Twenty thousand dollars? Even if she had said $200, they would have had to turn down the offer. They had gone into debt to buy their first car. Shirley grossed $53 a week working at the Mosaic Tile Company, where she was one of the top-paid secretaries in the city. Paul grossed $48 a week as a pottery inspector at Watts Pottery. Twenty thousand dollars sounded like an impossible amount. The long-term advantages of owning one of the city's historic sites didn't even enter their minds.

So they started their first search for a place to live. Little did they know this was just the prelude to a lifetime of searching, packing, moving, and unpacking.

One day Mary called. "Paul, I just got a job at the New Lexington Children's Home. Room and board comes with the job. If you and Shirley want to move out to the home place, you can have it rent free. All you have to do is keep the yard mowed."

To Paul it sounded like the perfect solution, especially since it was winter. "We won't even have to buy furniture. Mom's leaving hers." He scribbled some figures on a piece of scrap paper and showed them to his wife. "Look at all the money we can save if we don't have to pay rent."

But all Shirley could see was the path from the kitchen to the outhouse and the pump outside the kitchen door. No inside plumbing. No hot water. A tin bathtub. The figures on Paul's paper didn't glitter to her like they did to him.

But she was young and she was in love. So whatever made her husband happy made her happy . . . she hoped.

Order My Steps

Totally unaware of the sacrifice he was asking his little china doll to make, Paul whistled as he loaded the car with their clothes and household items and made several trips down #8 Hollow's gravel road. Familiarity and dollar signs blinded him to the discomforts of the old home place.

"A few months in the country," he told Shirley, "and we'll be able to make a down payment on a house of our own."

Winter in Ohio. A house in the country. A twenty-mile commute twice a day. No modern conveniences. A lack of things. But an abundance of love. They survived, even thrived.

Shirley shivered as she tore March from the calendar. A picture of spring brightened the kitchen wall. A big pot of bathwater boiled on the stove. Paul seated at the table looked up. Shirley had dark circles under her eyes.

"Are you tired, Charlie Brown?" he asked. When Grandpa Popp, Shirley's Hungarian grandfather, said "Shirley," he pronounced it "Charlie." Paul had picked up on it, added "Brown," and the pet name had stuck.

Shirley sighed as she dried the last dish. "A little. I'm tired of driving in snow and slush. I'll be so glad when spring comes."

"Hmmm, me too." He studied the figures on the tablet in front of him. "We haven't saved as much as I thought we would. The truth is, we haven't saved a penny."

Shirley stood behind him and wrapped her arms around his neck. "But we will."

Paul looked up. "It's cost more to live out here and drive to work than I thought it would."

Shirley looked at the old cookstove, the stand-alone cabinet, the washstand, and dreamed aloud. "One of these days we'll have a home of our own. It will be so much fun to decorate and clean and . . ."

Paul laughed as he pulled her onto his lap. "Only my Shirley would get excited about cleaning house."

Paul A. Dennis

A few days later a beaming Shirley sat down on the couch beside her husband. "I have some news for you."

Paul pulled her closer. "What?"

Shirley snuggled. "Guess."

Paul pondered. "You got a raise?"

"No."

"Your mother is coming for a visit?"

Shirley poked him in the ribs. "No! Guess again, Daddy."

"The car is—" Paul stared at his wife. "Wh—wh—whaat did you call me?"

Shirley snuggled closer. "Daddy."

Paul's heart did a flip-flop. He drew a deep breath. "Are you . . . are you?"

Shirley nodded. "Yes, I . . . we are expecting a baby."

A load of responsibility dropped onto his shoulders, while his heart danced. "Are you OK?"

Shirley laughed. "I'm fine, just a little tired."

Soon morning sickness struck with a vengeance, and they realized that the commute to work was too much for their baby's mamma.

Then the pottery plant laid Paul off. He went job hunting and was hired by the Gilbert Shoe Company as a manager-in-training. Five months after they moved to #8 Hollow, it was time to move back to Zanesville.

About this time Shirley's grandfather, because of poor health, decided to move to Pennsylvania to live with his son. Word was sent through the family grapevine that Shirley and Paul could have Grandpa Popp's furniture if they would go to Dillonvale and get it. Would they? Of course! It was an answer to prayer.

They found an apartment on Stewart Avenue, centrally located from both jobs, and moved in their new used furniture. As they piled their last load of personal items into the car and pulled onto #8 Hollow's gravel road, Shirley did not look back.

Sorrow Strikes

Paul dropped his jacket on a chair and hugged his ever-expanding wife. "Guess what?"

"Good news or bad?"

"Both," he answered. "Which do you want first?"

She pondered. "Bad, I guess; that way the good will be that much better."

"Larry has decided that he doesn't want to move, so I won't be managing the Zanesville store." For several weeks Paul had been in training for the manager's position.

Shirley's face fell. "Oh, I'm sorry, Paul. I know you were looking forward to being the manager. Now what's the good news?"

"I am being promoted to assistant manger in a new store."

Shirley squealed. "That's wonderful."

Paul held her a few inches away and looked into her sparkling brown eyes. "There's just one catch."

The sparkle dimmed. "What?"

"The new store is in Lima."

"Lima? But that's north of here. We'll have to move." Shirley looked at the pictures, the knickknacks, the curtains.

Paul's eyes followed hers. Since she had quit work when she was six months pregnant, she had spent hours turning their minuscule apartment into a home. Paul knew that having a home was important to Shirley. As he held her, he felt her shiver and choke back a sob. Paul could almost read her thoughts. *I love my home, but home is wherever Paul is.*

She sat down on the couch trying to absorb Paul's announcement and control her emotions. "When do we move?"

"September," Paul answered.

"A month from now," Shirley whispered.

Paul continued, "The first two things we need to do are find a church and a doctor. Pastor Howell can give us the name of the pastor in Lima."

"Doctor Elliott will refer me to a doctor in Lima. I'll have to get a new job."

"You won't have to work. You can stay home and take care of little Jeff," said her proud provider.

Shirley grinned, "Or little Allison. That reminds me. Aunt Teresa has a baby bed, a highchair, and a playpen we can have." She grinned weakly. "There's just one catch."

Paul was relieved to see that grin. For a minute she had looked like she was about to dissolve into tears. "What?"

"We have to go get them," Shirley said.

Paul sat down beside Shirley and put his arm around her shoulders. "That means a trip to Cleveland. I can't get away right now; too much to learn before we move."

"Mary and Sharon could go with me," Shirley suggested.

Paul frowned. "Are you sure you are up to a trip?"

Shirley poked him in the ribs. "Of course. It's still three months before Baby Dennis is due."

Paul placed his hand on her stomach. "Has *he* woken up yet?" A couple of weeks earlier Shirley had mentioned that the baby was not as active as it had been.

Shirley put her hand over Paul's. "*She* has been pretty laid back lately. Probably tired from all the kicking *she* did last month."

Paul chuckled. "*He's* just resting, getting ready to keep us up day and night." He stood up and stretched. "How about I take my favorite wife out for ice cream?"

Shirley held out her hand. Paul pulled her to her feet. "You're getting to be a heavyweight," he teased his tiny sweetheart. "It's a little cool outside. I'll get you a sweater, if I can find one big enough."

Order My Steps

Over Tom's homemade ice cream, they planned the trip to Cleveland. It would be a one-day there-and-back trip, provided Don's wife Mary and Shirley's sister Sharon could go with Shirley.

Life settled into a getting-ready-to-move routine—Paul prepared for the move and Shirley prepared for motherhood.

The Saturday before Labor Day the girls left early for the 300-mile trip to Cleveland. They arrived home around 10:00 PM. Shirley was worn out and Paul was on overload, but the next day was Sunday. And on Sundays they went to church; so, tired or not, they went to God's house.

Monday Paul kissed Shirley goodbye and headed for the shoe store, intent on catching the Labor Day shoppers. A little after 9:00 Paul was called to the phone.

"Paul, something is wrong," Shirley said. "I have to go to the emergency room."

Paul was confused. "Where are you?"

"At the neighbor's," she said. "I'm hurting and bleeding. I called the doctor. He said to come to the ER immediately."

Paul's mind whirled. "Don't panic! Stay calm! I'm on my way. I mean I'm coming," he yelled as he slammed down the phone. *Oh, Jesus, help us.*

It took him only a few minutes to get home. But the trip to the hospital took forever—through the streets of Zanesville and across the famous Y-bridge.

At the hospital, medical personnel whisked Shirley straight into the delivery room and directed Paul to the waiting area. He prayed. He paced. He struggled to replace fear with faith, to overcome panic with praise. The minutes turned into hours, and no one told him anything. He determined to find good in what was happening, but it was a losing battle. As soon as he erased one negative thought, another took its place.

After three hours Doctor Elliott entered. Paul's hopes died when he saw the doctor's tight smile. "Sorry, Paul, but your baby was stillborn."

Paul A. Dennis

Stillborn? The word squeeze Paul's heart. His brain froze. *Stillborn?*

"The best we can tell, the heart stopped beating two to three weeks ago," the doctor continued.

Two weeks ago? "Paul, I think our baby is getting lazy. She's not kicking much these days." Why didn't they know? They should have known something was not right.

Visions of an empty baby bed, a highchair, and a playpen filled his mind's screen. He stumbled back and collapsed into a chair. *They shouldn't have gone to Cleveland. I shouldn't have let Shirley . . . Shirley!*

Paul jumped up. "My wife! Doctor, how's my wife? I need to see Shirley. Is she OK?"

The doctor put a hand on Paul's shoulder. "She is fine, Paul, just a little groggy and tired."

Shirley is tired. She is hurting. I need to go to her. Our baby is . . .

"Doctor," Paul hesitated, inhaled and exhaled. "Doctor," he repeated, "was our baby a . . . was our baby a boy or a girl?"

"A boy," Doctor Elliott answered. "Do you want to see your son?"

Time stood still. *Am I ready for this? Can I do this?* Paul clenched his toes in his shoes. "Yes," he whispered.

Sympathy crossed the doctor's face as he explained what Paul would see—a small fetus, somewhat deformed, but he should be able to identify family features. Looking at that tiny form was the hardest thing Paul had ever done. Taking a beating from Rub, entering a fiery drill pit, staring at Audrey's twisted face—nothing he had ever experienced prepared him for looking at his stillborn son.

As Paul turned to leave the room, the doctor said, "I recommend that Shirley not see her baby. Before you go home, go by the office and sign the necessary forms. We'll take care of everything for you."

Order My Steps

Then Paul went to see his wife. She needed him. He needed her. As they held each other and talked about Jeff Allen, their firstborn son, the Comforter wrapped His arms around the grieving young couple. They were reminded that God also knew the sorrow of losing His Son. They held each other and wept for all that would not be, and prayed for strength to endure all that was.

Shirley squeezed Paul's hand. "This is another bridge. Together with God's help we will cross it, step by step."

Paul had never loved her more than he did at that moment.

Later in the office with a trembling hand, Paul signed the forms. Then he drove to Don's house. When his big brother put his arms around him, Paul's control crumbled. God's strength poured into him as his big double-brother (biological and spiritual) prayed for him. *What do guys do who do not have a big brother?*

Home Missions

"First Apostolic Church. Pastor Bryan speaking." The voice on the other end of the line was firm and warm.

Paul shifted the receiver to his other ear and smiled at Shirley who sidled closer, hoping to hear both sides of the conversation. "Pastor Bryan, this is Paul Dennis. I am being transferred to Lima by my job with Gilbert Shoe Company. My wife, Shirley, and I will be attending your church."

"Brother, that's great!" Pastor Bryan boomed. "Where do you live now?"

"Zanesville. We go to church in Crooksville and have a letter of transfer from Pastor Howell," Paul assured him.

A few minutes later Paul hung up the phone and turned to Shirley. "I like the sound of his voice."

"Why didn't you ask him how big the church is and how old he is and if they have children and—"

Paul laughed. "Whoa, Charlie Brown. Remember that was a long distance call. We'll soon know all of those things."

They packed some clothes and their Bibles. When Paul returned from carrying their suitcases to the car, he found Shirley standing beside the baby bed. He put his arm around her and she buried her face in his shoulder. Neither spoke. What was there to say?

They locked the door to their apartment and headed north. This time they were leaving behind family, friends, and their baby. They knew that no matter where God directed their steps in the future, a piece of their hearts would forever remain in Zanesville.

One hundred and fifty miles later they drove into Lima. Before they looked for a place to live or even a motel, they decided to check out the church. "It's at North and Pine," Shirley read the address Pastor Howell had given them.

Order My Steps

"That shouldn't be hard to find," Paul said. "North means north. Pine means there are other streets with tree names. We'll just find one and—"

Shirley held up her hand. "Paul, please just ask at a service station."

Paul frowned. He did not like to ask for directions. He glanced at his young wife. She was as lovely as ever, but the sparkle was missing from her brown eyes. She looked drained.

Shirley put her hand on Paul's leg. "Please, PD? It's getting late, and we need to eat and find a motel."

Paul's stomach growled; he conceded to reason, meaning Shirley and his appetite. He asked for directions, and soon they located North and Pine.

"But it's a house," Shirley said.

Paul pulled over to the curb and pointed at a hand-painted sign in the front yard: First Apostolic Church.

"Church in a house?" Shirley was surprised.

"No one told us it was a home missions church," Paul said.

"PD, you didn't ask," Shirley reminded him smugly.

They stared at the large old house situated on the corner of a busy intersection. Opening onto one street was an entrance that appeared to lead into the church. It resembled a storefront with a large glass window framing the steps leading up to the door. On the other street was the entrance to the house, or so it seemed. Only a ribbon of yard ran around the building. Diagonally across the street was an elementary school.

Paul cut the motor. "Let's see if anyone is around."

To their surprise they found several *someones* around—Pastor Bryan, his wife, and their six children. After introductions were made, the family proudly took their newest members on a tour. One large room adjacent to the "sanctuary" was a Sunday school classroom where children of all ages met. A small cutout area in the back of the sanctuary housed the horse-tank baptistery.

Paul A. Dennis

When the Bryans realized that the young couple needed a place to stay while they looked for a place to live, Pastor Bryan insisted that they had room for them.

"What's two more?" Sister Bryan laughed, as she rearranged the children's sleeping quarters. "The kids love bunking in together."

So the Bryan household increased to ten.

Monday Paul reported to his new job, and the search for living quarters started in earnest. The pressure was on to find a place quickly before they had to pay another month's rent on the apartment in Zanesville.

At night Paul and Shirley lay in their borrowed bed and talked in hushed tones. "It's so different," Shirley said. "From a church of 250 plus to a couple of dozen."

Paul linked his hands under his head and stared at the dark ceiling. "And from a church building to having services in a room added onto a house with a horse trough in the back for a baptismal tank."

"And Sunday school classes in the kitchen and living room," Shirley added. "Oh, Paul, will we ever fit in?"

"Of course we will. We are needed here." He pulled her into his arms.

A tear trickled down Shirley's cheek and landed on his shoulder. Unconsciously, she placed her hand on her flat stomach and choked back a sob. "Nothing is like it was supposed to be."

Paul knew she was thinking of the empty crib sitting in the dark apartment in Zanesville. "We are here for a reason, Shirley."

She sniffed. "Let's pray, Paul."

Quietly they knelt beside the bed and poured out their hearts to the One who was ordering their steps. Then they climbed back into bed and went to sleep, snuggled under a blanket of grace.

A few days after they moved in with the Bryans, they found a place to rent—a large two-story white frame house that had been divided into a duplex. "It's bigger than we need," Shirley said, as they wandered through the rooms.

"But the rent is right," Paul replied. "Better to get more than we need for the money than not enough."

The Saturday before their second Sunday in Lima, Pastor Bryan and Paul went to Zanesville in the pastor's car pulling a U-Haul trailer. Paul's Falcon was not up to the job. It was a get-there-get-loaded-and-get-back trip, as Pastor Bryan had to be back for Sunday service.

Pastor Bryan backed the U-Haul up to the apartment on Stewart Avenue. In went the Dennises' meager furnishings: a table and four wooden chairs, refrigerator, range, wringer washer, an iron bed with springs, and a burgundy mohair couch and chair, along with household items, bed and bath linens, and clothes.

As they drove out of town, Paul looked over his shoulder. Behind him was a memory trail of abuse and rebellion, acceptance and redemption. As he looked toward the horizon, he felt a twinge of anticipation. Where would God lead them?

Shirley's homemaking skills were soon evident as she turned another less-than-perfect apartment into a cozy castle. She was quite the economist too, keeping their finances in order, making sure that the firstfruits of Paul's checks went to God's storehouse. Little by little she learned to cook, although she never quite mastered the art of making gravy. Paul relaxed in his comfortable home, counted his blessings, and ate the gravy—thick or thin, black, brown, or white.

Paul's management skills were evident as he put his best efforts to work on the job. After two months he was promoted to manager. Although he had been trained for the position, he was surprised to advance so quickly. Bookkeeping, banking, inventory, hiring (and firing) personnel, arranging displays, training others, and public relations—the details of retail work energized him. He submerged himself in his job and enjoyed every phase of it.

Paul A. Dennis

They spent the raise that accompanied his promotion on necessary items for their home and sighed with relief when Paul learned that one benefit of being manager was insurance coverage. God, in His foreknowledge, knew this would soon be needed.

When the Lima newspaper conducted a contest to find the friendliest and most courteous salesman in the city, Paul won! The Gilbert Shoe Company was impressed. Not enough to give him a raise, but enough to pat him on the back.

The store was open seven days a week, and although Paul had a day off each week, his responsibilities were superglued to his shoulders.

Little did he know that everything he was learning would one day benefit him as he labored in God's kingdom halfway around the globe. In God's economy nothing is wasted.

The Dennises integrated seamlessly into the fabric of the church. They assumed responsibility without offending or slighting existing structure and status. Paul's energy, business savvy, and outgoing personality were powerful ingredients for revival. Shirley's gentle sweet spirit, vivacious talent, and glowing love of God permeated the congregation with grace.

Paul became the youth leader. One studious young man, Garry Truman, nephew of the pastor, lived with his mother and brother at the other end of the block. Garry's family had moved to Lima to help Uncle Clifford and Aunt Jean start the church. Paul was a great mentor for Garry, and Garry was a big help to Paul.

Shirley taught the children's Sunday school class. Her musical ability brought a new dimension to their worship services.

In addition they did outreach and anything else they were asked to do. Youth activities flourished, Sunday school blossomed, and the music was wonderful.

In Lima the Dennises got their first taste of missions—home missions. They learned many valuable lessons that in the distant future would carry them through some turbulent times in another kind of mission work in a land far removed from Ohio.

Insurance Claims

March 1962. They had been married seventeen months when Shirley again started calling Paul "Daddy." Their excitement was dimmed by memories of the dark pain following the loss of their son. Every day they prayed for their baby, not for a boy or a girl, just for a healthy baby.

They anxiously waited for the first kick. From that moment on, the baby's movements were their primary concern and the topic of many conversations every day.

Shirley pulled out the maternity clothes she had packed away. As she slipped into a skirt and top, a bittersweet feeling swept over her. A tear crawled down her cheek. She sniffed.

Paul turned from the mirror where he was striving to make a perfect knot in his tie. "Something wrong?" he asked.

She shook her head. "No. I'm just . . . I'm just feeling melancholy."

"Why?" he asked. "You look cute as a button in that parachute."

Shirley blew her nose. "I just . . . I just feel like I'm abandoning Jeff. Yet I'm so happy about this baby." She burst into sobs.

Paul forgot about his tie as he gathered his wife into his arms. "Shhh, Charlie Brown. Jeff is safe with God. It is time to move on with our lives and focus on this little one."

Gradually Shirley's sobs subsided. She gave Paul a watery smile. "I know. I'll be all right now."

Weeks became months. Shirley's figure ballooned. After each monthly visit to the doctor, she reported to Paul.

One month she told him, "I weigh 108 pounds!" She was horrified. Paul was amused.

Paul A. Dennis

"A spring breeze blowing through #8 Hollow could still carry you out to the cow pasture," he laughed.

Another month passed. "The doctor said the baby's heartbeat is strong. He kicks like a quarterback," Shirley reported as she placed a sandwich in front of Paul, who was on his lunch break.

Paul raised his eyebrows. "He? I think our baby is a she."

"But I thinks he's a he," Shirley argued.

They laughed. Paul bowed his head and gave thanks for his lovely wife, their baby, and the food. He glanced at his watch and started gobbling down his lunch.

"This Sunday is the annual church picnic at the park," Shirley reminded him.

"That should be fun," Paul said between bites. "Garry is helping me get the games together."

Shirley patted her expanded stomach. "I won't be playing many games this year."

Paul patted his expanding stomach. "I need to play lots of games," he grinned. "Your cooking is hard on my figure."

Shirley reached across the table and slapped his hand. "Don't make fun of my cooking."

Paul grinned. "Me? Make fun of your cooking? You know I'd never do that." Then he sobered. "Whatever you lack in cooking skills, you certainly make up for in decorating. You could work for *Better Gardens and Houses.*"

Shirley giggled. "It's *Better Homes and Gardens.*"

Paul shrugged. "Whatever. They'd be lucky to get you, but they can't have you. You're mine, and you make delicious sandwiches."

He stood, grabbed another sandwich, and gave her a promising goodbye kiss. Time to get back to the shoes.

Sunday was a made-in-Heaven picnic day. Shirley joined the serving crew, and Paul organized the games—baseball, horseshoes, and tether ball. He joined the tether ball gang.

Order My Steps

"Watch this, guys," he called, as he grabbed the rope and pulled the ball back as far as he could. Whop! His left shoulder fell into his armpit. His arm hung straight down his left side. A searing pain raced through his body. It consumed him.

Someone helped him into a car. Shirley climbed into the back seat beside him and started praying. Paul gritted his teeth and squeezed his eyes shut. He couldn't faint. He had never fainted in his life! Well, maybe he should pass out. It would block the pain. But it wasn't that easy. His shoulder throbbed. His arm screamed. His wife prayed, and somebody drove them to the hospital.

He thought the pain couldn't get any worse, but it did. They arranged him face-down on a table with his left arm dangling over the side. They attached heavy sandbag weights to his upper arm, forearm, and wrist.

Shirley answered questions, filled out the necessary forms, and produced their insurance card. Then she stood beside Paul, held his hand, and prayed, "Jesus! Jesus, help him. Are you all right, Paul? Paul! Jesus! Jesus!"

Paul didn't bother to answer. It took all of his energy to keep from screaming.

"Aren't they ever going to do anything?" Shirley looked around for help. "Oh, Jesus! Jesus, help us!"

Finally, a doctor came in and prodded Paul's shoulder. Yes, the pain could get worse! How much worse? Paul hoped he didn't have to find out.

"We had to put these weights on as soon as possible because all the tendons and muscles in your shoulder were stretched out like a rubber band. When the tendons and muscles went back into place, it left your arm out of the shoulder socket. We have to stretch the tendons and muscles again before I can set it. Are you ready for this?"

Paul wasn't, but he had no choice. Ready or not, here the doctor came.

Paul A. Dennis

He pulled a tall stool near the table and sat on it facing Paul. He lifted his feet and placed one on Paul's neck near his shoulder and the other under his arm near the socket hole. He pulled and he pulled and he pulled. After an unbearably long time, Paul felt a thud! His arm had snapped back into the socket.

"Don't move your arm!" the doctor warned. "Let me do it for you." He placed Paul's arm where he wanted it and taped it tightly to his body from his neck to his elbow.

"You can move your wrist and hand, but your arm has to stay immobile for six weeks," the doctor instructed.

As they left the hospital, Paul's very pregnant wife walked protectively by his side, thanking God for helping them. Paul groaned. "Thank Him for the insurance too, Shirley."

The sales ladies working for Paul became his arms. They arranged the displays, kept the racks full, waited on the customers, and ran the cash register. The stock boy expressed his sympathy, but he whistled while racking up extra hours. His boss's accident had been the answer to his prayers—more money.

August 10, 1962. The Dennises were taking care of the Bryan's six children, while their parents went to Ohio camp meeting.

"Time to get up, Shirley." Paul reached over and shut off the alarm.

Shirley moaned as she rolled over. *Why did we agree to babysit six children?* she wondered. *Must have been one of my weaker moments.* She was eight months pregnant, and she was tired. She trundled her bulky body out of bed and stood up. Something warm and wet rolled down her legs.

"Paul! Paul! My water just broke!"

Order My Steps

Paul shot up like a jack-in-the-box, throwing covers to the foot of the bed. "It can't! Not now! Not today! It's too early. You've got a month to go."

He looked at his wife standing there in her nightgown looking totally bewildered. His panic evaporated, and his emergency training kicked in. While Shirley dressed and fixed her hair, he got the older children up and told them that he was taking his wife to the hospital. He instructed them to call a relative to come and help them get to school.

At speed limit plus, the trip to the hospital passed like scenery before cataract-glazed eyes. But they made it without incident.

Once they were inside the hospital, things slowed to a crawl. No one, except the expectant dad, was a bit hurried. *Fill out this form. Answer these questions. Produce your insurance card.*

Finally, nurses prepped Shirley and took her to the labor room. Alone, Paul retired to the waiting room where he sat and prayed. He remembered the last time he had sat in a waiting room. He shuddered and wiped the sweat from his brow. It couldn't happen to them twice. Could it? A baby had a lot better chance at eight months than at six. Didn't it?

He paced and prayed. Then he sat and prayed. Then he took a nap.

His eyes popped open. *Where was... Oh, yes, the hospital. Shirley? What time?* He looked for the clock and saw the doctor peering down at him. Paul squared his shoulders and stood. The doctor smiled. Paul relaxed.

"At 12:10 your healthy daughter was born. She weighs six pounds and ten ounces. Congratulations." As he shook Paul's damp hand, he explained that the baby had been placed in an incubator as a precaution since she was a month early.

Paul wanted to shove the doctor out of the way and race to see his daughter, but courtesy prevailed. He thanked the doctor and followed him from the room.

Paul A. Dennis

Of all the amazing things Paul had seen in his life—sunsets, the ocean, his lovely bride—nothing had prepared him for his first glimpse of his daughter. His knees trembled. His throat tightened. His eyes misted. He couldn't touch the baby, but he stood paralyzed as he gazed in awe at the miracle in the incubator. His daughter—Paula Ann Dennis.

Shirley did not get to see their daughter until the next day. She kept asking Paul about their baby. All the proud daddy could say was, "She's perfect and beautiful, just like her mother."

A couple of days later, Shirley sat in a wheelchair holding their gift from Heaven as Paul pulled the car up to the hospital entrance. He loaded his greatest treasures into the car. Never had he driven as cautiously as he did that day.

Then followed a crash course in parenting—how to put nipples on bottles; how to heat milk to the perfect temperature; how to change diapers, making sure they kept their fingers between the diaper and the baby so they got the puncture wounds, not the baby. Oh, yes, and how to rinse out a dirty diaper.

Every extra penny went for things for the baby, plus the co-pay on the doctor and hospital bills. When Christmas rolled around, they wanted to take Paula Ann home to show their families, but money was too tight. Even so they had a lot to celebrate—their Christmas baby, a church family, and each other. Who could ask for more?

A Visit with Rub

"Come to Daddy, Paula," Paul stood an arm's length from his tottering daughter and held out his hands, almost touching her.

His little cherub with blue eyes and blonde hair hesitated for a moment, then took two wavering steps and fell into his arms. Paul whooped. "She did it, Mommy! Our baby is walking."

A grinning Shirley came into the living room drying her hands on her apron. She wrapped Paul and Paula in a hug. "Our baby is growing up too quickly."

"Maybe it's time to have another one," Paul suggested.

Shirley dropped the hug and stepped back. "You may have recovered from all those sleepless nights, warming bottles, changing diapers, walking the floor, soothing a colicky stomach, but I haven't."

Paul chuckled as he sat Paula down on the floor and backed up a few inches. "Come to Daddy, Baby. It looks like you're going to be the one and only, at least for a year or two."

Shirley had started back into the kitchen, when Paul's words stopped her cold. "The company is opening a new store in Bowling Green. They want me to manage it."

Shirley's shoulders straightened.

Paul cleared his throat and spoke to his wife's back. "They are impressed with . . . with the progress of the store here in Lima."

Silence.

Paul shuffled his feet. Deciding she was no longer the center of attention, little Paula sat down and crawled to her daddy. She tugged at his pants leg. Unconsciously he picked her up, never taking his eyes off his wife.

"They will pay our moving expenses, and I'll get a raise; granted, it will be a small one, but every little bit helps."

Slowly Shirley turned and locked eyes with Paul for a long minute. Then her gaze shifted as she scanned the room from the pictures to the knickknacks to the curtains. Paul saw the déjà vu look in her eyes. "Paul, do you realize that we have moved four times in three years?"

He winced. "Guess I haven't thought about it." He watched Shirley and held his breath.

She inhaled deeply. Paul could almost read her thoughts. *Will we forever be moving? Just when I get a place looking decent, we move.* She exhaled and smiled weakly; Paul's lungs kicked in again.

"It is a good thing I like to decorate. When do we move?"

"I don't have to give them an answer until next week. I know we are just getting comfortable here. Let's pray about it."

The week passed. They prayed. They decided—move and drive back and forth to church.

Paul started his new job in Bowling Green, a friendly, active college town. He commuted for a week until he found a two-bedroom house with a garage, ten minutes from his job.

"It's perfect for us," he told Shirley. "A house—not an apartment—and a garage. Just think; I won't have to scrape ice off the windshield every morning in the winter."

"How much is the rent, PD?" his accountant asked.

Paul gulped. He knew she would ask that. "Seventy-five dollars."

"Seventy-five!" Shirley's mental calculator whirred. "Paul, that is more than twice what we are paying now."

"I know, but the house is perfect for us. You're going to love it."

And she did. They moved. Paul hadn't factored in the utilities, which in the apartments had always been included in the rent. Their increased cost of living gobbled up his small raise.

Order My Steps

It was not feasible to drive seventy-five miles one way to church, so they contacted Pastor Fred Kinzie in Toledo and transferred their membership to the First Apostolic Church, about twenty-two miles from Bowling Green. On Sundays they drove to church for the morning service, hurried home so Paul could work a couple of hours, and then went back to church that evening. Wednesdays and most Fridays they repeated the trip.

Soon it was Christmas again. Because they had not been with their families the previous Christmas, they decided they were going to go home this year, no matter what it cost. Of course, they could not go empty handed.

The problem. No money.

The solution. Get a credit card.

Oh, what fun, buying for everyone!

Before they left for Crooksville, Mary called. "Paul, Rub is a very sick man. He has cirrhosis of the liver, kidney problems, and cancer. Unless God is merciful, he won't live long."

When Paul hung up the phone, he took a deep breath, remembering. After he returned from the military and before he became a Christian, he had seen Rub occasionally on the street or in a bar, but he had not visited with him. After Paul's conversion, he had not seen Rub.

"Shirley, we need to visit Rub when we go home for Christmas." It was not something he wanted to do; it was something he needed to do.

Shirley agreed.

Paul had trouble falling asleep that night. Memories he thought he had buried rose like specters from the grave: Dancing around Rub's legs while one of Rub's calloused hands grasped his arm and the other hand swung the miner's belt, stinging Paul's legs. Foul, dirty words Paul had not thought about since he had received the Holy Ghost echoed in his brain. Pictures of Rub's scornful face as he mocked his wife's faith.

Paul A. Dennis

Paul groaned and rolled over. As he did his memories shifted; Rub had not been all bad.

He was seven years old and the possessor of a vivid imagination. Ghosts, goblins, and monsters haunted his world, and big brother Don delighted in making little brother's life miserable.

Paul was outside playing, when he looked up and saw a brown ghost floating around the corner of the house. In terror he jumped up and ran behind the house, pausing only long enough to pick up a coal pick handle.

He scrunched against the corner of the house, holding the handle high over his head, ready to attack the ghost that was haunting him.

Big brother draped in a brown blanket stuck his head around the corner and moaned, "Ooooo."

Little brother came down with the handle. Thump! Right on top of the brown ghost's head. The blanket fell off, unmasking the ghost. Donald was out cold. Little brother ran for his life.

A small hole in the stone foundation was barely big enough for Paul to squeeze through. He curled into a ball in the dark hideaway.

Time passed as Paul shivered in fear; then he heard Donald's voice. "Paul, come out. It was just me. I won't hurt you."

But no amount of pleading by Donald could entice Paul to come out of his cramped cave. Then Donald went away, and Paul waited, hugging the cold, damp dirt.

"Paul! Paul!" Rub's voice rang through the hole. "Paul, come out. I won't let Donald hurt you."

Paul crawled out. That time Rub was his protector. Rub was the only dad he remembered.

Order My Steps

During the Christmas holidays, Paul took Shirley and Paula to meet his "dad." A woman came to the door; when Paul introduced himself, she invited them in.

Rub was wearing clean, pressed pajamas. Someone was taking good care of him.

"Dad, I wanted to come and see you so you could meet my wife and see your granddaughter."

Rub's eyes brightened as he smiled his *Shirkey* smile. Paul knew he was glad to see them.

Paul said, "I'm sorry you are so sick," but Rub wasn't inclined to talk about that or about his soul. The conversation bobbed on the surface—where Paul was working, where they were living, where they were going to church.

As they were leaving, Rub said, "I want to give my granddaughter something for Christmas." He looked around until he found two pecans. He handed them to toddler Paula, who in return gave him her precious smile. Paul wanted to cry.

It was a Christmas they would never forget.

Rub died on February 15, 1964; he was forty-six years old.

One day a couple of months after Christmas when Paul came home for lunch, he found Shirley sitting at the kitchen table, making an awful sound. She choked and sobbed and bellowed.

Fear gripped Paul. He had never seen her like this. "Shirley, what's the matter? Where's Paula?"

Shirley pointed toward the bedroom. "S-s-she's a-a-asleep. S-s-she's OK."

"Then what's wrong?" Paul looked around in bewilderment.

Shirley pointed at the open checkbook and piles of papers spread out before her. "When we . . ." She choked and tried again. "When we pay our b-b-bills, there's no money. . . ." Her voice rose several octaves. "There's no money left for food."

Paul A. Dennis

Practical Paul replied, "Then don't pay something."

"You don't understand. We have to p-p-pay them because we put them off last m-m-month."

Paul pulled out a chair and sat down beside her. He grimaced, bit his lip, and stared at the ceiling. *What are we going to do? Dear Jesus, I know we got ourselves into this whirlpool of debt, but would You please help us out of it?*

"I'll ask our landlord if we can miss one month's rent and make it up later," he decided.

But Mr. Donley decided not. "If you can't pay one month's rent now, what makes you think you'll be able to pay two months later?" he reasoned.

Paul did not have an answer for that kind of logic.

The landlord relented, "I'll tell you what I'll do. You are good honest renters. You take good care of the house, so I'll lower the rent by ten dollars."

Ten dollars wasn't much, but it would buy some groceries. They could manage. *Thank you, Mr. Landlord, and thank You, Jesus.*

Mr. and Mrs. Paul A. Dennis were not whiners. They agreed not to tell anyone about their problem. They tightened their financial belts and toughed it out. When they went to the grocery store, they first bought food for the baby. They were learning what most young couples learn the hard way: When outgo exceeds income, it spells trouble.

One evening Shirley handed Paul a dime, two nickels, and two pennies. "I went through all my purses and all your pockets. I found enough for a loaf of bread."

Another time Paul bought one pound of hamburger meat. Shirley divided it into portions to last a week.

They had to learn this lesson only one time.

The Announcement

With his free hand Paul reached for Shirley's hand. Paula was asleep in the back seat. "What a service!"

Shirley nodded, still basking in the afterglow.

Paul cleared his throat. "Uhhh, Shirley," he hesitated, looking straight ahead at the asphalt ribbon revealed by the headlights.

She turned her head and looked at his profile. The streetlights flashed yellow slivers of light into the car. She purred with contentment—a handsome husband, a darling daughter, a comfortable home, a loving church family. Who could ask for more?

Since they had moved into the apartment in Toledo, conquered their credit card, and Paul had gone to work for Newcomb Baker Shoe Store, their finances were back in the black. The Kinzies and the saints at First Apostolic Church had gathered them under their wings like a mother hen with her little chicks. Shirley felt secure and satisfied.

Paul cleared his throat again. "Honey, I need to tell you something. I probably should have told you this before we were married."

Beside him, Shirley stiffened. "PD, before we married I told you that you don't have to tell me anything about your life before Christ. I married the new Paul."

"It's not that. It's . . ." he swallowed and tried again. "Right after I received the Holy Ghost, I went to the Ohio camp meeting." He glanced at Shirley's profile. She stared straight ahead.

He continued, "Billy Cole, missionary to Thailand, was the main speaker."

Shirley nodded slightly. It was before they had started dating, but Paul knew she remembered that camp because they had often talked about it.

"At that camp, I . . . God . . ." Paul paused; then continued, his words spilling out. "While Brother Cole was preaching, I felt an electrifying shock go through me, and God said to me, 'Your salvation will require you to go back to Japan for Me.'"

Shirley froze. Paul waited. The car motor, the wind, and little Paula's steady breathing filled the silence. After several blocks, Shirley turned slightly toward him. Softly she said, "Oh, Paul, you were just feeling the emotion of the service. Brother Cole is a powerful preacher. When he tells about the revivals and miracles he has seen, it makes everyone want to be a missionary."

Paul made brief eye contact with his wife. "Shirley, God gave me a verse that night." He looked back at the asphalt ribbon as he quoted, "'And every one that hath forsaken houses, or brethren, or sisters, or father, or mother, or wife, or children, or lands, for my name's sake, shall receive an hundredfold, and shall inherit everlasting life' (Matthew 19:29)."

Shirley turned and watched the streetlights sail by. For several blocks she was silent; then she put on her kindest voice, "Paul, you aren't even a preacher."

Paul swallowed his Adam's apple. "I plan to talk to Pastor Kinzie about that."

As he waited for Shirley's reply, he could almost read her thoughts. He knew she was not surprised that he was feeling a call to the ministry. They already provided fingers for almost every hand of the church. It was simply the next step in their walk with God. But his announcement about Japan had thrown her off balance.

Shirley drew a deep breath and tried another tack. "Toledo is home, Paul. We belong here. We fit here."

Order My Steps

He was not surprised by this argument. Shirley was content, cocooned in her safe world, a church, a family, a home. She loved her life.

After that night the Dennises continued doing everything Pastor Kinzie asked them to do. In addition to her duties as wife, mother, homemaker, and Pastor Kinzie's secretary, Shirley taught Sunday school, assisted with the music, helped Paul lead the youth, and directed an annual drama. Paul worked long hours at the shoe store, rushed home, ate supper, and headed for the church to work on the construction of the new sanctuary. He also drove the church van and did outreach. His greatest joy was sharing the gospel, which he did every chance he got.

They had little time or desire to talk about Paul's call to missions. But it tickled the back of their minds, surfacing when they prayed and at unexpected moments, sending them into emotional spasms.

When Paul talked to Pastor Kinzie about his call to the ministry, Brother Kinzie smiled. He was not surprised.

"I need to go to Bible school," Paul told him. "There is so much I don't know about the Word of God."

Brother Kinzie studied the man across the desk from him: a disciplined young man twenty-eight years old, a faithful husband, a loving father, a superior salesman, a dedicated Christian, a man with potential to do great things in the kingdom of God.

"When you can come in here and tell me that God has spoken definitely to you and told you to go to Bible school, I will help you in any way I can. Meanwhile, keep doing what you are doing."

"There's one more thing, Brother Kinzie. I have a heavy burden for Japan. I feel God is calling me to go there."

Paul A. Dennis

Brother Kinzie weighed each word, then said. "I will help you pray about this, Brother Paul. Meanwhile, keep doing what you are doing."

So Paul kept doing what he was doing.

Hours at the shoe store were erratic and long. When he heard that National Cement would be hiring, he applied for a job. The cement plant was open eight hours a day, five days a week, with some overtime on Saturday. Paul applied and was hired.

The next church service, he was told, "Pastor Kinzie would like to see you."

In the office Pastor Kinzie waved him to a chair and got to the point. "Your employer at the shoe store called and told me that you got mad and quit your job."

Paul's chin dropped. "I don't know what she's talking about. I quit to accept a job with National Cement, but I didn't get mad."

Like molasses on a July day, a big grin spread across his pastor's face. "Just as I thought. I've known you for several years, Brother Paul, and I have never known you to do anything in anger." The grin grew. "She called back later and admitted that you didn't get mad; she did. She was upset about losing such a valuable salesman." The older man stood and extended his hand. "Congratulations on your new job." He chuckled, "Now that you will have so many free hours, maybe I can find something for you to do."

When the new sanctuary was complete, Pastor Kinzie offered Paul the job of maintenance man, complete with a house next to the church rent free.

Once again the Dennises moved, this time into a two-story white frame house with a basement and a garage. Shirley accepted each move with grace and enthusiasm, always making their house into a comfortable, attractive home. Life was good, but it was not without sorrow.

Order My Steps

Baby Dennis 3, a boy, and Baby Dennis 4, a girl, each arrived about three months prematurely and lived only a few hours. The medical field's inability to save the babies compounded the young couple's grief.

After the premature birth of Baby 4, Doctor Bradford told them, "We do not know why this keeps happening. We cannot find a medical reason. You have a beautiful, healthy daughter. I recommend that you enjoy her."

Paul and Shirley wrapped up their dreams of a brother or sister for Paula and stored them on their memory shelf. Then they placed their babies and their grief in the Comforter's arms and kept doing what they were doing—loving God, each other, and their adorable daughter.

One day when Paul was working at the church, he found the pastor's wife in the kitchen making her famous carrot juice drink. Vera Kinzie was a gracious lady, interested in everyone.

"Come in, Paula's daddy," she laughed. "Your little girl was so cute Sunday when the children's choir was singing."

The proud dad didn't argue. He hopped up on a kitchen stool.

As she poured juice into a glass, Sister Kinzie sang a line, "'If the sinner's in the way, we will stop. . . .'" She paused, then shouted, "Stop!"

Paul finished for her, "'And let him in.' I don't know why Paula won't say 'stop' with the rest of the children."

Sister Kinzie chuckled. "I do. She would never get that round of applause if she said it with everyone else. That two-second pause before she shouts 'stop!' gets everyone's attention. Would you like a glass of carrot juice?"

Paul managed not to turn up his nose as he politely refused.

The conversation turned serious when she asked how they were dealing with the loss of their babies and their dream of adding to their family. After they talked about pain and loss, Paul opened his heart and told her about his call to Japan.

Paul A. Dennis

Vera Kinzie saw the same man that her husband had seen. But with her woman's intuition, she saw something else. She saw the hand of God ordering the steps of a country boy from #8 Hollow, McLuney, Ohio.

"Brother Paul, I think that is wonderful. Draw close to God, and He will lead you step by step. In His time everything will fall in place."

Paul wanted to reach across the counter and hug her, but he didn't. "You are the first person who has believed me," he said. "No one thinks I am 'missionary material.' I am not a dynamic evangelist or a deep theological scholar. I don't have a college degree, not even a Bible school education. All I have is a passion to carry the gospel to Japan."

"God loves to make something out of nothing," she reminded him. "He is not looking for ability, but availability. He'll provide what you need, when you need it."

Under his first pastor Paul had learned submission and self-control. His second pastor had opened his eyes to the harvest around him. Pastor Kinzie wisely took what Paul had learned, built upon it, and prepared him for the ministry. Under Brother Kinzie's mentorship, Paul took a correspondence course and worked on the requirements for acquiring a ministerial license with the United Pentecostal Church International. When pastors called asking for someone to fill their pulpits, Brother Kinzie often sent Paul, giving him the opportunity to expand his pulpit ministry.

For six years Paul and Shirley worshiped and worked with the family of God at First Apostolic. Life was good, maybe too good, too consistent. Shirley sensed her husband's restlessness. She was not surprised when he said, "It's time to move."

They were going back to Lima, back to home missions work. As Shirley packed, she hummed, "Whither thou goest, I will go."

The Vision

Paul removed the key from the ignition, rubbed his eyes, and slumped behind the steering wheel. He was home again, parked in the drive at 629 West Grand Avenue, but how? He remembered getting in the car and starting home. After that, he drew a blank. Driving sixty-one miles from Lima to Toledo, working long hours, reversing the sixty-one mile drive, keeping up with church activities and responsibilities—all combined to drain him.

He pulled his sleep-deprived body from the car and crossed the grass-cushioned lawn with its manicured hedges.

Opening the front door, he called, "I'm home."

Eager footsteps and cheerful squeals greeted him. Hugs and kisses paid him in full for every long hour at the plant and on the road.

More and more Pastor Bryan was giving Paul pulpit time, so after supper he sat down on the sofa and picked up his study Bible. For a few seconds he closed his eyes and relaxed. His memory film rolled.

He was at the Ohio District conference as nervous "as a cat in a room full of rocking chairs," as his mother would have said.

Before the conference he had worked on memorizing the Articles of Faith and all the Oneness Scriptures he could find in preparation for applying for his local ministerial license. Every day his panic level had risen. His nerves had resembled a ball of yarn in a kitten's paws.

When we walked into that boardroom, he looked into the sternest faces he had ever seen. The only familiar face was Brother Kinzie's. He made eye contact with his mentor,

Paul A. Dennis

searching for hope. Brother Kinzie smiled slightly and Paul relaxed . . . slightly.

He sat down and mentally flipped quickly through his memorized material. He tensed, waiting for a barrage of questions.

"Tell us about your conversion."

That was easy. He loved to give his testimony.

Next question. One straight-faced board member leaned forward and asked, "Brother Dennis, when you get a church, will you let your people eat pork?"

Paul was blown away. He scanned every brain cell. No Scriptures. No answers. Just a blank . . . a blank blackboard.

Then he remembered facing another board, an air force board, answering questions to qualify for his second promotion. "Who is the best airman in your outfit?"

Good thing he had read the book. "I am, sir."

But the answer to the current question was not in the book, so Paul gave it his best shot. "If my people can afford pork, they can eat it."

The questioning board member smiled, while the other men roared.

Paul passed the test without quoting one Bible verse or referring to one segment of the Articles of Faith. He left that room a licensed minister of the United Pentecostal Church International and went downstairs to the fellowship hall to eat dinner feeling fifty pounds lighter.

As he was coming up the stairs after eating, he met George Christoff coming down. Paul stopped and stuck out his hand, "Praise the Lord, Brother Christoff."

The evangelist smiled and shook Paul's hand. "Praise the Lord."

"You don't remember me, do you?" Paul said.

Without blinking an eyelash, he replied, "Yes, I do. Your name is Paul. Your mother is Mary. You were sitting on the

Order My Steps

third pew near the front on the right side of the Crooksville church."

Paul was so surprised he grabbed the rail to keep his balance.

The evangelist continued, "The Lord spoke to me when you came into the building and told me to preach directly to you. So I did."

With that the evangelist continued down the stairs and Paul continued up, his head whirling. *So Mom didn't set me up that night; God did.*

On the couch, he opened his eyes and picked up his Bible. It was time to do the work of a minister and prepare a sermon. A few minutes later his eyelids drooped; the Bible dropped onto his lap.

A black screen flashed before his eyes; then it passed, and he was standing in front of a dingy white rectangular church building. A steeple drew his eyes up to the sapphire sky. He felt connected, as if he belonged there.

Then the image vanished.

His open Bible lay where he had dropped it. He shook his head to clear his brain. It was so vivid, so detailed. He had never seen that church before, yet it had gripped his heart. Was it a vision? If so, what was it all about?

For several days the vision of that church haunted him. Finally, one afternoon after he left the cement plant, he swung by the church. Pastor Kinzie's car was in the parking lot. Good. Paul needed to see his mentor and friend.

He found Brother Kinzie in his office and did not waste time on superficial greetings. "I had a dream or a vision. I don't know if it was from God or not, but I want to tell you about it."

Paul A. Dennis

Pastor Kinzie fastened his eyes on Paul as he described the church building in detail. When he finished, the older man smiled. "Would you like to see that church, Brother Paul?"

Paul nodded, speechless.

"It's an independent church here in Toledo, the Antioch Apostolic Church. The people contacted me to see if I knew of a UPC preacher who would be interested in becoming their pastor."

Paul leaned forward, chin in hands.

Brother Kinzie continued, "They have had nine pastors in three years. Some they did not like; some did not like them. I have been sending ministers there for a couple of months. I believe they already have someone scheduled for this coming Sunday evening, but I could tell them that you are available for Sunday morning. That is, if you are available."

Paul had yet to find his voice. He nodded. Pastor Kinzie stood. As he walked the younger man to the door, he said, "I'll call and let you know."

Paul cleared his throat. He had to say something. "Thanks," he mumbled as he stumbled out of the office to the church exit.

As he drove home, thoughts bombarded him from every direction—past, present, and future. His mind felt like Paula's toy box.

Him, pastor? Another move? What will Shirley say? But wait! He hadn't even preached there, let alone been voted in as pastor. But the vision? Surely it was from God. Or was it? Was it a sign of what was to come?

They had been in Shirley's dream house, minus the picket fence, for almost two years. The down payment had flattened their bank account. The loan stretched into eternity—the year 2000. But for once their home had their name on it, as well as Shirley's imprint.

As familiar patchwork scenery skimmed the edge of his vision, Paul took a mental tour of their white frame two-bedroom house. His favorite spot was in front of the fireplace. On

Order My Steps

cold winter evenings, it drew his petite, but complete, family of three into its warm embrace. The décor reflected Shirley's graciousness. The kitchen echoed with Paula's chatter and their laughter. It was home, their home.

They were settled and happy in Lima, just as they had been in Toledo and Bowling Green and Zanesville and #8 Hollow. Well, being honest, Paul admitted to himself that maybe Shirley wasn't as settled and happy in #8 Hollow as he had thought at the time. But he knew her roots went deep at 639 West Grand Avenue, and the fruit of her labors perfumed their home. How was he ever going to tell her that she might again be transplanted? How many transplants could she survive?

How could he tell Pastor Bryan? Their fingerprints were on every department of the Lima church. Paul groaned. Here he was doing what his mother had warned against—crossing bridges before he got to them.

He had to get to his prayer closet. He needed to talk to his Commander in Chief.

The next Sunday Paul and Shirley drove back to Toledo, this time to the Antioch Apostolic Church. Ten-year-old Paula spread her special brand of sunshine. Shirley's musical gift blessed the church. Paul preached. They connected.

After the service, the Dennises went home with a church family for dinner. They were asked to stay and minister that evening, as the previously scheduled preacher had cancelled.

As Paul preached that summer Sunday evening, Jan Tansel, the daughter of the lady in whose home the Antioch Apostolic Church had been birthed, heard the voice of God: "This is your new pastor."

Two weeks later Paul was voted in as pastor. He belonged there. But before they could sell their house and move, tragedy struck.

From Tragedy to Triumph

Another move? Paul was sure that if Shirley had known he had nomadic blood in his veins, she would have still married him, but she probably would have made him sweat a little more before she accepted his proposal.

A For Sale sign popped up on the lawn of Shirley's little white castle. The real estate agent assured them of a quick sale. Long before "staging" became a real estate marketing concept, Shirley practiced it. The Dennises' home was continuously staged—classy, charming, and cozy.

One Friday night after youth service, Mike and Jan Tansel, a young couple from the church, came home with the Dennises to spend the night. As the chattering group opened the front door, they heard the phone.

Paul hurried to answer it. As he listened to the messenger on the other end, his brain congealed. His heart choked.

"No!" he croaked. *Please, God, let it not be so.*

But it was so. New converts at Antioch Apostolic, Lois Cook and her six children plus a friend of one of the children (all between two and twelve years old), had been in a terrible accident. Their station wagon had left the road and rolled several times. The sole survivor, a small boy, was in critical condition.

As a former firefighter and crash flight responder, Paul instantly had flashbacks—a plane in flames, Audrey on a gurney. But seven lives, maybe eight, wiped out in a second, like a giant eraser swiping across a blackboard? It was beyond tragic. The shock threw the Dennises and Tansels to their knees, sobbing for the Comforter to come.

The thought of conducting such a funeral petrified this fledging shepherd who had never conducted a funeral. He sought refuge in the office of his mentor. As he drew from the quiet wisdom of this man of God, Paul's nerves calmed.

Order My Steps

With his spirit calmed and his wits collected, he went to the funeral home. "The funeral will be held here in our chapel," the director told him. "Mr. Cook has arranged for the pastor of their former church to be in charge and requested that you assist him."

The backpack of responsibility shifted. Paul could handle assisting; he was accustomed to assisting.

A couple of days later the little boy died.

The day of the funeral seven unopened caskets lined the front of the chapel. The Comforter carried the husband and father Dean Cook, as well as the church family, through the day.

An avalanche of grief swept down upon the Antioch Apostolic Church. Members of Pastor Dennis's new flock asked many hard questions that he could not answer. And he asked God many hard questions that God chose not to answer. Eventually, with agonizing prayer the congregation dug their way out of their sorrow and stood again in the sunlight of God's glory.

The Dennises had been on the pastoral roller coaster for two months when their house sold. If Shirley shed tears as she packed, no one but God knew it. She was not a whiner. Long before it became a popular slogan, Shirley Dennis knew how to bloom where she was planted.

They moved into a duplex a few miles from the church, as a family from the church lived in the parsonage.

Without missing a beat, the Dennises' intense on-the-job training continued. Paul juggled two full-time jobs—pastoring and working at the National Cement Company. His employer was not happy when Paul refused to work overtime, but the union supported his right to say no.

In September 1974, he requested a Friday off to meet the Ohio District board to apply for his general ministerial license. To Paul's surprise his foreman agreed to let him off, telling him that he would take care of his timecard.

Paul A. Dennis

Monday morning Paul stood before the time clock with a wrinkled brow. His timecard was not in the rack. He went into the office to report it missing.

The clerk on duty glared at him. "It's not missing. You no longer are employed here."

That was Paul's last secular job.

When he walked into the house in the middle of the day, Shirley took one look at his face and said, "Don't worry, Paul. God is ordering our steps. This is just a curve in the road."

That week they moved into the parsonage. Shirley's creative mind and industrious hands went to work. She got a secretarial job in the Crow's Rest Home office, and she taught piano lessons at the church. Paul pastored full time.

One Sunday night the ladies trio sang, "There's a still small voice saying to me, 'Closer, closer, draw closer to me.'" The husband of one of the saints sat on the back pew, head down. Conviction hovered, gently wooing him; but he did not respond.

A few days later Paul answered the phone. "What? Who? . . . Sister who? . . . Sorry, but I can't understand you. Please try to control yourself. . . . An accident? . . . The morgue? Yes. Yes. I'll do it for you."

With his heart cracked and bleeding, Paul went to the city morgue and identified the body of the unrepentant husband, who had been instantly killed in a motorcycle accident.

Tragedy followed tragedy.

One glorious Saturday in June, Edith Forgy was killed in an auto accident while on her way to buy snacks for her teen Sunday school class. She was one of the founders of the church, a close friend and faithful supporter of the Dennises.

Pastoring is real life and it hurts.

Antioch Apostolic Church placed a strong emphasis on missions. They treated visiting missionaries like royalty. These missionary services stirred up the coals of Paul's calling, which continually smoldered in his soul. No matter how awesome the

Order My Steps

move of God at AAC, Japan was forever at the back of his mind, calling out to him.

The church/pastor honeymoon was in full bloom. Attendance was up from the 20s to the 40s and 50s. Then a searing wind blew across the congregation—a clique formed. Their mantra: "We want a new pastor. We want a new pastor." After all, these people were accustomed to changing pastors on a regular basis. Paul Dennis was too settled.

One day one of the leaders of the clique stormed into Paul's office intent on blowing to shreds the doctrines he preached. But Pastor Dennis stood firmly on the Word of God. Speaking in tongues, the gifts of the Spirit, baptism in the name of the Lord Jesus Christ, and a holy lifestyle—these biblical truths could not be shaken by any wind of false doctrine, certainly not by a whirlwind of hot air.

Another day. Another man. Paul was at his desk when the office door burst open. In marched a member of the rebellion. His face was red; his fists clinched.

"You're leading my wife astray with your false doctrine," he screamed. With each word the volume rose and his fist swung higher. "I'm going to put a stop to your nonsense and give you a fat lip."

A holy indignation exploded somewhere in the region of the former firefighter rescue worker's stomach. Paul jumped to his feet. Matching volume for volume, he yelled, "When I get on the other side of this desk, you had better be ready, because I am going to wipe the floor with you!"

The enraged pastor started around the desk. But before he could reach other side, the tornado blew over; the guy was out the door.

The astonished pastor backed up and collapsed into his chair. What had he done? He pulled a clean handkerchief from his back pocket and wiped the sweat from his brow. In his memory echoed Brother Kinzie's voice quoting Mark Twain: "It's not the size of the dog in the fight, but the size of the fight in the dog."

End of that windstorm, but not the end of the tempest.

Paul spent many hours on his knees asking God how to control the raging storm. One evening God told him what to do. Paul got up, not understanding what he was about to do, but knowing he had heard from God.

Saturday he went to the church, took anointing oil, and anointed above every door, pew, musical instrument, and piece of furniture in the name of Jesus.

Sunday morning his mind was blank. No sermon. Not even an idea. Then during the service, God handed him his sermon outline.

He went to the pulpit, opened his Bible to Luke 15, and preached.

Part I: The Parable of the Lost Sheep. Emphasis: repentance. No response.

Part II: The Parable of the Lost Coin. Emphasis: repentance. No response.

Part III: The Parable of the Prodigal Son. Emphasis: repentance. No response.

Pastor Dennis gave the altar call. No response.

Then the Lord put words in his mouth. They vibrated through the sanctuary and pierced the hearts of the listeners. "Yesterday the Lord told me to anoint every doorway, every pew, and every piece of furniture in this church in the name of Jesus. You are sitting under God's anointing. You are not fighting against me. You are fighting against God."

The altar filled with repentant saints, crying out for forgiveness and mercy. The rebels got up and walked out.

When the whirlwind passed and the damage was assessed, attendance was again in the 20s. But revival winds blew in, bringing the sunlight of God's love and sinners seeking salvation. Soon the pews filled; the walls bulged. It was time to build.

Order My Steps

One problem. No money.

So Paul paid a friendly call on the banker.

"Sorry, Pastor Dennis, but we have not made a building loan in over a year." The banker hesitated; then drew a deep breath. "But go ahead and fill out an application. I'll submit it. I don't know why because I know it will not be approved, but I just feel like I should."

A week after the application was submitted, the banker asked Paul and the church board of trustees to come to his office. He told them, "I don't understand this. We have not granted a building loan in a year, but you have been approved. And we are still in 'no loan' mode."

Work began immediately on the new addition to the sanctuary. They poured the foundation and braced the wall frames; they were ready for the roof joists. The exhausted men went home one evening, excited about the progress they were making, expecting to put up the roof joists the next day.

During the night Paul was awakened by a howling wind, flashing lightning, and booming thunder. *I hope everything at the church is OK,* he thought as he covered his head with a pillow.

But things were not OK. The walls had toppled and several studs had to be replaced. "Just a test," Paul told the men, as they thanked God their losses were not greater. The walls went back up. The roof went on, and the work continued.

In an amazingly short time the building program was complete. The church pulsated with excitement. Attendance was well over 150. Paul had a new car. Shirley had a new piano. Paula had a large circle of friends, and something else she had always wanted: a puppy. Cricket, a smart white-and-buff cockapoo, was one of her best friends

They had gone from tragedy to triumph.

Life was good, maybe too good, too consistent. The Dennises were on spiritual alert. What next?

Section III
Missionary Paul

1987 - FUPC - McFarlands leaving Okinawa

1988 - FUPC - Paula the music director

1987 - FUPC - Ministers of the FUPC Okinawa

1989 - FUPC - Paul and Shirley Dennis

1988 - FUPC - Dennises departing for deputation

1988 - FUPC - Dennises leaving

1987 - FUPC - Welcome Back Pastor (coming from Burma)

1989 - FUPC - The Dennises and Townsleys

1992 - FUPC - A Military Church

1992 - Regional Field Supervisor and Sister Garry Tracy

Hokkaido Church

Koto and Kunio Fujibayashi
Kyoto, Japan

Bicycles bought by the Okinawa FUPC for Burma

Paula Townsley, Missionary Kid

The Dennises with Fred Kinzie after meeting the Foreign Missions Board

George and Margaret Shalm

Shio

Charter members of Okinawa FUPC

A Conference Call

Louisville, Kentucky, 1975 General Conference of the United Pentecostal Church International.

Paul and Shirley sat electrified by the power of God during the foreign missions service. The cry of the lost came from far across the Pacific and crashed on the shores of their hearts. When the call was made for those who were willing to dedicate their lives to carrying the gospel to the lost in foreign lands, the cry of the Japanese compelled them to leave their seats.

Hand in hand they made their way to the front. Step by step they followed their Lord.

Shirley whispered, "Paul, are you sure? How will we know?"

Paul squeezed her hand. "God will show us the way."

With hearts melting and tears flowing, they raised their hands in surrender. Veteran missionaries mingled with the hundreds who packed the front of the auditorium. As Paul and Shirley committed their lives to missionary service, they felt hands placed on their heads.

When the prayer ended, they looked into the faces of the missionary couple that had prayed for them.

"Thank you for praying for us," Paul said.

The missionary lady wiped her tears as her husband shook Paul's hand and said, "We're Claude and Helen Thompson, missionaries to Japan."

Tears gushed from Paul's and Shirley's eyes; they grabbed the Thompsons and hugged them. When the sobs had subsided, Paul made eye contact with his wife. He didn't say a word. He didn't need to. The same words were echoing in the chambers of their hearts. *How will we know? God will show us the way.*

After that service Paul asked for and received an application for foreign missions appointment.

Home again they quickly melted into their busy, productive schedule. They placed the application in a desk drawer to be filled out "later."

December rushed in, bringing its demands for a program, a banquet, parties, caroling, shopping, and family time. The church celebrated New Year's Eve in the new sanctuary. Loud, joyful voices overpowered the faint voice calling from the desk drawer.

A few days later Paul was in his office praying and studying, when God spoke to his spirit. "Are you ready to go to Japan for Me?"

The application in his desk flashed before his closed eyes. Paul got to his feet and pulled it out of the drawer. He laid it before God. "I am ready."

Then he went home to talk to his wife.

"Shirley, it is time to fill out the foreign missions application."

His creative, committed wife, who loved her home and her church family, but loved God and her husband more, smiled and said, "PD, if you feel that is what we should do, it's OK with me." This time she didn't even glance at her perfect *Home and Garden* house. She could make a home for her family anywhere in the world.

They sat down at the kitchen table, filled out the lengthy form, prayed over it, and mailed it to headquarters.

Then they went back to doing what they had been doing.

God added to the church monthly. Tears polished the altar. Sins were washed down the drain, as new converts were baptized in the name of Jesus. The sanctuary rang with the joyous cries of babies being born into the kingdom of God.

The windows of Heaven were wide open. Financial blessings rained down on the church on Rall Road, Toledo, Ohio. Mortgage payments were paid three months in advance. The church owned a 48-passenger bus, a large van, and five acres of

Order My Steps

cleared land. The saints worked, worshiped, and played together. All was up, running full steam ahead.

About two weeks later, Paul picked up the mail and carried it into his office. Sitting at his desk, he flipped through the stack. An envelope with a St. Louis return address momentarily paralyzed him: Foreign Missions Division, United Pentecostal Church International. His heart flip-flopped; his breath quickened.

He picked up the phone and dialed the parsonage. "Shirley, it's here."

"What's here?" she asked.

"A letter from the Foreign Missions Division. I'm coming home so we can open it together." He hung up.

When they sat down on the couch to read the letter, Cricket yapped and jumped into Shirley's lap. Shirley automatically scratched Paula's pet's ears, as Paul opened the letter. They read silently. Then they fell into one another's arms, crying and laughing at the same time.

"Can you believe it, Shirley? They've accepted us. We're going to Japan."

Shirley pushed him back a few inches and gazed into his eyes. "Wait a minute, Paul. Our application has been reviewed and accepted. This is just the first step."

Paul's countenance darkened for a second and then brightened. "But it's a big step. When do we meet the foreign missions board?"

Shirley picked up the letter and held it above Cricket's head. "January 19."

The next few days the Dennises went into fast-forward mode. So much to do. Tickets to purchase. Arrangements to make for someone to take care of Paula and Cricket while they were out of town. Piano lessons to reschedule. Dozen of details.

Paul A. Dennis

Stressed and stretched, Paul and Shirley snapped at each other, apologized, fretted, worried, and prayed that they would survive. By the time they boarded the plane in Toledo, they were two balls of tangled nerves bouncing against each other.

The flight was too short and too long—one hour and five minutes. Dorsey Burk met them and took them straight to World Evangelism Center, where they waited. *Reminds me of the air force,* Paul thought. *Hurry up and wait. Walk through a door into the unknown. Answer questions. Hope your answers are correct.*

Paul tapped his foot impatiently.

Shirley reached over and took his hand. "Relax, Paul. If God wants us in Japan, we will go. If not, we can go home and keep doing what we love doing."

"Brother and Sister Dennis, the board will see you now," an anonymous voice announced.

After they walked though the double swinging doors, Paul surveyed the room. Seeing those serious men of God around that table completely unraveled him. Then he made eye contact with his mentor, and a peace enveloped him. He remembered the day four years ago when he had met the Ohio District board. Brother Kinzie's presence had calmed him that day too.

T. F. Tenney, foreign missions director, invited Paul and Shirley to be seated. He was introducing them to the board members, when suddenly the doors swung open. Ernest Jolley, a rotund man whose name perfectly matched him, bounced in and pointed at Brother Tenney: "I'm going to get even with you." Then he was gone.

Laughter filled the boardroom. Brother Tenney put his head in his hands. "What an introduction to the board!"

The tension oozed out of Shirley and Paul. They didn't know what was going on, but it didn't matter. Ernest Jolley had saved the day for them.

Order My Steps

The introductions were finished and the interview started. Tell us about your family. Your home life. Your church. Your previous ministry. Your gifts. Your education. Your missions involvement, both personal and financial. Your burden. Your experiences in Japan. The questions went on and on.

When Paul and Shirley thought the interview would never end, Director Tenney fastened his eyes on them and asked one more question. "Brother and Sister Dennis, do you know that Japan has been called the graveyard for missionaries?"

That challenged Paul. *That will not happen to us,* he promised himself. Little did he realize all that statement entailed, but it stirred in him a determination that held him steady during some turbulent times on the mission field.

Paul straightened his shoulders and looked straight at Brother Tenney. "Sir, before I was in the church, when I served in the air force in Japan, I was deep in sin and stooped as low as a person could stoop in the depravity of the flesh. God has promised me that He will take all those stones of sin and make a safe walkway for us, so we can do His work in Japan."

Before the end of the day, Pastor and Mrs. Paul A. Dennis were approved and appointed as United Pentecostal Church missionaries to Japan. As they were leaving the boardroom, Brother Kinzie said, "Brother Paul, if you give this board any problems, I will skin you alive."

Paul and Shirley boarded the plane that evening, relieved and terrified.

The next step? Go home and tell Paula they were moving again—this time halfway around the world.

A New Home for Cricket

"But what about Cricket?" Paula's blue eyes changed to green when she was upset. Paul couldn't look at his daughter. He stared at his shoes. Thirteen-year-old Paula was seated between her parents on the couch with Cricket snuggled in her arms.

Cricket? Ah, yes, Cricket. What were they going to do about Cricket? He couldn't go on deputation with them. Not many pastors' wives would appreciate a missionary family with a dog traipsing through their homes.

Paula Ann hugged Cricket so tightly that the little dog yapped. Shirley waited. As Paul's memory film rolled, he reached over and scratched the cockapoo's head.

Paul remembered the day he was teaching Paula how to bat.

Paula stood with a bat on her shoulder, watching the ball as instructed. No one noticed Cricket standing behind Paul. Cricket loved to play ball. When Paula threw the ball, Cricket's eyes would follow it as he ran to catch it, often in midair; then he would return it to her. His eyes would beg, "Do it again. That was fun."

That day Paul wound and pitched. In a flash Cricket was after the ball. Paula swung the bat just as Cricket jumped. The bat missed the ball and hit Cricket's head. Clunk! Their little buddy collapsed, stiff legged, quivering like a dying dog.

Paula ran to Cricket screaming, "Pray, Daddy. Pray for Cricket. Don't let him die."

Paul had never prayed a more earnest prayer in his life. After a few minutes, the stunned dog opened his eyes and staggered to his feet.

Paula grabbed the bewildered dog and hugged him tightly, crying over and over, "Cricket, are you OK? I'm so sorry I hit you." Whether Cricket was dying or stunned, they never knew. But that little experience taught his daughter she could trust God for anything. A valuable lesson for a future missionary kid.

Paul pulled his thoughts back to the present problem—Cricket. He bit his lips. "We'll . . . we'll have to find a new home for him."

Paula sobbed. Shirley sniffed. Paul gathered his girls, and one boy, into his arms. "We'll make it. The next few months will be the hardest, but we'll make it."

"I don't mind giving up my bicycle and bedroom furniture and all that other stuff," Paula sobbed. "But Cricket is my best friend!" She gulped, "Well, one of my best friends."

Paul's heart cracked and bled. Then he heard it again, the cries of the lost Japanese. It drowned out his daughter's wails. No matter what it cost, they were committed to Japan.

Paula pulled out of her daddy's arms and looked up at him through gushing tears. "Will you get me another puppy when we get to Japan, Daddy?"

His daughter's face blurred. "Absolutely, baby. Absolutely." As Paul cradled his family in his arms, Cricket licked the tears off his chin.

When Paul announced their missionary appointment to the church, a shocked silence blanketed the congregation, followed by sniffs and sobs and applause. The saints were grieved to lose the pastor who had brought them through church troubles and family tragedies, and led them into awesome revival. But they were honored to know that their pastor and his family had been chosen by God to carry the gospel halfway around the world.

The church began the search for a new pastor. Paul took care of a hundred details. Shirley dismantled their home, dis-

Paul A. Dennis

posed of furniture, and packed stuff. Paula hunted for a new home for Cricket.

One day she danced into the house, side-stepping the boxes Shirley was packing, calling, "Mom! Dad! I found a home for Cricket."

Paul looked up from the kitchen table where he was sorting through papers, deciding what to keep, what to toss. Shirley stood and straightened. Left. Right. Left. Right. Roll. She eased the tension from her shoulders. "Where?"

Paula picked up Cricket who was jumping around her feet. "Margie Whitcomb said she would love to have Cricket."

A load lifted from Paula's parents' hearts. Margie was the perfect answer to their problem. She would love Cricket almost as much as Paula had.

As Shirley polished her piano for the last time, she willed herself not to cry. Over the years she had told Paul, "I don't want a piano at home until I can have a new one." That dream had materialized the year before when she had received a small inheritance from her grandmother.

When the men came to move her most cherished "thing" to the church, she watched in dry silence until the door closed behind them. Then she disappeared into the bedroom. Later when she came out, her eyes were swollen, but her face was glowing. Pride and pity squeezed Paul's heart. Shirley Dennis was missionary material through and through.

As he wrapped his arms around her, he quoted, "And every one that hath forsaken houses, or brethren, or sisters, or father, or mother, or wife, or children, or lands, for my name's sake, shall receive an hundredfold, and shall inherit everlasting life."

Six months after they met the foreign missions board, the parsonage was empty, waiting for the new pastor's family. The Dennises' furniture was sold, and all the personal items they could not take on deputation were stored at Donald's in Zanesville. Foreign missions paperwork was complete.

Order My Steps

They had only one other thing to do before they started down the deputation trail—deliver Cricket to his new home. It was the hardest thing they did.

Roads, Rubber, and Rewards

June 1976 with $200, an LTD Ford, and a 6' x 13' Shasta trailer, the three missionaries-to-be pulled out of the parking lot of Antioch Apostolic Church headed for their first deputation service. Their goal was to raise, as quickly as possible, their budget of $6,300 a month. It seemed an insurmountable goal.

They didn't need a map to direct them to their first service, as they simply went across town to the First Apostolic Church.

At the end of the service, Pastor Kinzie signed their PIM card and handed them a check for $1,000. This offering filled many gaps in the next ten months. This was their second PIM; their first was Jack Leaman, director of promotions and publications for the Foreign Missions Division, a friend from their days at Crooksville Apostolic Gospel Church.

The Dennises' calendar filled quickly. Most weeks they were in service Tuesday through Saturday, with two services on Sunday. Keeping track of where to be when and the pastor's name required an efficient secretary, and Paul had the best riding in the front seat beside him.

Mondays were usually long-distance days. Often they traveled four hundred to six hundred miles to get to where they needed to be Tuesday night.

Most nights were spent in the pastor's home, evangelist's quarters, or a room at the church. Nights in a motel were a rare treat.

"When in Rome do as the Romans do," became their favorite saying. Each district and church added a new dimension to their deputation collage. Paul's air force training clicked in: Eyes and ears open. Mouth shut.

Order My Steps

In August they pulled up in front of the pastor's home in Rock Hill, South Carolina. More strangers, soon-to-be friends, LaDean and Betty Erickson came out to greet them.

After they had exchanged the pertinent get-acquainted information, LaDean asked, "Do you like to fish? Lake Wylie is only a few miles from here. It's a great fishing spot."

"Love to," Paul answered.

"Then let's take tomorrow off and catch our supper. How about it, girls?"

"We can't all fit in your two-man boat," Betty reminded her husband.

"Why don't we take lawn chairs and books?" Shirley suggested.

"Great," Betty agreed. "We can sit on the shore, soak up the sun, and read while the men bring in the bacon, oops, I mean the fish."

"Can we swim?" Paula asked.

Betty shook her head. "It's not a good place to swim, but we can wade around the edges."

The next day the ladies settled contentedly on the shore while the men loaded their fishing gear into the boat and headed out to bring in "supper."

All was well until, in the middle of the lake, the motor died and refused to be revived. Cranking and choking, pleading and praying did not impress it.

"Must be out of gas," LaDean snorted. "Rule #1 for all boaters—check the gas tank. Looks like we'll have to paddle back to the shore. Would you please get out the oars, Paul?"

Paul's search of the boat took only a few seconds. "What oars?"

LaDean winced. "No oars?"

No oars.

The pastor-fisherman's face turned red, and it wasn't from the sizzling August sun. "Rule #2—always pack the oars."

Paul A. Dennis

Paul chuckled. "Looks like we swim and pull the boat."

They pulled off their shoes and socks and plunged into the lake. The cool water soothed their sun-baked skin. For the first hundred yards their unexpected swim was a treat. After that, yard by yard, they slowed to a crawl, pulling the ever-growing boat. Paul's memory film rewound.

He and his cousins, Clifford "Bugs" and Billy "Froggie," were skinny dipping in Myron Taylor's watering hole again, squishing the mud between their toes, changing the sky blue water to earth brown. Red-faced Mr. Taylor burst over the rise, screaming, "How many times do I have to tell you hoodlums not to—"

The delinquents jumped out, grabbed their clothes, and made a mad dash for the woods.

"—swim in my watering hole? That water is for my horses and cattle, not bored boys. You'd better not let me catch—"

His ranting and raving faded into mumbles as the boys scurried into their hideout built from scraps of tin, lumber, and cardboard. There they lay on old blankets and talked about things they knew nothing about.

Paul chuckled. Ugh! He spat out the dirty lake water. Welcome back to Lake Wylie.

His water-soaked clothes and the drag of the boat turned each lap into a weightlifting exercise. He longed for the freedom of skinny dipping. But times had changed. He was a missionary on deputation, and the ladies were on the shore watching.

Finally, host and guest were close enough to put down their feet and walk. The ladies, who had been so worried minutes before, hooted. But when the men collapsed on the shore, the laughter died.

Order My Steps

"Are you all right?" "What happened?" "You could have drowned!" "What are we going to do now?"

When the men finally got their breath and the ladies lost theirs, it was decided that LaDean would drive to the marina to buy gas. The others would stay with the stuff.

While he was gone, a luxurious cabin cruiser pulled near the shore. The captain leaned over the rail and shouted, "You folks need help?"

Betty called back, "We ran out of gas. My husband has gone to the marina to get some."

"Want a ride to the marina?" the gentleman asked.

Paula, jumping up and down, begged. "Oh please say yes. I want to ride in *that* boat."

Paul grinned, "You girls go ahead. I'll boat-sit until LaDean gets back, and we'll pick you up at the marina."

So, assisted by the jauntily dressed stranger, three sunbaked, sand-caked women climbed aboard the polished cabin cruiser, sprinkling sand on the plush pillows and dripping water on the polished floor.

Later around the supper table, the Dennises and Ericksons hilariously recounted their adventure. As LaDean, the perfect host, handed the green beans to his wife, he dropped the bowl. No fish. No beans. But lifelong friends and memories. Rock Hill, South Carolina, a bright spot on a long road.

In Florida while making new memories, Paul stumbled onto an old, painful one. Orange Blossom Trail, Orlando. The burned-out shell of a building.

He pulled into what was left of the parking lot and turned off the motor. Shirley and Paula waited quietly while memories engulfed Paul like a tsunami. He gripped the steering wheel and groaned.

After a few minutes he cleared his throat. "This was where . . ." He choked, paused, and tried again. "This was the nightclub where I worked in the late fifties, after I got back from Japan . . . after Audrey's accident. This place was filled with vice and wickedness. I . . ."

He looked over his shoulder at Paula Ann. Her eyes were wide. She was drinking in every word. He had to be careful.

As memories of past deeds swept over Paul, a heavy weight smothered him. His soul cried out, "Oh, God, forgive me!"

I have.

Two words, but it was enough. His grip on the steering wheel relaxed. His shoulders straightened as the memories receded back under the blood. God did not remember his past sins; neither should he.

He started the car, determined to focus on making new memories, not reviving dead ones.

Paula Ann's bubbly personality paved the way everywhere they went. She jumped right into whatever the youth group was doing, making friends at every church.

Occasionally a church would give her an offering to buy whatever she wanted. She had no problem deciding how to spend these bonuses. "I am going to buy a new dress that is *not* on sale." It was her gentle way of rebelling against her parents' economics.

The road ate up the summer months. It was September and time for Paula to go back to school. So with a heavy heart Paul pointed the LTD toward Zanesville, where they stopped in front of his brother's house. Donald and Mary had agreed to be surrogate parents to Paula during the school year. The problem? Paula wanted her real parents, and they wanted her.

They unpacked Paula's stuff, visited awhile, said goodbye, and headed down the road. After a few miles Paul pulled the car to the side of the road, and Shirley fell into his arms. Heaving sobs shredded their hearts. Up to this point, they had not

Order My Steps

considered anything they had given up—their church, their home, Shirley's piano, Cricket—to be a sacrifice. But leaving their daughter was a sacrifice. There was no other way to describe it.

A few days later two lonely parents sat side by side as the mile markers appeared and disappeared. A hurting mother said, "I can't stand it, Paul."

"I can't either," the dad answered.

"Then do something, Daddy," Shirley begged.

So Mr. Fix-it Dennis, heartbroken dad, contacted the American School and arranged for their daughter to take correspondence studies. By December the LTD rang with the laughter of a reunited family, as three missionaries to Japan traveled the deputation trail.

After 55,000 miles and 350 services, the slides of Japan were dilapidated, but the Dennises' passion had not dimmed. In each service their vision coupled with the saints' provision renewed Paul's and Shirley's energy and kept them rolling down the road, closer and closer to Japan. Offerings ranged from $14 to $300. The $1,000 offering was never matched; running a distant second was one for $500. PIMs of $5, $10, and $15 piled up until they conquered that seemingly insurmountable budget.

From coast to coast the Dennises made memories and friends. The road stretched long and the rubber grew thin, but the rewards were eternal.

The Land of the Rising Sun

May 1977. After sixteen months of cutting strings, counting miles, and cultivating friendships, Paul, Shirley, and fourteen-year-old Paula Ann walked down the concourse to the Northwest Airlines gate at the Columbus airport. They had one more hurdle to cross before leaving their homeland for four years—saying goodbye to family and friends.

At the gate Shirley's and Paul's families and Ohio District Secretary George Thompson gathered around them for prayer. Brother Thompson spoke a blessing over the excited, but apprehensive, outgoing missionaries.

Hugs. Kisses. Tears. Promises. Goodbyes.

As the plane lifted off the runway, Paul's soul sang, his heart ached, and his mind whirled like a milkshake in a blender. Darkness blanketed him. A verse flashed on the screen of his memory.

"And every one that hath forsaken houses, or brethren, or sisters, or father, or mother, or wife, or children, or lands, for my name's sake, shall receive an hundredfold, and shall inherit everlasting life" (Matthew 19:29).

Suddenly, the plane pierced through the clouds and sunlight filled the cabin. He got the message. They were taking Sonlight to those "that sat in darkness." Light always drives out darkness.

He smiled at Shirley and winked at Paula. They, directed by their Commander in Chief, were headed for one awesome adventure. Why was he worried? God was ordering their steps.

After a layover at Chicago, they were in the air again going west—this time for about eighteen hours, flying over Canada and Alaska to the other side of the world—to the "Land of the Rising Sun."

Order My Steps

On May 16 around 10:00 PM, seat-weary Shirley, Paula Ann, and Paul debarked at the Northwest Airlines terminal in Osaka, Japan.

"Where did all these people come from?" Paula asked as they were meshed into the mob.

"Welcome to Japan," Paul told her. "Hold my hand."

Paula grabbed her dad's hand, and Shirley linked her arm through her husband's. "I'm glad you've been here before and know what to do."

"Yeah," Paul muttered. Arriving on a ship, falling in line, boarding a bus to air force housing, having each step ordered by a barking officer was somewhat different from the present situation. He sent a silent prayer heavenward for the unseen hand to guide them.

"See that sign?" Paula pointed. "It's in English. Customs is that way."

A Japanese customs official speaking heavily accented English shot rapid questions at them. Paul relived his first day in school. It was his language, but he didn't understand. "Huh? . . . What? . . . Pardon me, sir. I do not understand. What did you say? . . . Passports? . . . Yes sir, right here."

Inch by inch they worked their way through the process into the land of their calling. Next step—collect their luggage, fourteen suitcases, three carry-on bags, and the ladies' handbags.

"Count them, Shirley. Are they all here?"

All accounted for. "Now let's find carts to carry them."

Finally, each pushing a cart loaded with their compressed belongings, they headed to the waiting lounge eager to meet missionaries Claude and Helen Thompson, their prayer partners from the Louisville General Conference.

"Where are they, Daddy?" Paula asked as they scanned the lounge.

Paul wrinkled his brow. "I'm sure they are here somewhere. Look for Americans."

Paul A. Dennis

"Are you sure they knew when we would arrive?" Shirley asked.

"Absolutely," Paul declared. "In his last letter Brother Thompson said they would be waiting. They're just running late."

Shirley sighed. "We might as well sit down." She looked around, "If we can find a seat."

An hour later the Dennises were worried. Had there been an accident? Were they in the wrong lounge? Were the Thompsons at a different airport?

Shirley dug in her purse and pulled out an address book. "Here's their phone number, Paul. Please call."

Next step—find a telephone. There was not a black telephone in sight, but they did find a green contraption with three slots for coins. It had to be a telephone.

Next step—find some Japanese coins.

Paul was weary. Shirley was exhausted. Paula Ann was fascinated.

Eventually, they found a place to exchange their American dollars for Japanese yen, and someone to show them how to deposit the yen and call the number in Shirley's little black book.

As the phone on the other end rang, Shirley fretted, "What if they aren't home? What if they got the date wrong and have gone out of town? What if . . ."

With his right palm, Paul covered his open ear. "Shhhh, Shirley, I can't hear."

"Hello?" A man's sleepy voice answered, an English voice.

"Is this Claude Thompson?"

"Yes?"

"This is Paul Dennis. We are at the airport in Osaka."

"You're not! Now? But I thought you were coming in later this week."

Order My Steps

Paul looked at his watch. It was . . . no, it wasn't. His watch was still set on Central Standard Time. He didn't know what time it was. He just knew it was late, and they were bone tired.

". . . do have the address, don't you?"

Paul realized he had missed part of the conversation. "Sorry. I was distracted. What did you say?"

The voice on the other end repeated, "It would take too long for us to get to the airport. I know you are tired, so get a taxi and come to our house in Kyoto. You do have the address, don't you?"

"Yes, we do. Sorry about the mix-up, Brother Thompson. We'll be there soon." Paul didn't realize that he was speaking optimistically.

"You girls stay with the luggage while I look for a taxi," the weary traveler instructed. No sense in pushing three heavily laden carts who knew where.

Finding a driver who could understand even a few words of English required determination, but Paul did it. When he showed the driver the address, the little man raised his eyebrows and shook his head.

Paul nodded firmly.

The driver shrugged. Using a combination of broken English and hand maneuvers, he asked about their luggage. Paul led him to where Shirley and Paula were standing guard beside a small mountain of suitcases.

The driver's almond-shaped eyes formed circles. He shouted, "Two taxis! Two taxis!"

Paul figured they could stuff it all into one, until he saw the taxi. The Japanese taxi was not an LTD. So he relented and agreed to pay for two taxis. Surely it would not be too far. But it was.

Does this guy know where he is going? Is he taking us for a ride to run up the cost? Will both taxis get to the same address? What a night!

Paul A. Dennis

In the dark before dawn two taxis pulled up in front of the Thompson's home. Lights pouring from every window spread a welcome mat through the darkness. The minute the taxis pulled up, the door opened. The Thompsons' bright smiles drove away the gloom that had hovered around the new missionaries.

"I'll pay the drivers," Claude said. "You can pay me back later."

The drivers calculated the fares, "Fifteen thousand yen."

The veteran missionary translated for Paul, "That's about one hundred dollars."

The men grabbed suitcases and followed the ladies into the house. A wonderful American aroma embraced them.

"I know you are exhausted, but how about some vegetable soup and Jell-O?" their gracious hostess invited.

The Dennises would eat a lot of exotic Japanese cuisine in the years to come, but nothing ever tasted better than that simple American comfort food.

Laugh and Learn

Paul had never expected to attend Yale University, but he did in Kyoto, Japan. As soon as he had made arrangements to rent the Thompsons' house and taken care of postal and banking business, his family enrolled in the language school—*Kyoto Nihongo Gakko*, a branch of Yale University. The school motto was "We have to be cruel to be kind." That gave the Dennises a hint as to what was ahead. It was intense: three hours a day, five days a week, plus homework, reading, writing, and speaking.

The first day the teacher surveyed her class of four: one student from Canada and a family of three from the United States.

She introduced herself as Mrs. Masuda and asked their names.

The Canadian replied, "My name is Paul."

She turned to the father of the family. "My name is Paul." The teacher smiled and nodded.

She looked at the daughter, who said, "My name is Paul-a." The teacher's smile faded.

She raised her eyebrows at the mother, who said, "My name is Mrs. Paul."

By then the four students were laughing hilariously, and the teacher was thoroughly confused. They may have had the first laugh, but she had the last laugh many times over.

One day Mrs. Masuda put her hand behind her ear and said, "*Kiite Kudasai.*"

Her students stared at her. She wiggled her hand behind her ear and repeated, "*Kiite Kudasai.*"

Shirley whispered to Paul—her Paul, "What do you think she wants us to do?"

Paul had no idea; neither did Paula nor Paul from Canada.

Paul decided to make a guess. "Maybe she wants us to put a hand behind our ear like she is doing."

So each student gave her a big smile and mimicked her.

The teacher looked down her nose and said emphatically, "No! No! I am saying 'please listen'."

It sure didn't sound like "please listen" to her students. Then she said something they never did understand. When they repeated it, the teacher said, "*Dame. Dame,*" what sounded like "dumb."

Shirley frowned and tightened her lips. She did not appreciate the teacher calling them "dummies." Later she learned that *dame* means "not right."

They asked questions in English, and the teacher responded in Japanese. The words bounced back and forth until the teacher reluctantly translated. They were not forbidden to use English, but it was discouraged.

A couple of months into language study, the teacher informed them, "Paula will be the first to speak good Japanese. Shirley will be second." She paused and pointed at Paul. "You will be last."

So much for the power of affirmation. Oh, well, sometimes a challenge motivated Paul more than affirmation.

While he struggled with the language, Shirley did well, most of the time; and Paula excelled, although they never caught her picking up a book. At the same time she continued her high school studies by correspondence from the American School.

Before leaving for their new assignment, the Thompsons had introduced the new missionaries to the superintendent of the United Pentecostal Church of Japan, Pastor Kunio Fujibayashi, and his wife, Koto. By virtue of his appointment as a missionary of the UPCI, Paul was an official board member of the UPCI of Japan. However, he chose to "sit below the salt" until being asked to take a higher chair of the organization. He submitted himself to and worked closely with Brother Fujibayashi and the Japanese brethren.

The Dennises started attending Pastor Fujibayashi's church *Kamigamo Fukuin Kyokai* (Kamigamo Gospel Church) and soon developed a firm friendship with his family.

Order My Steps

They had been in Japan for about a month when Pastor Fujibayashi asked Paul to preach at the welcoming service for his family. With some trepidation, Paul agreed.

At the beginning of the service, he followed protocol and gave honor to the superintendent, board members, and visiting pastors. Knowing the gift-giving tradition of the Japanese, he gave, first to the pastor and then to the other dignitaries, a bright new 1976 silver dollar. Before leaving the States, he had purchased forty of these from a bank, commemorating the year of their appointment as missionaries to Japan.

Soon Paul and Shirley were immersed in the Kamigamo church, doing what they had always done in the States—submitting to the authority of the pastor and fulfilling every request made of them. They were faithful in attendance, worship, ministry, tithing, teaching, preaching, and outreach. Paula joined the choir and youth group. The language and culture were different, but the spirit was the same.

Koto had attended Christian Life College in Stockton, California, and had a good command of the English language. One day at church Shirley decided to utilize her language skills. Greeting the mother of a small baby, she said in Japanese, "You have a very cute baby." Surprise flashed across the mother's face. Shirley assumed that the young lady was amazed at her mastery of Japanese.

Her bubble burst when Koto asked, "Do you know what you said to her?"

Shirley nodded. "I told her that she has a cute baby."

Koto giggled. "No, you didn't. You told her that she has a scary little devil." Shirley had changed the vowels in the words: cute is *kawai* and scary is *kowai;* baby is *akachan* and devil is *akuman*.

"Oops! Quick, Koto. Tell me, how do I apologize in Japanese?"

Interpreting for Paul presented challenges. Once when teaching a Bible study, Paul said, "In the church that I pastored in the

States, one lady would come in and sit in the service like an old bull."

This stretched Pastor Fujibayashi's language skills, so in Japanese he said, "Brother Dennis had this church member that sits in church like a 'he-cow.' I don't know how a he-cow sits, but please laugh."

The congregation complied and laughed. The Bible study continued.

When the Fujibayashis and the Dennises were together, laughter filled in the gaps where language failed.

Pastor Fujibayashi often referred to himself and Paul as "David and Jonathan." No one asked who was who. It didn't matter. They were great friends. Such good friends, in fact, that when they traveled together, the pastor let the American drive his new Toyota.

Koto taught Shirley much about flower arrangements, the tea ceremony, the koto musical instrument, and other things important to the Japanese culture. They often sat together in church, where the language lessons continued. Shirley would write down a word from the sermon, and Koto would write the Japanese word beside it. What fun they had, learning from one another. Often a stern glance from their husbands squelched their giggles.

The parents were not the only ones who enjoyed and profited from their families' relationship. Often Isaiah, 13; Mona, 10; Mina, 8; and Timothy, 7, stayed with the Dennises while their parents took care of church business in other areas.

"Sister Dennis, may we have some green pudding," was a familiar request. Soon the Dennises had to write home ordering more packages of pistachio pudding to match the supply with the demand.

It was give and take. The children learned to enjoy western foods and speak English, and the Dennises learned a lot about the Japanese language, manners, and customs.

Order My Steps

One day Pastor Fujibayashi, Koto, Paul, Shirley, and Mamoru Hashimoto, the director of the Japan Gospel Pentecostal Organization, dined at a local restaurant.

Paul ordered barbecued ribs. He told the Japanese, "This is the way to eat spare ribs." He picked up a piece of meat and put it in his mouth; then he licked his fingers, smacked his lips, and said, "Finger-licking good!"

Mamoru grinned and imitated Paul, saying in his broken English, "Finger-lickin' good."

The simple comic act produced laughter and created a memory, bonding people whose nations had once been enemies. Such was the ministry of missionaries Paul and Shirley Dennis, ambassadors of Christ, bringing laughter and goodwill from the United States to Japan.

Pushed by dreams of reaching a nation with the gospel, Paul felt as though he were crawling. His spirit screamed, "Run, Paul, run," but the Holy Spirit and missionary administrator Edwin Judd said, "Walk. You'll learn a lot more about the city and its people walking among them, than buzzing past them."

The Dennises' home was near the foot of Mount Heia. Before they got their Sheaves for Christ car, they took a bus or taxi to school. After class, Shirley and Paula, along with whatever packages they had accumulated on the way, usually took public transportation home. Paul walked, using the cap of Mount Heia as his signpost.

As he walked he saw small white square signs with black Japanese lettering posted in the yards of many homes.

Paul asked some friends what these signs were, and they told him, "The people in those houses are communists."

One day in language school, he asked Mrs. Masuda why there were so many communists in Kyoto.

She tightened her eyebrows. "How do you know that?"

Paul A. Dennis

"As we walk around our neighborhood, we see signs at the entrances to the houses."

"What do the signs look like?"

Paul drew the symbol. As his teacher watched the design take shape, her perplexed look exploded into laughter lines. "That does not mean 'a communist lives here.' It means 'we have a dog.'"

Laugh and learn. That's what the Dennises did every day in their new world.

For efficient, organized Shirley shopping in Japan was a delight. Even the fish in the market were lined up with their heads pointing the same direction. Many shopping days she put on a church dress and her high heels, jumped on her bicycle, and pedaled to the market, just like the Japanese ladies. Paul was amazed at how well his petite, precocious Shirley adapted to life in Japan. The culture fit her like the gloves she wore when she went fishing.

The Ladies Ministry of the United Pentecostal Church International, through a special offering called Mothers Memorial, provides every missionary with a washer, dryer, stove, and refrigerator. Paul and Shirley had elected to purchase theirs after arriving on the field. And it was a good thing they did. The electricity was only 60 hertz. American appliances would have required separate converters. Even the American-made clocks ran hours behind time.

Everything was a learning experience, and the Dennises, with their love for knowledge, loved almost every minute, even though they often felt like their American clock.

One lesson was a bit expensive—translating yen to dollars.

As a lover of ice cream, Paul kept a constant supply in the small freezer compartment of their Mothers Memorial refrigerator. One day while grocery shopping with his wife, he looked twice at the price. "Shirley, how much does that translate into dollars?"

Shirley ran her mental calculator. "About $16."

"Sixteen dollars!" Paul shouted, as he looked at the container, smaller than a half-gallon.

Shirley looked around. "Shhh! Don't create a scene."

Order My Steps

Paul lowered his voice one notch. "Don't tell me we've been paying $16 for this itty-bitty container of ice cream."

Shirley shrugged. "OK, I won't tell you."

Paul quickly lost his appetite for ice cream.

Fruit-loving Shirley developed a craving for cantaloupe. One day when shopping, Paul discovered a display of six cantaloupes artistically arranged and packaged.

In his best Japanese, he asked, "*Oikura desu ka?*" (How much is it?)

The clerk responded, "*Hasssen yen desu*" (eight thousand yen).

By then Paul had learned to use his mental calculator so he did some fast figuring. Eighty dollars? Incredible! That couldn't be right.

He repeated, "*Oikura desu ka?*"

"*Hasssen yen desu.*"

That quashed Shirley's craving for cantaloupe.

One steaming summer day Shirley reminded Paul, "We're going to need some heat this winter."

Paul wiped sweat on his work shirt sleeve. "If we can figure out a way to bottle some of today's heat and use it next winter, we'll get rich. Then we can let someone else have our PIMs," he joked.

Shirley didn't laugh. "Seriously, Paul, if we buy a heater now it will be cheaper than it will be this winter."

Paul nodded. It made sense. His economy-minded wife's ability to plan ahead often saved them dollars and cents—make that *yen*.

The next day they set out, via the cram-and-pack public transportation, to find a kerosene heater.

In every shop they met the same response—an astonished look and "A heater? Now? It is hot enough without a heater. If you want a heater, come back this winter."

Paul A. Dennis

Another lesson learned. If you want winter goods in Japan, you shop for them in the winter. They are not even in stock, much less on sale, in the summer.

One day Paul and Paula decided to take some father/daughter time and stroll in a hereto unexplored part of their neighborhood.

As they walked and talked, Paul stopped and sniffed. "What's that I smell?"

Paula wrinkled her nose. "Gingerbread maybe?"

"I think it is," Paul's stomach rumbled. The scent transported him to #8 Hollow. He shut his eyes and saw his mother pulling gingerbread cookies out of the oven of her four-lid coal and wood cookstove. He opened his eyes and turned to his daughter, "We've got to have some. Let's find it."

Paula giggled and pointed, "I think it's coming from that way."

So they followed their noses until they came to a building on a little side path. Was it a shop or bakery? They couldn't tell. But the smell was definitely coming from behind the wooden sliding door.

Driven by a passionate longing for a taste of home, Paul said, "I'm going to go in and see if I can get some."

Paula was horrified. "Dad, you're not!"

"Yes, I am."

Paula turned and fled to the main street. She didn't know that snoopy American. Paul slid the door open and stuck his nose into someone else's business. It smelled wonderful.

No one was in sight, so he continued sniffing his way into the next room, which was the kitchen. A baker stood at a table making yatsuhashi, a hard cinnamon cookie. He took a bit of dough about three inches long, pressed it over a mold that resembled half of a half-inch pipe, forming a bridge.

The baker looked up and froze. Paul started to explain that he had been pulled in by the smell, but the baker did not understand English. So Paul rubbed his nose and stomach, and then took some money out of his pocket. The baker relaxed. Now the foreigner was talking Japanese.

Paul exited with a taste of home, fresh-from-the-oven cookies. Paula ran to meet her dad and home they went with a tasty surprise for Mom.

Every Friday night after the Dennises went to bed, a weird, creepy horn sound sent misshapen music notes through their open bedroom window.

"Maybe it has something to do with the Buddhist or Shinto ceremonies," Shirley guessed.

"Or perhaps it is a funeral," Paul added. "The next time this happens I am going to find out what it is all about."

A week later Paul lay awake listening for the sound. When it crashed through their window, Shirley put her hands over her offended ears. "I wish they would at least play something melodic."

Paul jumped out of bed and into his clothes. He burst out of the house and raced down the side street. By the time he got to the main street, the source of the sound was about five blocks away. He shifted into high gear. As he gained on the creeping vehicle, he saw the outline of a house-shaped structure on wheels. He was sure it was a hearse.

A few feet away from the contraption, he realized it was a mobile shop. He watched in amazement. As it rolled slowly through the neighborhood, tooting its cranky horn, doors flew open. People ran out carrying empty bowls. The driver stopped and filled them with his special brand of Ramen noodles. The people paid him and went back in to eat their middle-of-the-night meal.

"Shirley will never believe this," Paul muttered. He persuaded the noodle man to return to his house. He got Shirley and Paula out of bed, handed them bowls, and sent them out to buy noodles. Like all good Japanese, they had noodle soup at midnight.

Another mystery of Japanese culture solved.

Paul A. Dennis

As Paul and Shirley explored their mission field, they fell in love with Kyoto, the third largest and the oldest city in Japan. Kyoto means "capital city." Home to 1.4 million people and as many as 3,000 Buddha and Shinto shrines, it is thought of as the heart of Japan. The city is one of the academic centers of Japan, home of the Doshisha, Kyoto, and Ritsumeikan Universities, three of the best in Japan.

Kyoto was a wonderful place to learn the Japanese language and culture. But as the Dennises walked and later drove the streets of Kyoto, the spiritual sirens deep within them sounded. The ancient cultural and historic landmarks impressed and oppressed them. The *Kyomizu-dera,* a magnificent wooden temple, *Kinkaku-ji,* Temple of the Golden Pavilion, *Ginkaku-ji,* Temple of the Silver Pavilion, and *Ryoan-ji,* the famous rock garden, turned men's eyes and hearts to false gods.

In the Temple of Thousand and One Gods, each idol had a different expression on its face, but each one was made the same way. Standing in this temple, Paul pondered Acts 17. Under his breath he paraphrased, "Ye men of [Kyoto], I perceive that in all things you are too superstitious.... Whom therefore ye ignorantly worship, him declare I unto you [as soon as I learn your language]."

Oh, Lord Jesus, how do we reach them? Order our steps according to Your Word.

Fitting In

As Paul leaned down and tied his black dress shoes, he caught a glimpse of his wife's spiked high heels. "How you keep your balance in those ridiculous shoes is beyond me."

Shirley pirouetted around the bedroom laughing, "How you can pick up your feet wearing those heavy shoes is beyond me. Walking in your shoes one block would exhaust me."

Paul chuckled, "Tell you what, you wear your shoes; I'll wear mine." He grabbed her in a quick hug. "Agreed?"

"Agreed." Shirley put the finishing touches on her hair. "What time does church begin?"

"In a little over an hour. We'll be OK if we catch the right train. Are you about ready?"

Shirley put down her brush. "Ready. I'll check on Paula." She headed down the hall calling, "Paula Ann, time to go."

"Just a minute," their teenage daughter replied. "As soon as I put on my shoes."

Paul stood at the front door for several minutes, tapping his feet and staring at his watch, before Shirley appeared. "All set," she said. "I'm excited about seeing Sister Hirata again. Remember when we met her?"

"I sure do," Paul said. "It was last year at general conference in Anaheim. We were her hosts while she was in the States."

"Remember the foreign missions service?" Shirley asked, as she slipped her hand through his arm.

"How could I forget?" Paul chuckled. "Remember how shocked Sister Hirata was when she saw that you were going to wear *getas* (men's shoes) during that service?" He shook his watch. "What's keeping Paula?"

Shirley ignored the question. "Sister Hirata rushed to her hotel room and got her *zoris* (ladies shoes). She insisted that I wear them. She said that I could not wear getas with my kimono. She is a precious lady."

"And doing a wonderful job pastoring in Uji," Paul raised his voice, "Paula Ann! We're going to miss the train."

"Coming, Dad," Paula's voice floated down the hall ahead of her.

As he locked the door behind them, Paul said, "So much has happened in the last year." He grabbed his girls' hands. "Run, girls, run!"

His stomach tightened as they neared the train station. "Hold on tight," he ordered.

Paula rolled her eyes. "We know, Dad. We go through this every time we ride the subway or train."

"See that you remember," he said sternly. "If you get separated from us, you'll be on your own until we can find you and that could be miles down the line."

At that moment the train roared to a stop in front of them; the doors slid open, and they jumped on and grabbed the nearest unoccupied handrails. Quickly, the doors slid shut, and the train sped smoothly down the silver tracks.

After several stops and shuffles, they were able to sit down. "Whew! This feels good," Shirley said, as she wiggled her toes inside her cramped shoes.

Paul glanced at the stilts she was wearing, but wisely didn't say anything. As he settled into the thinly padded seat, he remembered a few weeks earlier when, hot and tired after a day at school, they waited for a bus. Like all public transportation, the buses were always crammed. They usually were lucky to find a standing place in the aisle.

That day when the bus door swung open, they joined the throng of commuters, pushed their way in, and discovered two empty seats in the center.

Order My Steps

Paula said, "Dad, you and Mom sit down. I'll stand."

They rushed to the seats, glad to rest their aching feet. At the next stop an elderly couple got on. They glared at Paul and Shirley, who smiled at them. The glares intensified.

Paul looked at Shirley and whispered, "Why are they mad at us?"

A young man turned to the ignorant foreigners and said kindly, "The seats you are in are reserved for the elderly and handicapped."

Paul's lips formed a circle. "Oh. We didn't know. Thanks for telling us."

They stood the rest of the way home.

"Always read the signs" is good advice, but it helps to be able to read the signs.

Public transportation was grueling, but educational. Surprises were plenteous, humorous, shocking, and often embarrassing.

One day they were on a train when a man about four seats in front of them stood and started taking off his shirt.

Paul said quietly, "Girls, remember the rule about not looking?"

Puzzled, Shirley and Paula turned to him. Paula said, "Do you mean the unwritten one about not looking directly at someone else?"

"Yes," Paul answered. "This is a good time to not look in front of you. Look out the window or at me."

Curiosity tempted them, but courtesy won. They stared out the window until Paul said, "OK. It's safe to look now."

Shirley leaned over Paula who was sitting between them and whispered, "PD, what in the world was that all about?"

Paul motioned with his eyebrows. "That guy just changed his trousers."

Shirley and Paula bit their lips to stifle their giggles.

Paul A. Dennis

Invitations to preach and teach at the local churches flooded in as the pastors learned the missionaries were available for special services. Everywhere the Dennises ministered, they were loved and respected because they loved and respected the Japanese. Graciousness bonded to graciousness.

Coming home from their first Japanese wedding, Paul erupted in chuckles every few minutes. Shirley glared at him, but he kept chuckling.

"Well, how was I to know that in Japan everyone wears black at weddings? And how was I to know they would want us in their wedding picture?" Shirley fretted, "There I was in a blue dress. . . ."

Paul's shoulders shook as he looked into his wife's intense brown eyes. They always shot sparks when she was upset; sometimes it was the prelude to tears. He decided it was time to quell his laughter and redirect the conversation.

"Remember the first wedding I performed? I was so humiliated."

Shirley nodded and smiled slightly. "The groom and best man, the bridesmaids and matron of honor were in place at the altar."

As their memory film rolled, Paul said, "I looked at the people packed in the church, cleared my throat, and said in my best professional voice, 'Ladies and gentlemen, we have come today to join together this man and woman in holy matrimony. If anyone knows any reason why they should not be joined, speak now or forever hold your peace.'"

Shirley giggled. "Then you saw the bride in the back of the church waving her arms and pointing at herself."

Paul guffawed. "Simultaneously I suffered a hot flash and a cold chill."

Shirley continued, "So you motioned for me to start 'The Bridal March.' With the first chord all eyes went to the bride at the back of the church."

Order My Steps

"That's when I took out my handkerchief and wiped the sweat. No one seemed to realize my goof, and I certainly never told them about my freezing and melting sensation."

Shirley laughed, and then her expression sobered. "We can laugh because that was then; this is now."

Paul put his arm around her shoulders, "In time you will laugh about today. Besides you looked adorable in your blue dress. You were lovelier than the bride."

Shirley knew that wasn't true, but who was she to argue with her husband?

Funerals brought another surprise. A church member died who did not have any family, so Pastor Fujibayashi asked Paul to act as the family member. After the service they went to the crematory where Paul discovered that the family members (in this case, him) picked out of the remains any bones they wanted to store in a cremation urn. This was put in the *Haka* (tomb or vault) on the church grounds.

Picking out a human bone for preservation was not Paul's favorite thing to do, but "When in Rome do as the Romans do."

Fitting in required flexibility and focus.

After four months of riding buses, subways, and trains, the Dennises received their first Sheaves for Christ car, furnished by the youth of the United Pentecostal Church International. Learning the laws and driving was a snap. All that was required was that they have good vision and know *migi* (right), *hidiri* (left), *ue* (up) and *shita* (down).

After he got his driver's license, the hardest part for Paul was driving with a driver on his left hand and one in the back seat. Driving in Japan was the opposite of driving in the U.S. All Paul had to do was tune out his girls and reverse his mind, a task he found fairly easy to do.

One week in January so many ministers from the States came to visit that Pastor Fujibayashi called it "International Preachers Week." It was revival time in the Kyoto churches and

Paul A. Dennis

for the Dennises. Time spent with their mentors, the Kinzies, along with other friends refreshed their spirits.

Soon after their guests left, at her husband's request Sister Koto Fujibayashi approached the Dennises about starting an English class as an outreach for the church. She found them a lovely room on the third floor above a Christian bookstore. It was furnished with blackboards, tables, and chairs.

They purchased English workbooks, announced the class, and young Japanese eager to learn English came. They had one hour of grammar and one hour of conversation. Koto assisted with the translation. After class the new missionaries served green tea, soda, and snacks. In addition to enabling the Dennises to develop their language skills, the classes gave them one-on-one contact with Japanese who did not know Jesus. This helped to satisfy Paul's, Shirley's, and Paula's intense passion to share the gospel. Out of this class at least four young people were born again.

Finally, the Dennises felt as though they were fitting in and doing what they came to do.

Back to the Future

Paul burst through the front door, calling, "Shirley! Shirley! Charlie Brown, are you home?"

Shirley came from the kitchen. "I'm right here, Paul. What in the world has happened?"

He pulled her into his arms and swung her around a couple of times. "There is a language school in Hokkaido and an American International School that Paula can attend."

Shirley gasped for air as Paul released her. Her mouth fell open, "But we were told that there wasn't. If we had known that we would have gone to Hokkaido a year ago."

They moved into the kitchen and sat down at the table. Paul puckered his lips. "I know. That's where we are called to go, back to the island where I spent three years in the air force."

Shirley tapped her fingernails on the tabletop. "Then why . . .?"

Paul stared at the ceiling for several seconds before he looked at his wife. "All I can say is that we have built a strong foundation of friendships with the ministers of the United Pentecostal Church of Japan. It has been a time of bonding. I have a feeling we are going to need that in the future."

Shirley nodded thoughtfully. "We have learned a lot about the culture, the language, and the people. And I love the church here." She stood up and pushed her chair under the table. She grinned, "So you are telling me that we are moving again."

Paul looked guilty. "But I didn't say that."

She laughed as she stroked his day old whiskers. "Oh, no? That's what I heard."

Paul chuckled. She knew him so well. "Have you got a good cup of coffee and a cinnamon roll, Charlie Brown? I'm sick of tea and tea cakes."

Paul A. Dennis

"That's the price you pay for bringing this Ohio girl halfway around the world," she teased, as she put on the coffeepot. "This afternoon I'll type up a letter to headquarters, asking for permission for us to move to Hokkaido."

On May 18, 1978, a year after they arrived in Kyoto, permission was granted. They decided that Paul should go first and find a place for them to live.

As the plane lifted off the runway in Osaka and headed north to the island of Hokkaido, missionary Paul Dennis leaned his head back and closed his eyes. His memory film rolled.

He was young. He was invincible. He was uninhibited. He was foolish. He rushed into the inferno in the drill pit without a thought of Hell. He drove the crash rescue truck like the devil was after him, and he was. He caroused. He reveled in sin. He lived as though there were no tomorrow.

Paul opened his eyes and looked down. Cloud pillows were scattered across the sky like Shirley's décor pillows on the sofa. Through them he watched as the outline of the mainland took shape and then disappeared. Blue sky and ocean blended until he could not separate them.

Then as the outline of Hokkaido took shape, Paul's soul sang and wept. Twenty-three years earlier he had come to this island as an airman under orders from the United States Air Force. This time he was coming as an ambassador under orders from his Commander in Chief, the Lord Jesus Christ. He felt as though he were going back into the future. A different man with a different mission.

Reverend Kunihiko Yamaki, pastor of the local UPCJ, met Paul at the airport and took him to check into his hotel. Then

Order My Steps

they went to the Yamakis' house, which was also the church, for dinner and fellowship.

The next day they went house shopping. Brother Yamaki knew that a mission house owned by the Lutheran organization was for rent. That day Paul closed the deal on the house. He rejoiced as he remembered the Quonset huts at Chitose Air Force Base. He sent up praise to his present Commander. "You certainly provide better for your servicemen than Uncle Sam does."

"The last two years I was stationed at Chitose, I served as the station captain and training instructor," he explained to the Japanese pastor. "I trained both military men and Japanese nationals. I would like to see if anyone I trained is still there."

Pastor Yamaki volunteered to take Paul to Chitose City the next day to visit the base, which had been turned over to the Japanese.

When they arrived in Chitose, Paul was astounded. It was much different from the country village of the '50s. Paved streets, pharmacies, department stores, supermarkets, and offices had replaced dirt roads, open sewers, tacky shops, and bars. He did not see one rickshaw. They could have been in any city in the States.

After several hours, it looked hopeless. They were not going to be allowed on base. Finally, on their third stop they were granted a pass, and an escort was appointed to take them to the base and fire station. Paul was surprised to see some of the same trucks they had used in 1955-1958. After visiting with numerous guys, he realized that no one remembered him.

Discouraged, they returned to the car. About a half mile from the gate, a military car drove up behind them honking furiously. Their driver pulled over and waited for the driver of the other car to come to them. Instead, a passenger jumped out of the back seat and ran around to Paul's open window. He stuck his head in it and shouted, "I am Beebee."

Paul A. Dennis

Beebee? Paul jumped out of the car, grabbed the Japanese's hand, and shook it vigorously. Their words tumbled over each other. Kamitani "Beebee" had been one of Paul's two hundred on-the-job trainees.

"You trained me well," Beebee said. "I am now the civilian fire chief working with the Japanese Air Force."

Paul told him that he was returning to Hokkaido to live and why.

"Many of your friends have moved away or died, but some are still here," Beebee said. "I will make arrangements for you to see them when you return with your family."

As Paul climbed back into the car, praises filled his soul. The past and future had met, and he was in the middle.

The Family Grows

On June 14, 1978, at 8:20 AM, the movers knocked on the Dennises' door in Kyoto. Two hours later the loaded moving truck and workers headed to the ferry dock. Paul, Shirley, and Paula followed in their Sheaves for Christ car.

The girls were embarking on a new adventure—a sea trip from the mainland to their new home, Hokkaido, the second-largest Japanese island. Paula chattered all the way to the dock, asking dozens of questions, and one question dozens of times, "Will I get my dog in Hokkaido?"

After the truck, car, workers, and family were safely on board, the Dennises explored the boat. Their cabin was furnished with hard wooden bunks with small futons for sleeping. Meals were eaten in the shared dining room.

Breakfast was not the traditional American one they had been having in their home in Kyoto. It consisted of a small bowl of rice and *miso* (soup); the soup resembled hot coffee with sour cream in it. Knowing that looks were not the taste, they simply stirred the soup before each drink. While in Kyoto the "Ohio transplants" had learned to like the red miso, even after they discovered it was made from fermented soy beans. But the soup on the ship was the white Hokkaido miso.

Paul stirred the soup with his chopsticks; then he picked up the bowl and slurped. Uggggh! Pssst! Too fishy for him.

Breakfast concluded with a lettuce salad topped with a scoop of mayonnaise. Shirley asked for a cup of coffee, but settled for green tea.

Later as they walked the deck, Paul filled his girls in on what to expect on the island of Hokkaido.

"It's a lot like Ohio with four seasons," he said. "In winter it is a sportsman's paradise—skiing, sledding, snowboarding.

Paul A. Dennis

Every year they have the spectacular Sapporo Snow Festival, *Yuki Matsuri* in Japanese."

Paul paused. Looking into the past he pictured the snow-covered Quonset huts on Chitose Air Force Base. "In Hokkaido snow is measured in feet, not inches," he told his family.

"Feet?" Shirley repeated.

"Yes. Ten to twenty feet of snow in the winter."

Paula's mental calculator whirred. "Wow! That's a lot of inches."

Paul pointed at a dark blue line following the horizon. "Hokkaido is a beautiful collage of mountains, fields, and lakes. In the summer we can climb and hike. And there are hundreds of natural hot spring baths for health and relaxation."

"Hot spring baths?" Shirley repeated

"They spring from the active volcanoes," Paul informed them.

"Active volcanoes?" Shirley was starting to sound like an echo. "Are you sure it is safe to live there, Paul?"

"Absolutely," Paul answered. "Some day I hope to take you to the far north to an Ainu village, where I—"

"Oh, look!" Paula interrupted. She pointed at the flying fish that had erupted from the surface. Some were gliding; others were flapping and flying. "Awesome!"

Thirty-six hours after they embarked, the Dennises debarked at Sapporo, the capital city of Hokkaido. They were thoroughly rested and ready for the challenges ahead.

Several hours later the moving truck and SFC car pulled into the driveway of their new home at 34-8 Higashi Tsukisamu, Toyohira Ku, Sapporo 061-01, Hokkaido, Japan.

After their tiny home in Kyoto, the Lutheran mission house looked like a mansion.

"A lawn? A real lawn!" Paula squealed. "We haven't had a lawn since we left Ohio."

Order My Steps

Paul ruffled Paula's hair. "We'll have to buy a lawnmower right away."

"There's even a little garden plot," Shirley observed. "This is perfect for us."

Shirley and Paula were ecstatic as they explored the oversized living room with a huge fireplace, kitchen, three bedrooms, maid's room, office, laundry room, bathrooms, garage, and huge boiler room. As soon as the furniture was unloaded and boxes appropriated to the right rooms, they went to work settling in—painting walls, hanging curtains and pictures, adding Shirley's décor.

In Kyoto the Thompsons had guided the new missionaries through the settling-in process. In Sapporo they were on their own. So Paul set out to tackle the business of becoming foreign residents—getting the utilities turned on, making arrangements to get their mail, setting up an account at the bank, and transferring the car registration from Kyoto to Hokkaido.

One evening as Shirley and Paula unpacked dishes, Paul sat at the kitchen table, grumbling, "Can you believe I have to draw a diagram of the garage to prove that we have a place to park our car? I have already filled out one thousand and one papers."

Paula giggled, "I thought you were more a teacher than an evangelist, Dad."

Paul's brow wrinkled. "Why do you say that?"

His sixteen-year-old daughter laughed, "Because you are speaking evangelistically about those papers. Surely it hasn't been one thousand and one papers, maybe more like nine hundred and ninety-nine."

Teasing and laughing about obstacles was the Dennises' way of overcoming, and it worked most of the time.

As Shirley unpacked the elegant, full-dress Japanese kimonos given each one of them by the Kyoto church at their going-away service, Paul handed her the tissue box. He knew she was recalling the kind words, the tears, and the laughs they had shared with the Fujibayashis and the saints.

Gently she put away the *tabis* (socks), undergarments, middle garments, outer garments, belts for men and *obis* (sashes) for the ladies. Each complete kimono cost several thousand dollars, but the real value of these treasures was the love and memories woven into them.

After a few weeks of searching, they found a small private language school and made arrangements to continue their studies with Mr. Yamade.

The first class was devoted to getting acquainted. The Dennises answered the usual multitude of questions. After which, Mr. Yamade said, "I want you to know that I know one thing. You are going to try to convert me to be a Christian. I have taught many missionaries language and culture and all have tried. However, I am still what I believe and that is *Sokka Gakkai*."

His students did not pursue the matter. They knew that Sokka Gakkai, an eclectic mix of religions, was a militant movement, the third power in the Japanese government. Their first goal was to make Mr. Yamade their friend; then they would introduce him to their Savior.

Going to language school three days a week cost about $900 a month, so before long they reduced their schooling to one day a week.

One evening Mr. Yamade and his family showed up at the Dennis house. The teacher was carrying a snowball of fur.

"A puppy for Paula," he said proudly, as he handed the bundle to her.

Holding the bundle of life under her chin, Paula crooned, "Oh, Dad! Mom! Isn't he adorable?" It was love at first sight.

Paul looked at their visitor. "It is a male?"

"Yes! Yes. This is a very special dog, from a pedigreed line of Ainu-Ken dogs. These pups usually cost about 30,000 yen."

Order My Steps

Paul mentally translated that into $150–$200. Too much money. He shook his head.

Mr. Yamade held out his hands, palms up. "It is free, free to you. The owner is my good friend. This dog is the runt of the litter, so he gives it to you as a favor to me."

During this conversation, Paula was giving her heart to the pup.

Mr. Yamade continued, "These dogs are trained to hunt bears, but this dog will be too small. He would never make a good hunting dog."

Paul realized that a gift was being extended to them. It was the ultimate of rudeness to refuse a gift. He reached for the puppy. Paula reluctantly handed it to her dad. "Isn't he precious, Dad?" Love glowed in her eyes.

Paul flipped the puppy over for an examination. He was a she, but it was too late. He could not break his daughter's heart.

As soon as the door closed behind the Yamade family, the search for a name for the newest family member started.

"Not Snowball or Whitey," Paula declared. "Those are too American."

"Salt! He is as white as salt," Shirley suggested.

"That's better," Paula said, "but it's still not quite right. How do you say 'salt' in Japanese?" She thought a minute then answered her own question. "*Shio?* That's it!"

"Shio is perfect," she declared, as she christened her new friend. "Your name is Shio."

Shio never reached the size of a hunting dog, but from 1978 until 1996 she guarded her beloved family. Her courageous spirit later saved them from loss, harm, and possible death.

Reaching Out

The UPCI missions director had told the Dennises to plan to spend their first term learning the language and the culture, and use extra time, if any, on church work. So they devoted that "extra time" to assisting the local churches of the Japan United Pentecostal Church. In Sapporo they immediately got involved in the church pastored by Brother Yamaki.

Shirley and Paula conducted English classes before the services, worked in the Sunday school, and taught the ladies new hairstyles. When word circulated that the missionaries were teaching the children to sing in English, the Sunday school grew. The saints helped the Dennises learn the Japanese language and culture. The teacher/student roles often reversed.

Soon after arriving in Sapporo, Paul called Beebee. He told Paul that he had located seven or eight men from the crash unit that remembered him, so he had arranged a reunion party the second of July in Chitose City.

Not being familiar with the address, Paul asked Pastor Yamaki to accompany him, Shirley, and Paula.

Etiquette. Shaking hands. Bowing. Shaking hands. Bowing.

Reminiscing. Telling stories. Sharing laughs. Repeating jokes.

Hospitality. Drinks—beer, sake, and whiskey—were abundant. Luckily for Pentecostal missionaries, Coke is available around the world.

"Coke? You, Paul, are asking for a Coke? What has happened to you? You always had a drink in your hand."

Paul was delighted to tell them, "I am no longer a firefighter, but a *senkyoshi* (missionary)."

Bother Yamaki stepped in with his fluent Japanese and explained, "Paul is not like a Buddhist monk or Shinto priest. He is a Christian, a follower of Jesus Christ."

Order My Steps

After that Paul could only guess what Brother Yamaki was saying. He just grinned as his old buddies rolled their eyeballs and nodded their heads as if they understood. What they did not understand was the new Paul. No drinking. No smoking. No wild partying. Astounding.

End of the party.

Every day that Paul was cooped up learning to conjugate verbs, he battled sheer frustration. He was still in translator mode when speaking, and it was slow going. His preaching and teaching ministry was severely limited. He longed to run with the gospel; instead, he crawled.

One day he came home from language class feeling like a kindergartner in college with Mrs. Masuda's voice ringing in his memory, "You will be last one to learn." Looking for a hiding place, he went out to his garden patch and plopped down behind the six-foot-high tomato-less tomato plants.

Tears flowed down his face, dripped onto the ground, and watered the unproductive plants. *I am just like these plants. No fruit.*

He cried out, "God, why don't You give me this language? You have allowed me to speak in unknown tongues. Why don't You give me the ability to speak Japanese?"

A clear voice rang in his spirit. *Why should I give it to you? Everyone before you has worked and studied to obtain it. You can too.*

Instantly, the tears stopped. Paul got up. If those before him, the Thompsons, the Halls, and others, could learn Japanese, then he could do it too. He would do it.

The next Sunday evening as he sat holding the songbook and singing with the little Japanese congregation, he suddenly realized what he was doing. "*Shu ni mamiyuru, sono hi ni wa.*" ("It will be worth it all when we see Jesus.") He was unconsciously reading and singing in Japanese. Praise God! Faith lifted him above the shadows. In the future he would still struggle with the language, but in that service the gloom dissipated.

Their goal was to start a church in their home. Sapporo had a population of 1.5 million and one United Pentecostal Church. Daily they asked God to help them find someone to work with them as a translator.

"I'm going to town, Shirley," Paul called. "Is there anything you need?"

"Toothpaste."

"Got it," Paul replied. "I'll be back in a couple of hours."

Downtown he walked, thinking, *Don't forget the toothpaste. Where shall I buy it? The kusuriya* (drugstore) *or the maketto* (food market) *or the depato* (department store). He chuckled. Even in his thoughts, he practiced Japanese.

But what he wanted more than toothpaste was an interpreter. *Oh, God, please guide my steps to the right person.*

He looked in the window of a small weather-beaten store. No need to go in there. They wouldn't have toothpaste.

As he turned to walk away, he felt the Spirit nudge him. *Go back and go in.*

He kept walking. *Go back and go in.*

He shrugged the feeling aside and walked on. *Go back! Go in!*

So he did. The shop appeared empty. He snooped around, looking for toothpaste, until a tiny, antique Japanese lady with a humped back hobbled up the aisle.

"*Irasshimase.*" (Welcome. Come in.)

"*Konnichi wa.* (Good afternoon.) Do you have toothpaste?"

She frowned and shook her head. Paul realized she did not speak English. So he mimicked brushing his teeth.

She frowned and shook her head. She still did not understand.

Paul searched his mental Japanese vocabulary. Not one word for toothpaste did he find. Not even two words for tooth paste.

Order My Steps

Meanwhile, the little lady stared at him with question marks in her eyes, a universal language.

Paul was about to give up and leave, when she went to the stairway leading to the second floor. She called out something Paul did not understand.

Muffled footsteps vibrated the ceiling above him, and then moved to the staircase and down. A young lady appeared at the bottom of the stairs. She walked over to him and said in perfect English, "How may I help you?"

Paul's frustration vanished. "You speak English?" Well, of course, she did. Hadn't she just offered to help him? "I need toothpaste, please."

"*Hamigaki* (toothpaste); it's right over here," she said, as she moved to another aisle and returned with a tube. "Are you an American?"

"Yes."

In a friendly tone, she asked, "What are you doing in Sapporo?"

"My wife, daughter, and I are here to do missionary work."

Her eyes lit up. "What! Are you a Christian?"

Paul grinned. "I am."

Her almond eyes crinkled. "Wow!" Then Atsuko, a twenty-six-year-old college graduate, told him that she had recently returned from Israel where she had gone to live in a kibbutz and learn about God. But it was nothing like she had expected. She had returned disillusioned and hurt.

"Just before my mother called me to come and help you, I was in my room praying, 'God, if You are real, send someone here today to teach me about Christianity and You.'"

Paul's grin pushed his earlobes out. "I was walking and praying, asking God to help me find someone who would help us start a house church. We need a translator."

They locked eyes. Atsuko smiled, "I am your answer to prayer, and you are mine!"

Paul A. Dennis

On August 4, 1978, the Dennises started having church in their home with Atsuko translating. At their first meeting they had seventeen in attendance, plus Paul, Shirley, and Paula. These were not members of the Sapporo church, but high school and college students or graduates, interested in learning English and more about Christianity. Friendships were molded as they studied the Bible, fellowshiped, enjoyed snacks, and played games.

Yusuki, a twenty-seven-year-old Buddhist, first heard about Jesus Christ about a month before coming to the Dennises' home. His cousin asked him to come to practice his English. After he came several times, he decided he would continue because he said, "I find the teachings of Christ to be very useful to one's life."

Maya, a twenty-two-year-old college student, said, "The lesson I liked best was I learned God's name, Jesus."

Yoko, a twenty-nine-year-old college graduate, came to see how an American family lived in Japan. She said, "I learned about the foundation Jesus." Her favorite lesson was "I am the way, the truth, and the life."

A few weeks after they began services, Atsuko told her new missionary friends, "I studied Christianity in college, but was not interested, only to pass the exam. I went to Israel and met Christian people, and my mind was changed. In the kibbutz I had studied Marxism, which is communist thinking, but my mind changed on this because Marxist ideas are good in books, but relationship is bad. Christian people are equal between reality and ideas, because they live Bible principles, and I am looking for truth."

(In 2006 when Paul and Shirley returned to Hokkaido they met with Atusko and her husband. She had been baptized and received the Holy Ghost. All seed does not bear fruit in one season.)

Order My Steps

Services at their home were conducted on Mondays, so the Dennises could continue attending the Sapporo UPC. Often the young people from their Bible study also attended the services.

Then winter roared in. Temperatures dropped to as low as -10 degrees Centigrade (14 degrees Fahrenheit). Winter invited itself in and settled down to stay. The Japanese called it *nai yuki* (sleeping snow). The heat from the buildings escaped through the roofs. As the snow melted, dangerous gigantic icicles formed.

Paul put spiked tires on his car and carried a set of chains in case of an emergency. When he ventured out, he discovered that he was driving on two to three feet of packed snow. He quickly learned to stay in the tracks.

When weather permitted, they had church, but there were lots of "snow days," as ten feet of snow fell that winter. The Dennises made the best of these days and weeks—studying, reading, and enjoying each other. They often gave thanks for the 300-gallon fuel tank outside their boiler room and their 747 furnace, so named because it sounded like a jet on takeoff. The noise meant heat and that meant comfort. They were thankful.

When Paul could get out, he helped Pastor Yamaki paint the church building. No hot water, no carpet, cracks in the walls that the winter winds howled through. The *ofuro* (bathroom) had a cold-water shower. The *gofujo* (toilet) had a curtain for a door, giving flies free access. These same flies buzzed the sanctuary.

Paul was impressed by this young couple's dedication. While Shirley was adjusting to church in their home, Sister Yamaki had adapted to home in their church. As Paul cleaned paintbrushes and washed his paint-colored hands in icy water, he thought of something his family could do for the Yamakis and their baby—purchase a hot water heater. This would benefit both the Yamakis and the church. That simple act of kindness forever bonded their families.

According to Japanese custom, everyone took off his or her shoes at the door and put on thin slippers. Often the back door of the church was iced open, and the cracked wooden floor felt like a hockey rink. As the biting wind whistled through the cracks around her feet, Shirley played the pump organ by automation, because her frozen feet barely felt the pedals.

"Maybe we should carpet the floor, Brother Yamaki," Paul suggested.

The young pastor agreed that it would be nice, but he had a problem. No funds.

"I will see what I can do," Paul promised. His PIM account at headquarters was in good shape, so he requested permission to carpet the sanctuary and the foyer. Thanks to the faithful giving of the saints in the United States, the request was granted.

The Yamakis chose a gold carpet. The first time Pastor Yamaki's aged parents came to church after the carpet was down, *Obaasan (*Grandmother) Yamaki asked to testify.

"I have prayed many times and thanked God for our church and asked Him to bless this poor little church with good things, and now I want to thank God for not making me wait until I get to Heaven to walk on gold. I can walk on gold here in my own church."

A year later *Obaasan* Yamaki was walking on streets of gold.

Life in Hokkaido was good. Paula had Shio. Shirley was extending hospitality to the young people who often visited their home, both for church and for fellowship. Paul was getting comfortable preaching and teaching in Japanese. The Dennises were doing what missionaries do—reaching new people, sowing the seed of the Word, and blessing the saints.

The snow was melting. The trees were budding. Paul was thinking about planting a garden in their little plot, when they received a shocking phone call that sent them to their knees.

A Giant Step

Rinnnng! Riiiinnnggg!

"Paul! Paul!" Shirley shook her sleeping husband's shoulder. "Paul, the phone is ringing."

"Huh?" Paul snorted and rolled over. "What time is it anyway?"

Rinnnng! Riiiinnnggg!

"I don't know, but it's early. Get the phone. It must be an emergency."

Paul groped in the dark for the insistent intruder on the nightstand.

Rinnnng! Riiiinnnggg!

"*Moshi moshi.* Hello?"

"Brother Dennis?"

"Yes."

"This is Paul Cook in St. Louis."

Paul covered the receiver with his hand and whispered to Shirley, "It's headquarters. Brother Cook." Paul Cook was their regional field supervisor.

After a formal greeting and asking after the Dennis family, Brother Cook got to the point. "I'm sorry, but I have bad news for you."

Paul's heart skipped a beat. He sat motionless as he waited for the next line.

"The Japanese church has nationalized and no longer needs a UPCI missionary in Japan."

Paul swung his feet over the edge of the bed and sat up ramrod straight. Shirley jumped up and came around the bed, sat down beside her husband, and grabbed his free hand. Paul held the phone a few inches from his ear so she could hear.

Paul A. Dennis

The voice from halfway around the world shattered their world, "The foreign missions board has decided that you can stay where you are and finish your four years, or you can return to the States to pastor, or you can transfer to another country."

The conversation continued for a few minutes, but little registered with Paul. When he hung up the phone, Shirley fell into his arms sobbing. Their tears mingled. They had never felt so lost and alone.

It was May 25, 1979. They had been in Hokkaido three hundred and forty-five days.

The next few days Paul and Shirley staggered around in a mental and spiritual daze. They cried. They struggled. They prayed.

Option 1: Stay here where they were not needed. Not needed? What about Atsuko, Maya, Yusuki, Yoko, and the 1.5 million other souls in Sapporo? What about Beebee? Paul had planned to contact him again. If they were not needed in Japan, why all the money and energy spent on language school? Nothing made sense.

Option 2: Go home to the States and then what? Pastor a church? Where? Start a church? Where? Pack up and ship their furniture? Return the Mothers Memorial appliances and the Sheaves for Christ car? Explain to their partners in missions why they were home? "Sorry, we made a mistake. We're not called to Japan." But that was not true. Paul knew they were called to Japan. Then why?

Option 3: Ask for reassignment to another country. But where? Japan was the land of their calling. How many more moves must they make before they found their place? Would they ever find their place?

Paul fell to his knees again. *Oh, God, remember Your promise that You will take all the stones of sin from my past and make*

Order My Steps

a safe walkway for us, so we can do Your work in Japan. I am clinging to that promise, God. Please show us the way. Order our steps according to Your Word. We are so confused.

Then the memory film rolled back two years. Paul and Claude Thompson were on the island of Okinawa, visiting the military work. Missionary Thompson said, "Brother Dennis, there is a great need for a missionary to work with the military. Men are here from everywhere. This is a harvest field that has the potential to reach the world."

Something clicked in Paul's spirit. He jumped to his feet and ran to find his helpmate. "Shirley! Shirley! I know what we are to do."

Shirley raised her eyebrows and waited.

"We are going to apply for appointment to the military work in Okinawa."

Sunlight poured across Shirley's face, driving back the clouds that had covered her countenance for days. "Oh, Paul, that's it! That's it! We can stay in Japan, after all."

Paul held up his hands. "Don't get too excited yet. Our transfer has to be approved by the foreign missions board."

As Paul prayed, he reviewed his steps from #8 Hollow to Hokkaido, Japan. A picture was forming; it was not complete, but it was starting to take shape.

Their request to transfer was granted.

Paul, Shirley, and Paula sank into their seats on the Northwest Airlines flight from Sapporo to Okinawa; exhaustion and elation flooded them. The last month as they had packed, their emotional pendulums had swung from panic to peace.

As the plane taxied down the runway, Paul glanced at the date on his watch—June 19, 1979. During the three-hour flight, Shirley napped; Paula read; Paul reviewed the last month.

Paul A. Dennis

It was a Monday morning in May after they had been reassigned to Okinawa. Paul sat down at his desk and called Jim Laughter, a staff sergeant in the United States Air Force, whom the Foreign Missions Division had appointed to oversee the small group of believers. Paul had never had any contact with Brother Laughter, although they had met his wife, Wilma, a few months ago in Toyko at the Thompsons'.

"Hello?" the voice on the other end said.

"Brother Jim Laughter?"

"Speaking."

"This is missionary Paul Dennis in Hokkaido." Paul thought he heard a gulp on the other end.

"Brother Dennis? The missionary?"

"Yes. My wife and I have been reassigned as missionaries to the military in Okinawa. We—"

"Wait! Wait!" Brother Laughter said. "I am trying to absorb this because I have $20.15 in my pocket for you. Yesterday in our service we took you as our partners in missions. We drew your name out of a bowl. We—"

"Wait! Wait!" It was Paul's turn to ask for time to absorb what he was hearing. "You took an offering for us yesterday?"

"Yes. We have been praying for God to send us a missionary. God asked me, 'Why should I send you a missionary when you are not supporting a missionary?' That was a hard-hitting question," Brother Laughter continued. "So I determined that we would take a step of faith and start supporting a missionary. Each one put in a bowl the name of a missionary he or she knew. My wife put your name in the bowl, and our little boy Samuel drew out your name. Where do I send your $20.15?"

"Just hold it," Paul said. "We should be in Okinawa in a few weeks. You can give it to me then."

If Paul had any doubts about whether it was God's will for them to move to Okinawa, that call settled them.

Order My Steps

Brother Laughter agreed to look for a house for the Dennises. He called a few days later rejoicing. "I found you a lovely house in the Country Club Heights district, not far from the base. And it is affordable!"

Paul shifted in his restricted, rutted seat and gazed out the window. The outline of Hokkaido was blending into the past as they flew into the future. Perfect peace enveloped him; he knew that this step from Hokkaido to Okinawa was ordered by the Lord.

As soon as their feet hit the walkway at the Naha International Airport, a hot humid blanket smothered them. They had taken a giant step—from the far northern island of Japan to the most southern one, and the change in the weather was overwhelming. Okinawa was hot plus hot; the humidity was 100 percent. After a few minutes, the Dennises felt as if their bodies had been painted with a sticky substance.

"These winter clothes we are wearing are headed for the mothballs," Shirley promised.

At the baggage claim area, they were met by the gracious Laughter family and reunited with Shio, who had ridden second-class at the Dennises' personal expense. They claimed their luggage and piled into the Laughters' car.

"We're going to the McFarlands' home for a short service," Jim told them. "Charles is a marine stationed at Makiminato Marine Base. He and his wife, Anna, have one son, Wayne. The other members of our little group will be there to greet you too."

Soon they pulled into a driveway and everyone, including Shio on her leash, tumbled out of the car. The McFarlands rushed out to welcome them with six-year-old Wayne in the lead.

Paul A. Dennis

Shio, still recovering from an unpleasant flight, decided that the little boy was a threat to her family. She lunged. Wayne screamed and ran to his dad. Charles picked up his son, and Paula pulled Shio back to her side.

It was not the best introduction, but soon the Dennises and their new church family, the Laughters, McFarlands, Jacksons, and Tim Long, were laughing and rejoicing as they thanked God for bringing them together. Everyone bonded quickly, except Shio and Wayne. That took a little more time.

After the service Jim took them to see their new home at Awase 14 Country Club Heights, Shimabukuro, Kita Nakagusuku Son. Shirley loved the cozy two-bedroom house. It had about 1700 square feet of living space, just right for their family of three, make that four.

Shio went wild in the front yard, sniffing and yapping, running from one side to the other. In a land where every foot of ground is premium, their 30' x 10' yard was a mini-paradise; even their dog appreciated space to run. A row of red hibiscus separated the yard from the street. Cement walls fenced the rest of the yard.

Three days later their furniture arrived and they moved in. Their next-door neighbor, Luther Watness, was the pastor of the Lutheran Military Church.

"Our church has been meeting in homes," Paul told him. "Would there be any possibility of us renting the meeting room on the first floor of your church?"

Pastor Watness agreed to rent it to them for their weeknight services. On Sundays they continued meeting in homes.

One Sunday when the saints met in Arthur Jacksons' home, Jim Laughter approached Paul. "Brother Dennis, last night I felt like the Lord gave me a definite message for the church. I know this is an unusual request, but would you surrender the pulpit to me this morning?"

Order My Steps

Since Paul had assumed the pastorate of the church, Jim had worked with him as the church secretary. Paul had no problem with allowing him to speak to the saints.

Jim's message was one of hope and affirmation, assuring the saints that they were in the will of God, and that God was leading them into a new dimension of growth and ministry. As Jim spoke, Paul wept.

When the service was over, they compared notes. They were identical—Scripture references and side notes. The Lord had given both men the same message. What an awesome confirmation of God's will!

On July 13 Paul baptized marine Harold Goings in the name of the Lord Jesus Christ in the Pacific Ocean. It was the largest baptismal tank Paul had ever used.

Part of the time they had a building. Souls were being added to the church. It was forward march! But Satan had held this island for centuries. He was not about to relinquish his territory without a fight.

"I'm sorry, Paul," Luther Watness said, "but the Lutheran headquarters has told me they do not want me renting any part of our building to another group, especially not a Pentecostal group. So by the end of August, you need to move."

Put on the whole armor of God, Paul. The battle has begun.

A Bottle of Oil and a Hammer

In World War II more people died during the Battle of Okinawa than all those killed during the atomic bombings of Hiroshima and Nagasaki. Before the Dennises were in Koza long they realized that Okinawa was still a battlefield—a spiritual battlefield.

One night Paul had just dropped off to sleep when he was suddenly awakened and gripped by an intense fear.

Turning toward the window, he saw the shadow of someone walking by the window, stopping at the corner of the house, and peeking through the side of the drapes. Many American military personnel lived in their neighborhood, so he knew that break-ins were common. For a long time he lay tense and ready to spring up to defend his family, watching and listening, not wanting to disturb Shirley. Quietly he got up and crept through the dark into Paula's room to check her windows and make sure she was safe. Shio was sound asleep at the foot of Paula's bed.

Finally, Paul drifted into a restless sleep. The next morning the incident rested heavily on his mind.

This happened night after night for two or three months. As Paul lay tense and alert, he pondered the religious history of Okinawa.

The Okinawan native religion was Animistic and Shamanistic. Animism is the belief that all objects in nature have a conscious life. Shamanism is the belief in an unseen spirit world of gods and ancestral spirits that respond only to the Shamans. Over the centuries these beliefs have been influenced and transformed by Shintoism, Buddhism, Taoism, and Christianity. It is a weird mix.

Many Okinawans believed that everything has a spirit—ancestral spirits, water-well spirits, house spirits, literally everything. All these spirits are considered sacred and supernatural. Religious rituals are practiced diligently to appease the gods, ward off misfortunes, and invoke blessings.

Every year in September the *obon* (the all souls day meaning "to loose") festival is celebrated. The worshipers believe that on this day they send the spirits of their dead ancestors back to wherever they came from.

One night Paul awoke with a start. A huge black figure stood over him, choking him. Paul gasped for breath. He tried to reach over and shake Shirley, but his arms and legs were shackled to the bed. He shook his head violently, fighting for the next breath. When it came, he cried out, "Jesus!"

At the sound of that name, the evil presence released Paul's arms and legs. The darkness overshadowing him vanished. Shaking and sweating, he rolled out of bed and went into the living room. It was time to pray.

The shadows that had passed their window night after night were not figments of his tired mind. The dark spirits of evil were attacking his home.

"For we wrestle not against flesh and blood, but against principalities, against powers, against the rulers of the darkness of this world, against spiritual wickedness in high places" (Ephesians 6:12).

But Paul had a weapon that the enemy could not conquer—the name of Jesus.

"And these signs shall follow them that believe; In my name shall they cast out devils" (Mark 16:17).

After that night the Dennis home was never again under evil surveillance. The name of Jesus covered them.

Later Paul and Shirley received a call from a church member who lived in their neighborhood.

"Sister Dennis, I'm frightened. My husband is working nights, and I keep hearing sounds. Someone is walking in the

Paul A. Dennis

house during the night. Pictures are falling off the walls; doors are opening and closing of their own accord. I don't know what to do."

Paul and Shirley, armed with a bottle of anointing oil and the name of Jesus, went to that home. They went through the house anointing every door, doorjamb, window, and cupboard in the name of Jesus, commanding the evil spirits to depart. They did.

Missions work is a combination of spiritual battles, hard work, and the nitty-gritty of daily life.

When Paul's landlord heard they had lost their meeting place, he came to Paul with an offer.

"We have an apartment complex with a large dining hall; we will rent you the dining hall for $300 a month."

The complex had been built during the time of the U.S. occupation of Okinawa. After checking out the dining hall, Paul decided that with some repairs it would work as a church. A plus was the location, not far from their house. They signed a rental agreement, picked up their hammers, and started to work.

The wooden windows were rotting; paint was peeling off the walls; floor tiles were missing, broken, and multicolored. Termites, geckos, and cockroaches had long ago moved in. But the saints had a mind to work.

They shopped yard sales and secondhand stores for chairs, tables, and other items. An old wooden cupboard with the top removed was transformed into a pulpit. Used carpets were sewn together to cover most of the floor. Every time it rained or a typhoon swept in, they ran to the church and rolled back the carpets to save them from leaks. The new church even had a 747 air conditioner that reminded the Dennises of the furnace in their Hokkaido home.

After they had been in the dining-hall-turned-church a few months, the landlord came to Paul with a business pitch. "We are going to sell this apartment complex and want to give you the first chance to purchase it."

Paul's mind went into overdrive. Immediately he started visualizing the building with partitions removed and added.

"We are asking only $50,000," the landlord said.

Just $50,000? Paul knew it was a reasonable price, but $50,000 was $50,000 more than their little congregation had.

"Brother Cook will be here in a few days," Shirley reminded Paul. "Perhaps the Foreign Missions Division will help us."

When Brother Cook, regional field supervisor for Asia, arrived, Paul eagerly showed him the property, spreading his vision out before him like the land of milk and honey.

Brother Cook was not impressed. "I can't ask the FMD for that kind of money without having something to show them that you are serious about buying this building."

In the next service Paul presented the need to the handful of saints. "We are doing this not only for ourselves, but for those who follow us, those who come after we move on," he said.

Jim Laughter's oldest son, seven-year-old Samuel, pledged the money in his piggy bank—$29. The ball was rolling. On the spot the saints pledged over $7,000 from their personal savings and income tax returns. One man borrowed money to pay his pledge.

Brother Cook was impressed. He approached the FMD board on behalf of the saints in the military work in Okinawa. They agreed to loan them $50,000 if they would repay it in two years. The saints agreed to this plan. The building became property of the Military First United Pentecostal Church.

Armed with a bottle of oil and a hammer, the Dennises worked to bring "righteousness, peace, and joy in the Holy Ghost" to the bloodiest battlefield in the Pacific.

Adding to the Church

One Sunday morning when Paul stepped outside the church after greeting the departing saints, a taxi drove up. A tall, young, black man dressed in a suit and tie got out and paid the driver.

He strode over to Paul. "Are you the pastor?"

"Yes, sir, I am."

"Is this the First United Pentecostal Church?" Paul refrained from rolling his eyes and pointing to the white sign with black and blue letters that boldly announced the church name.

The young man shook Paul's hand and introduced himself. "I am David Thompson. I'm in the marines with the Echo Battery. I'll be here for a year. Does this church teach the Apostolic doctrine?"

"Yes we do."

"Do you baptize in the name of Jesus Christ, receive the Holy Ghost speaking in tongues, and preach holiness?"

"Yes."

"Then this is the place."

Paul invited him in to visit. Once they were settled, David continued, "I have been here in Okinawa for about a month and have been attending another denominational church. The fellowship is great. The music is good. Emotions are high. But something is missing in the preaching. The preacher never mentions repentance, baptism, the Holy Ghost, or living a holy life. There is no anointing or response to the preaching."

David paused. Paul nodded and waited.

"This morning I was sitting in church when the Lord spoke to me. 'Get up and go to the First United Pentecostal Church.' So I got up, went outside, and flagged down a taxi. The driver could not speak English, and I can't speak Japanese. When I

Order My Steps

told him I wanted to go to the First United Pentecostal Church, all he understood was 'church.' So we've been going from church to church for two hours! I know the Lord spoke to me and here I am."

Paul chuckled. This guy was determined and considerably poorer than he had been two hours before. *Better invite him to dinner.* Paul did, which gave them more time to get acquainted.

The next Wednesday night Bible study was a typical revival service—enthusiastic worship, intense prayer, and exciting testimonies, followed by the anointed ministry of the Word.

After the service, David approached Paul. His black face was beaming. "Brother Dennis, I did not know that white people received the Holy Ghost. I am so excited to know this."

After David's first year, he extended his time in Okinawa another year. He was a good and faithful servant of the Lord Jesus, always in church, giving tithes and offerings, storming the gates of Hell with prayer.

Never had Paul heard anyone pray like David. In prayer he was shut in with God. He interceded for every request, quoted God's promises, and entreated God to add to the church. That was not all. At the end of this prayer he prayed for his needs, some personal and some normal cares of life. It mattered not if the whole church eavesdropped. He talked to God in private publicly.

After his second year in Okinawa, he returned to California, joined the Pentecostal Assemblies of the World, married, had two sons, and served as the youth pastor.

One night David and his wife had taken several young people home after a youth gathering, when the church van ran out of gas. About forty yards down the road was a telephone booth.

"You wait here. I'll go call the church and ask someone to bring us some gas," he told his wife.

Paul A. Dennis

As his wife watched, he jogged to the phone booth. As he placed his call, three thugs came up and demanded his wallet. As he handed it to them, they shot him.

In his memory Paul still hears David Thompson's prayers bombarding Heaven, and Heaven hears them too.

The church roof was leaking again. Paul, dressed in his old jeans and work shirt covered with tar, paint, and cement, was fixing it. As he came down the ladder to get a drink of water, a taxi stopped in front of the church and a young lady got out.

"I am looking for Reverend Paul A. Dennis," she said. "Do you know him?"

Paul was tempted to say no. Instead, he acknowledged that he was Reverend Dennis and apologized for his appearance.

Brenda Alexander smiled and graciously said, "I understand." Then she told him her story.

The night before she was to leave for Okinawa to join her husband who was in the military, she was baptized and received the Holy Ghost. As she went through the boarding gate at the airport, someone (she did not see who) shoved a small brown paper bag into her hand and said, "Find this man."

"On the plane I pulled the bag out of my purse and found a wrinkled piece of paper with your name 'Paul A. Dennis' on it. That was all. We have been on the island for a couple of weeks, living in the billeting quarters.

"Today I checked the base phone book and found your name and this address. I am looking for a church for myself and my three children. My husband does not attend church."

About a year later Paul took Lester Alexander to the East China Sea and baptized him in the name of Jesus Christ. For five years the Alexander family faithfully served the Lord in the FUPC of Okinawa.

Order My Steps

Some who came had been baptized in the name of Jesus and filled with the Holy Ghost before arriving in Okinawa; many others received their Acts 2:38 salvation on the "Rock," the island's nickname. One by one, one person, one family at a time, the Lord added to the church.

Saying Goodbye

August 17, 1980, is written on the Dennises' memories with a permanent black marker.

From the moment they had stepped foot on Japanese soil they had tried to shove this day into the future, but it had stalked them until suddenly it pounced upon them. What they feared had come upon them. They could no longer push it away.

After a tearful goodbye to Shio, Paula, who had celebrated her eighteenth birthday seven days earlier, followed her parents to the loaded car. After cramming two years' worth of schooling into one so she could graduate with her classmates from Ohio, Paula was leaving for Jackson College of Ministries. Her goal was a degree in music.

Selling their home, leaving their friends and extended family, moving halfway around the world—no sacrifice, no loss, no pain—compared to what Paul and Shirley felt that day. As Paul checked their only child in at the ticket counter, a vise clamped down on his stomach.

Paula, clinging to Shirley, was surrounded by Japanese friends who had come to say goodbye, not knowing when, if ever, they would see her again.

Tears threatened as Paula asked, "Mom, what will I do when I get to Chicago? I don't know the airport."

One of her friends spoke up, "Paula, all you have to do is read the signs. They will be in English."

Duh! The light moment eased the pain.

In Japan Paula had traveled all over the country with her parents and by herself, reading and following Japanese directions. The Japanese language and culture had oozed into her soul. Now she was going back . . . back to the future, just as

Order My Steps

her dad had done three years previously when they had come to Japan.

As the gate attendant announced Paula's flight, panic threatened to overwhelm her parents. "It's only for a year," Paul's voice cracked. "We'll be home for deputation in a year."

In those pre-email, pre-Skype days, halfway around the world was . . . halfway around the world. A five-minute phone call cost as much as $50. Fears assailed Paul and Shirley. *What are we thinking, letting our baby go back to the States without us? What will happen to her?*

As they gathered for final hugs, kisses, and prayer, Paul's soul cried out, *Oh God, order her steps.*

As Paula turned and walked down the jetway, her parents' hearts shredded. They watched as the plane taxied to the runway and took off. Then it lifted into the clouds and turned into the future. They did not move until the last stream of vapors dissipated.

Silently they walked out of the airport and climbed into their Sheaves for Christ car. As they drove home, they reviewed the past year, anything to keep from thinking about what had just happened.

"One year ago to the day the typhoon struck," Shirley reminded Paul. "August 17, 1979, seven days after Paula's seventeenth birthday party."

"August 17 seems to be a black-letter day for us." Paul swallowed; then he admitted, "I hate to go home. It's going to be so lonely without Paula." The cars approaching them blurred. With the back of his hand, he wiped the tears from his cheeks.

Shirley drew a deep breath. "Paul, I'm trying. Please help me. Let's talk about something else, something pleasant, like the typhoon." Anything was pleasant when compared with releasing Paula.

Paul honored his wife's request. He quoted the military typhoon instructions. "'Remove all moving objects from your yard or tie them fast. Be sure to have three days of food supply, batteries for the radio, and filled water containers in case the water main is off. Tape your windows with a big X across each one and stay indoors.' What a hassle it was; three days of hard work."

"But it was worth it," Shirley remembered. "Typhoon Judy was an angry gal. What a temper tantrum she threw. The power and water went off. Remember how the rain blew in around the doors and windows. And the wind stripped our beautiful hibiscus bushes. It has been a year, and they still haven't recovered." She choked back a sob. "How long will it take us to recover from our baby growing up?"

Paul reached for her hand and squeezed it. "We probably never will."

Shirley gave him a wobbly smile. "I feel like I have been through an emotional typhoon. It only took a couple of weeks to get the church back in shape. But parents' hearts aren't as easily patched as church walls, are they?"

Silence intruded and shared their sorrow. All they could do was go back to doing what they had been doing—praying, studying, working, teaching, preaching. Only time could heal their broken hearts.

Open Windows

"The windows of Heaven are open; God's power is falling tonight."

Sunday evening. Angels hovered above the growing congregation as the saints sang and marched, bringing their tithes and offerings. They were giving cheerfully, and God was blessing abundantly.

Under the missionaries' leadership, in the past year the small church had made enormous progress. Major renovation had transformed two of the apartments into a beautiful church. Before the remodeling was complete, the people who had sold the building to them for $50,000 offered $70,000 for it. Paul replied, "We will accept no less than $150,000." (The church is now the headquarters for the Asian Military District.)

By the summer of 1980 the military church of Okinawa was making a building payment, renting a building across the street for a church office, and paying utilities on all of the buildings. They had purchased a used van to transport people to church. In addition they had taken on several UPCI missionaries as PIMs. Two of the apartments were rented out to military families, which added to their income.

Missionary Dennis's goal was to build a missions-minded church, so he continually emphasized prayer, giving, missions, and outreach. An annual detailed financial report of the First United Pentecostal Church of Okinawa was sent to the Foreign Missions Division. The goal was for the church to become indigenous as soon as possible, which is what happened.

After the baptism of Marine Brian Spann (Paul's second baptismal service in Okinawa), revival winds swept through the military church. They were reaching all branches of the United States military—the air force, marines, navy, army, and coast guard. In addition, Okinawans were being reached with the gospel.

For their watch-night service in 1980, God gave Paul three watchwords for the church from Psalm 27: believe, courage, and wait. Every Sunday night, this chapter was read aloud at the beginning of the service; the saints memorized it. It was their tower of strength.

Many were baptized and received the Holy Ghost. Those bound by addictions were delivered from alcohol, drugs, and tobacco. The sick were healed. Marriages were fortified with new commitments. Children regularly received the Holy Ghost in Sunday school. Departments like the ladies auxiliary and men's fellowship were set in place.

God was calling young men into the ministry, so Paul started a ministers training program, using the combined UPCI and Asia Military District requirements for ministers.

"What did you say, Brother Dennis? Did I hear you right? Did you say I have to clean the restrooms?"

"That's right. Doing janitorial work is part of your ministerial training. Have you not read Mark 10:44, 'Whosoever of you will be the chiefest, shall be servant of all'?"

One evening as Paul taught aspiring ministers, a blank look settled on every face. One brave young man raised his hand. "Brother Dennis, did you say I have to buy a set of china for my wife?"

Paul grinned. "Yes, sir, I did."

"But . . . but . . ." the young man was speechless.

Paul enjoyed the class's bewilderment for a few seconds. He stood and paced. "You guys are here from all over the world. You could be assigned to anywhere at anytime. Wherever you go, you are ambassadors of the Lord Jesus Christ. Like the apostle Paul, you could stand before kings or sit at the table with heads of state. Don't laugh. I am not joking. In this class are men with the potential to reach people from all walks of life with the gospel. You

Order My Steps

do not know who will walk through the door of your home. You and your wife need to know how to entertain in a way that will bring honor to the kingdom of God."

So each married man who graduated from Paul's ministerial training class purchased a set of china from China Pete's, which sold name-brand china at bargain basement prices. Shirley, the first Martha Stewart, taught the military ministers' wives how to entertain par excellence.

The trainees received hands-on experience teaching Sunday school classes, giving Bible studies, doing outreach, and filling the pulpit. They were taught the beginning steps of church administration, personal relations, ministerial ethics, teamwork, and leadership. They worked in the altars, on the streets, and at the different bases bringing new souls to Christ. They were challenged to be totally committed to soulwinning and were shown by example how to work as a team to accomplish kingdom goals.

After Paula cut the apron strings and Paul and Shirley released her into God's hands, they jumped back into the whirlwind of activity. They realized that the year would go a lot faster if they kept busy.

For a while they worried about Shio. "She's grieving. She misses Paula so much," Shirley told Paul, as she cuddled the growing dog on her tiny lap.

Paul sighed. He knew exactly how Shio felt. Releasing Paula into God's hands was a daily exercise in faith.

One night Paul was awakened by Shirley shaking him. In the background Shio was barking furiously. "Paul! Paul! Shio wants out."

Paul groaned and tumbled out of bed. *Paula, get back here and take care of your dog.*

He stumbled through the dark to the door where he expected Shio to be waiting.

Paul A. Dennis

No dog.

"Shio! Get in here and I'll let you out."

Toward the back of the house, Shio growled.

"Shio! If you want out, get in here now."

No dog. Just a lot of barking and growling.

"OK, if that's the way you're going to act, I'm going back to bed. So hush!"

The next morning Shirley came into the living room. "Paul, why did you leave the washroom window open?"

Paul looked up from reading the morning paper. "I didn't."

"Well, I didn't either," she said. "But it's open."

Paul dropped the paper, and followed by Shirley and Shio, went to check. As they neared the washroom, Shio sniffed the floor and whined.

Paul walked over to the open window. "Look! The screen is missing, and what's that out there on the ground?"

"What?" Shirley peered over his shoulder and out the window. "Oh my! That's my laundry products."

"So that's what Shio was telling us last night. Someone broke into our house. If it hadn't been for Shio, there's no telling what the thief would have done."

Shirley's face blanched. "Shio must have stood guard and refused to let the intruder get beyond the washroom door. He probably ran when he heard you get up and call Shio."

After that incident Shio became the Dennises' heroine. Unfortunately, she had developed a dislike for the Japanese, which led to a few difficult encounters. But no matter whom she threatened, Shio was a firm member of the Dennis family until she died in 1996.

"Shirley, I'm going to the bank," Paul said. "Do you need anything from town?"

Order My Steps

"No. Just hurry back. We have a lot to do this afternoon," she reminded him, as he brushed her cheek with a quick kiss.

After Paul finished his business at the bank, he decided to save time and take a shortcut, a one-lane side road. When cars met, one driver had to find a wide spot and pull over so the other could pass.

As Paul drove around a sharp turn, a little boy ran across the road in front of him. Instantly, Paul's reflexes kicked into gear. He swerved to the right to miss the child. Right move. Wrong time. He slammed head-on into a car coming around the curve from the other direction. Everyone stopped but the child. He kept running.

After a few seconds of stunned silence, the other driver jumped out. Paul recognized him as the city tax collector. They had met a few months ago when the man had collected taxes on the church property. Paul had invited him to church.

Mr. Tax Man's red face and clenched fists told Paul that his anger level was high. It didn't take a professional body language reader to figure that out.

As soon as the irate driver recognized Paul, he shouted in perfect English, "Where is your God now?"

An on-the-scene policeman who witnessed the accident responded, also in English, "You are alive, aren't you?"

Those few words knocked the hot air out of the tax man. He calmed down, and the drivers gave the officer the needed information.

In Japan when an accident happens, the person who caused the accident is 80 percent at fault and the other person is 20 percent at fault. In this case, the thinking was that if the tax man had not been there, Paul would not have hit him. Both cars were still drivable, so the men parted peaceably.

As Paul drove cautiously down the shortcut to the main road, he sang, "The windows of Heaven are open; God's power is falling tonight. There's joy, joy, joy in my heart, since Jesus made everything right."

Coming and Going

PCS is a military term that means "permanent change of station" and moves people like pawns on a chessboard. A fact of pastoring a military work is that people are always coming and going, based on Uncle Sam's whims. With heavy hearts the Dennises said goodbye to Jim and Wilma Laughter and their children.

Soon after the Laughters left, the Dennises' landlord called. "Mr. Dennis, I am selling the house you are renting. I am giving you two months' notice."

When Paul told Shirley, she didn't even flinch. Moving was a constant for them. They had lived in their present house for almost two years; that was longer than average. "What are we going to do? We leave in April for deputation," she reminded him.

"I will talk to the church board about turning the two rented apartments into missionary quarters. Our furlough replacements can live in it while we are gone. Then we can live in it when we return."

"That's a good idea," Shirley agreed, "but you don't have much time."

From that point everything went into cyclone mode. The renters moved out. Paul and the church men went to work—knocking out walls, replacing windows, adding partitions, moving water and gas lines, pouring a new concrete floor, putting up ceiling tiles. Contractors were hired only when the men of the church could not do a particular job. Workers were coming and going day and night.

In addition to working on the building, they had church on Sunday, Wednesday, Friday, and Saturday. The other days they had Bible studies or services at various military outposts.

Order My Steps

In all they had fourteen outreach ministries going. When the Dennises weren't coming from one meeting, they were going to another.

"Paul, you need to take a day off," Shirley urged one morning. "Working on the building plus taking care of the church business, preaching, teaching, getting ready for deputation—it's too much. If you don't slow down and rest, you're going to be sick."

Paul grabbed Shirley and gave her a quick hug. "I love doing everything I'm doing, Charlie Brown, and I love you." He picked up his electric drill and Bible. "See you tonight."

On April 9, Regional Field Supervisor (RFS) Paul Cook arrived, along with the Dennises' furlough replacement, newlyweds Harold and Renee Hoffman. The apartment was almost ready, but not quite. The carpet had to be laid and the walls painted. Ten days later the Dennises' furniture and household items were moved in. The next day the Hoffmans moved into the gleaming, smelling-like-new missionary quarters. Paul and Shirley camped out in their rented house with one bed and their personal belongings.

The Dennises took the Hoffmans through a crash course in life on Okinawa.

Paul told Harold, "Last year we had ten receive the Holy Ghost, and we made twenty-three trips to the East China Sea for baptisms. It's the most beautiful baptistery in the world. As an evangelist, you're going to have the time of your life in Okinawa. This church is alive and growing." He grinned the infectious Dennis grin as he handed the young man a typed list three pages long. "Here are some things you can do in your spare time."

On May 2, Paul and Shirley boarded a plane for Kyoto via Osaka to attend the Japanese National Conference. Six days later they were thirty-four thousand feet above the Pacific going home.

Paul A. Dennis

Paul reached for his wife's hand. Flying at some six hundred miles per hour, he stopped for the first time in months. "Four years, Shirley. Four wonderful years. The Lord has . . . zzzzz." Exhaustion finally caught up with him.

The next afternoon they arrived in Chicago. Four hours later they were in Columbus in the arms of their family.

The next week was filled with speaking engagements, orientation at headquarters, purchasing a car, getting back in the swing of life in the States. Finally, they turned the car south, counting down the miles separating them from their daughter. Ten months that had seemed like ten years were about to end. *Paula, Mother and Dad are coming.*

June was family month, catching up on four years of separation. In July they hit the deputation trail, starting in Missouri, then Indiana, Michigan, and back to Toledo on July 27, where they crashed at the home of their friends Bob and Jo Hensley.

"Shirley! Shirley, wake up," Paul groaned. "Shirley."

His wife muttered and burrowed deeper into the pillow.

"Shirley, wake up. Ooohhh!" Paul gasped. "Ooohhh!"

His wife shot up like a released helium balloon. Reaching for the switch on the table lamp, she asked, "What's wrong, Paul?"

"My chest. My back. I can't breathe."

"Bob! Jo!" Shirley called as she grabbed her robe. "Something is wrong with Paul."

The Hensleys rushed into the room, pulling on their robes. Combining prayers with actions, they sped to the hospital.

Immediately, the medical staff started testing Paul's heart. Two hours later the doctor told them, "He is not having a heart attack, but I would like to keep him overnight for observation."

As Paul twisted and turned on the narrow, antiseptic hospital bed, he watched his wife sleep, all curled up in a chair. She looked about as comfortable as he felt. He knew she could have said, "I told you so," but she didn't. He appreciated that.

Order My Steps

The next morning Doctor Bradford bounced in with a cheerful grin and turned their lives upside down. "Mr. Dennis, I don't want to scare you, but we have found a dark mass in your right lung. We have reason to think it could be cancer; we need to run some tests."

Shirley called Pastor Kinzie, who came and prayed for Paul and for Shirley. What a comfort it was to have their mentor and friend walk alongside them as Paul endured one test after another.

Another day passed. "We have to run one more test. If it does not tell us anything, we will have to tap your lungs to get a specimen to check before we do surgery," the doctor reported.

The medical team took Paul into the examination room and enclosed him in a clear plastic tent with oxygen pumped into it. "We are going to spray a chemical into the tent," the technician told him. "You will not be able to see, smell, or taste it, and you won't feel a thing."

That was good news. At least, Paul hoped it was good news.

They set up a monitor. "Watch this," the tech said. "You can see your lungs."

As Paul watched, thousands of little silver dots went into his lungs, filling his left lung. But only a small portion of the silver dots went into his right lung. An ugly black blot filled the rest of it. It looked evil to Paul.

The tech made notes on a clipboard, but he did not comment. Then they took the worried patient back to his room.

A few hours later Doctor Bradford came in. In a calm voice he crashed their schedule. "I have good and bad news for you. The good news is that you don't have cancer. The bad news is that you have walking pneumonia."

Together Paul and Shirley exhaled. "That's easy to treat, isn't it?" Shirley asked.

The doctor hesitated. "Yes, normally, but this is not a normal case. In fact, we have had only four cases like this." He

Paul A. Dennis

looked straight at Paul. "You are drowning in your own blood because your heart cannot pump the blood fast enough to drain it. We're starting you on a special medicine right away, and we need to run a few more minor tests."

"How long will I be in the hospital?" Paul asked.

The doctor tried not to grimace. "That depends," he answered, as he bid them good day and walked out.

Paul learned later that three of those four cases had died. "But prayer was made" for Paul.

On August 2, a week after Paul entered the hospital, Doctor Bradford sat down on the edge of Paul's bed, clipboard in hand. After flipping through a few papers, he nodded. Through squinted eyes, he stared at Paul. "I'm going to release you today if . . . number one, you promise that you will take the rest of the month off and rest . . . and number two, if you will take your medicine faithfully, as it is drying up the blood in your lungs."

Thinking about their deputation schedule, Paul shot a question mark at Shirley. Thinking about Paul, Shirley bounced an exclamation mark back. "Agreed!" she told the doctor.

Doctor Bradford chuckled. "I know you go to Reverend Kinzie's church," he hesitated, and then continued. "Just don't get too excited."

Paul followed the doctor's orders as much as possible. August was down month. In September they were back on the deputation trail. It was difficult not to get "too excited" as he shared with his PIM churches the wonderful things God had done in Japan in the last four years. And he rejoiced with them as they shared with him their revival stories. General conference was definitely a test of Paul's willpower. Who can worship with thousands of God's people and not get too excited?

A warm blanket of God's grace enveloped the Dennises that Christmas as they laughed and ate and celebrated with Paula and their extended families. More than ever, they valued each day and their moments together.

Order My Steps

As March ended, Paul and Shirley said goodbye again to their daughter, but this time it was much easier. Paula was coming to Okinawa in a couple of month to spend the summer as an Associate in Missions.

On April 1, 1982, second-term missionaries Paul and Shirley Dennis landed at the Naha airport and stepped back into the sweltering island humidity. After a winter in the States, the bone-baking heat felt wonderful.

Harold Hoffman met Paul with a big smile and handed him the three-page typed list. Every item had been marked off.

Paul chuckled, "I was just teasing."

Teasing or not, the Hoffmans' short term in Okinawa had been great training ground for future pastoral work. In their ten months on the island, they had taken only two days off.

Within a day Paul and Shirley were settled into the missionary quarters and back in work mode, coming and going, doing what missionaries do.

Family Matters

April 15, Shirley answered the phone. Her heart flipped when she recognized her sister Sharon's voice on the other end.

"Shirley, Mom fell down the back porch steps and hurt her hip. She's in the hospital. We're not sure how badly she is injured."

Phone calls were expensive, so the conversation was kept to a minimum—the barest details and a promise to keep in touch. Suddenly, the 11,600 miles separating Shirley from her family stretched in front of her like an unfathomable chasm.

When she hung up the phone, she burst into choking sobs. Paul held her and prayed for healing for Ann and peace for Shirley. Being separated from family in time of tragedy and sickness is one of a missionary's deepest pains.

Soon the comforting presence of the Lord swept into their living room. Shirley smiled through her tears. "I'll be all right now, PD. The same sweet Spirit that is here with us is in Ohio with Mom. I will trust God."

Tests revealed that Shirley's mother's hip was not broken. Three days later she went home from the hospital. Shirley's smile returned. Not knowing is often worse than the facts. That's a reality that missionaries live with all the time.

Soon Paula was back in Okinawa, taking care of the office and directing the church's music. Paul and Shirley determined to enjoy every day with their daughter and not let the looming date of August 15 shadow the summer. The days swirled by like a paper plane in a whirlwind.

Order My Steps

On August 10 Paula celebrated her twentieth birthday. Five days later she was back at Naha airport, waiting for her flight to Jackson. Releasing Paula from that final embrace was not quite as difficult as it had been two years ago.

One afternoon Paul came bouncing into the house. "Shirley, this morning I got a great idea."

Shirley turned from the kitchen sink to give Paul her full attention. She had learned to listen carefully to his "great ideas."

"If I had a motor scooter, I could get around a lot easier than driving the car. Think how much time I waste looking for parking spots. Besides, we could save a lot of money on gas."

Shirley's countenance dropped, so Paul looked elsewhere.

"I found a used scooter in excellent condition for a remarkable price. I figure I—" He paused, as Shirley started shaking her head.

"Paul, you are too old and your reflexes are not fast enough for you to ride a motor scooter."

That hurt his feelings. He certainly was not too old! Who was she to tell him that his reflexes were bad?

"Besides," his wife said gently but firmly, "the Foreign Missions Division will not approve funds for a motor scooter."

By now Paul was seething. "Then I will buy it myself." He stormed out of the house and bought the scooter.

For three days he felt like a teenager as he varoomed around cars and whistled into the wind. What fun! And he was saving a multitude of yen on gas . . . well, at least, a few yen.

Day four. The scooter flipped and Paul flopped. He came up with a damaged arm and shoulder, plus scrapes and stings everywhere. As he limped into the house with his shirt torn, his trousers dirty, and his countenance fallen, alarm flashed across Shirley's face. "Paul, what happened?"

Paul A. Dennis

"I had a wreck."

Alarm was replaced by disgust. His wife put her hands on her hips and in her sternest motherly tone said, "You are a wreck! I told you not to buy that thing, that you would kill yourself. So just suffer. See if I care," her voice broke, as she marched down the hall to the bathroom to get the first aid kit.

A few days later Paul sold the scooter. He hated it when Shirley was right.

Another Christmas came. As was their custom, the Dennises invited military men far from their own families to the Dennises' house for dinner and gifts and games. Togetherness diminished their loneliness.

PCS, *permanent change of station,* the ever-present nemesis, struck in February 1983, with a vengeance. The McFarlands, the last of the original families who had greeted the Dennises when they moved to Okinawa in 1979, were assigned to a new station.

Charles McFarland was one of fifty-eight men who answered a call to the ministry while stationed in Okinawa. Paul realized that the military work was a training station, but every time a family moved on, he and Shirley felt their heartstrings stretched nearly to the breaking point.

Ministers and officials from the States flew in and out, leaving the Dennises and the saints enriched by their ministry. Missionaries from the area retreated to the Dennises' home where they were refreshed by Paul's jovial attitude, Shirley's sweet spirit, and the Dennises' superb hospitality.

Military families moved in and stayed until PCSed. Young men were called by God and trained by Paul. The heartbeat of this church was souls. The new converts were many and the

Order My Steps

enthusiasm was high. Opportunities abounded; it was every young minister's dream.

The Dennises were starting the second year of their second term when a family matter arose that consumed their thoughts.

In March, during one of their rare and expensive phone calls, Paula said, "Howi Tiller has an assignment to photograph a unique tribe in the Philippines. Keith is going along as his assistant. They want to stop back by Okinawa to visit you."

Lately the name "Keith" had come up more and more in Paula's letters and phone calls.

Paul's noncommittal answer, "Oh? Really?" did little to warm Paula's heart. In desperation she said, "Dad, you've got to like him. It's a matter of life and death."

Paul felt a hand squeeze his father's heart. Apparently, Keith Townsley's visit would be more than a friendly, I-just-dropped-in-to-see-you visit. It was.

Keith was in Okinawa, Japan, on a mission—a mission to gain the hand of the girl he loved. His principles demanded that before he asked Paula to marry him, he had to have her parents' permission, even if it meant flying across the Pacific Ocean to get it. Paula's parents were impressed.

After several days of services, sightseeing, and a lot of talking, Paul and Shirley granted Keith permission to propose to their daughter. He left Okinawa one happy young man. And the Dennises returned to work, assured once again that God was ordering their daughter's steps.

Not many days later Paula called bubbling, "We're getting married August 13."

After that call, Mom and Dad struggled not to cry, but lost the battle. They respected Keith and felt he was the right one for Paula. But, oh, how hard it was to give their daughter to him! Joy and sorrow whirled in their souls, much like chocolate and vanilla in a hot fudge sundae. Paula's news was good, but almost too much.

"Four and half months to plan a wedding!" Shirley fretted. "Paula's in Jackson, we're here, and the wedding is to be in Ohio. How will I ever get it coordinated?"

"If anyone can do it, you can," Paul consoled her. "But how can I ever pay for it?"

Shirley grinned, "If anyone can do it, you can."

They laughed and went back to work, putting wedding plans on hold until summer, when Paula was coming again as an AIMer. No need to make plans now anyway; Paula would change them when she came.

Meanwhile, a special guest from Burma was coming.

From Missions to Missions with Love

"Brother Buai, you and Sister Dennis go ahead and eat," Paul said as he came into the living room. "I have an errand to run and I could be delayed. So eat while the food is hot."

The superintendent of Burma, Ral J. Buai, was spending the week with the Dennises. He had come to Japan for the Kyoto United Pentecostal Church of Japan campmeeting. When Paul learned that Pastor Fujibayashi had invited Superintendent Buai to Kyoto, he extended an invitation for him to come to Okinawa and speak to the military church.

Paul and Brother Buai had met in 1981 when Paul accompanied Paul Cook, RFS for Asia, to Burma for a national conference. Superintendent Buai had introduced them as "the two Pauls from Ohio." Paul's first experience preaching in a third world country had been an eye opener.

The sanctuary of the church was the remodeled living room of the Buais' home. The room was large but not adequate for the crowd. The men sat in chairs; the women and children sat on mats on the floor. Paul recognized the officials and pastors, and opened his Bible to read his text. A baby's wail pierced the silence. The mother seated front and center rocked back and forth, trying to calm her baby. That didn't work, so she pushed aside her blouse and nursed her baby. The baby hushed and Paul blushed.

Right before that service began, RFS Paul had asked missionary Paul, "Do you think you could preach the rest of this conference?"

Paul replied, "If I had to I could."

Paul A. Dennis

Brother Cook said, "Well, you have to. My house is for sale. My wife called and said I am needed at home to sign some papers. So I am going home."

After the service they took Paul Cook to the airport, and Paul Dennis stepped into the RFS's shoes. Little did he realize that he was again getting on-the-job training.

As Burma had been a new experience for Paul, so Okinawa was a new experience for Brother Buai. Fellowshiping with the American military personnel showed him a side of America that surprised him. He discovered that the soldiers were men of strong convictions and dedication, who loved God, their families, and their country.

As Paul rushed out to take care of business, Shirley called, "Lunch is ready, Brother Buai."

Brother Buai sat down at the cheerfully decorated table covered with a crisp linen cloth and set with simple, but elegant, china. A warm, appetizing aroma drifted around the browned Cornish hens and the complementary dishes dominating the table. It was one of the nicest table settings he had ever seen. Brother Buai was awed by the abundance of food available in Japan.

His hen was cooked to perfection, so tender that it fell off the bone when he touched it with his fork. He enjoyed every bite. When Brother Buai finished his lunch, he heaped lavish praise on Shirley's cooking.

Later Paul came in and sat down to eat. "I thought you baked Cornish hens for lunch, Shirley," he said, emphasizing the plural "hens" as only one was on the table.

Shirley smiled. "I did. I gave Brother Buai one hen, and he ate the whole thing."

Paul chuckled and said, "He must like chicken."

Order My Steps

Sunday morning when Paul introduced Superintendent Buai to the church, he teased, "Brother Buai is a true Pentecostal preacher; he loves chicken. In fact, for lunch he ate the whole thing," making it sound like they had only one chicken, not a Cornish hen for each person. He left it to Brother Buai to explain.

That morning Brother Buai's stirring testimony of how he became a Christian touched everyone. When he presented the needs of their brothers and sisters in Burma, the saints in Okinawa opened their hearts and wallets. The visiting minister was astounded. He received money for nine Coleman lights, three church roofs, three horses, and seven bicycles. The native preachers would use the horses and bicycles to reach the northern hill country of Burma.

By the time he left for home, the saints had also provided for his personal needs: shirts, trousers, shoes, handkerchiefs, travel items, and many other things.

As tears tumbled down his cheeks, he told the church, "Never have I had so much at one time. I am very humbled. When I came, I had only one white handkerchief. I did not use it in Burma, as I saved it for my trip to Japan. Now you have given me many packages of handkerchiefs. I will share them with the pastors at home."

When the church in Burma had a need, Brother Buai knew whom to call. Over the years the Asian Military District gave funds to build three country churches, helped build the Bible school and dorms, and purchased appliances for the Buais' home. One offering of $8,000 was given to pay off the loan on their headquarters church.

Paul had a burden for the sinner, the new convert, the young minister, and the missionary alike. Not only did he teach the saints to work, he taught them by example to give. From time to time he sent those in training to neighboring countries to hold revivals for missionaries. He paid the fare for the evangel-

Paul A.Dennis

ist and his family, and sent an offering for the church, so the evangelist would not be a hardship on the missionary.

The military work in Okinawa, which began as a foreign missions church, had matured into a foreign missions giving church—from missions to missions with love.

Here Comes the Bride (and Groom)

"Where are we supposed to eat?" Paul growled. "Look at this table, flowers from one end to the other."

Paula giggled. "Dad, you don't scare me. I see that smile in your eyes. We thought you could fast until the bouquets are finished."

Paul joined his girls at the kitchen table. He shook his head. What a summer! Ever since Paula had graduated from Jackson College of Ministries in May and returned for her second term as an AIMer, their world had been in total chaos. Even so, it was wonderful having their girl home again.

The bride was committed to her responsibilities as an AIMer, utilizing the things she had learned at Bible school, directing the music, teaching Sunday school, and doing anything else that her pastor asked. She loved the church in Okinawa and working for God, but it was evident that she had left a good portion of her heart (and mind) in the United States.

The mother of the bride was doing double time—helping her daughter plan a long-distance wedding and keeping up with her regular duties, which were multiple.

The father of the bride was suffering from emotional somersaults. *Am I bipolar?* Paul wondered.

Every spare minute, and there were few, was devoted to making ribbon flower bouquets and boutonnières, planning the ceremony, choosing dresses, and taking care of a hundred other wedding details. Liz Carey, Paula's friend, gave her a personal bridal shower and helped with wedding plans.

The church gave a wedding shower for the bride and groom, sans the groom. Shirley placed a photo of Keith in a prominent

Paul A. Dennis

place; it was the nearest to the real thing they could get. Everyone laughed when Paula said, "It reminds me of a funeral."

Paul and Shirley had missed their daughter's graduation from Bible college, choosing rather to return to the States for her wedding. In August the Dennis family of three left for Zanesville. Paula and Keith had chosen to be married at the church pastored by Paula's uncle, Arthur Potts.

Coming back to Zanesville opened a chest of memories for Paul—courting Shirley, their first apartment, the pottery plant, Gilbert Shoe Company, Jeffrey Allen. Twenty-two years had passed since a piece had been cut from his heart and buried here. In a few days he was going to give away another piece of his heart in this same city. For Paul it was a bittersweet trip.

Paul and Shirley loved and respected Keith. They were thankful that God had blessed their daughter with a godly bridegroom and them with a son. They knew Paula and Keith belonged together, but parents are never emotionally prepared for the day their daughter changes her last name.

On August 13, 1983, Paul walked his beautiful treasure down the aisle to meet the love of her life.

"Who giveth this woman to be wed to this man?" asked Reverend Terry Erwin, Keith's brother-in-law.

Paul swallowed his Adam's apple twice. He looked at his mentor, Fred Kinzie, standing beside Terry. Once again he drew courage from his friend. He cleared his throat and answered, "Her mother and I." He placed his baby's hand into the hand of another man. He hugged her and gave her a watery smile; then he sat down beside his bride and took her hand in his.

The ceremony. The kiss. Congratulations. Hugs and kisses. Laughter. Pictures. Gifts. Punch. Wedding cake.

The bride and groom, rich in love, left for their honeymoon, and Keith's final year at Jackson College of Ministries. The mother and father of the bride left, poor in pocket, to return to the harvest field.

Order My Steps

On September 18, they had dual celebrations: Paul's forty-eighth birthday and the burning of the church mortgage. When the FMD had loaned them $50,000 to purchase the apartment complex, they had agreed to repay it in two years; instead, it had taken three. But that did not dim the rejoicing that night. The Asia Military District was the proud owner of a mighty nice piece of property in Okinawa, Japan, thanks to the generous saints and their hard-working, thrifty missionary pastor and his wife.

The next May AIMers Reverend and Mrs. Keith Townsley arrived. What a great addition to the First UPC team! Keith jumped in like a pro, teaching a series on the Book of Acts. Paula took charge of the music program, taught Sunday school, assisted Shirley with the ladies ministry. In Paula's words, their pastor-dad gave them "leeway to grow; create; become; fail; succeed; experiment; learn; live." Never was Paul's and Shirley's calling as "ministry makers" more evident than in their son-in-law's and daughter's ministries. Their fingerprints were stamped indelibly on Reverend and Mrs. Keith Townsley.

In September Paul, waving a welcome sign, stood on tiptoe peering through the crowd at the Naha International Airport. Shirley held a beautiful bouquet of fresh flowers. As Richard and Jean Lucas, newly appointed missionaries to the American Military in Japan, exited the jetway and saw the Dennises, sunny smiles brightened their faces. After a few days' R&R (rest and recovery) in Okinawa, the Lucases would move on to Tokyo.

Four days before leaving for Japan, Richard and Jean had discovered they were expecting their first baby. They arrived

Paul A. Dennis

physically and emotionally exhausted. Their ten days in the Dennises' home acclimated them gently to a new culture.

Paul and Shirley gave the Lucases the same royal treatment they gave every guest in their home—the morning tea tray, delicious meals at home and at the DaiRai restaurant, put-your-feet-up hospitality.

They even made shopping fun as they taught the Lucases how to recognize common household items by the familiar packaging. The new missionaries' spirits were revived by the lively worship at church and Friday all-night prayer meeting.

When it was time for the Lucases to move on, the Dennises went with them to help them find an apartment and take care of the complicated business of getting settled in a foreign land. They left the Okinawa church in the capable hands of the Townsleys.

The holiday season rolled around, and Paula immersed herself in producing a children's musical, "The Late Great Potentate," which they presented to the church on December 8.

After the program Paul stood at the door greeting departing guests. "That was awesome," said a lady. "I am the Kadena Air Force Base representative for promotional activities. I have been looking for something special for this year's old-fashioned Christmas program. Could the children do this program for us?"

Paula was consulted and quickly agreed. What an opportunity. The civilian church was not permitted to pass out tracts or witness on base. This children's musical opened the door for the First United Pentecostal Church of Okinawa—free PR. The program was advertised on FEN-TV (Far East Network TV) and printed in all the base activity schedules. Paula repeated her mantra, "God works in mischievous ways."

Order My Steps

After the final production of "The Late Great Potentate," the missionaries settled down to planning their *family* Christmas dinner. As always, military families and singles, far from home, gathered at their house for a special time of celebrating Christ's birth and their friendship. Color, race, and culture were not important—blacks, whites, Asians, Hispanics, UPC, PAW, AMF, air force, army, navy, marines—all blended into one caring church family around the Dennises' table.

Shirley's hospitality and Paul's humor, assisted by Paula's and Keith's helping hands, made 1984 another memory-making Christmas.

In April 1985, Paul and Shirley traveled to Osaka, where Paul met with RFS George Shalm and the new Japanese superintendent, Akimoto Okura. Then it was on to Kyoto for the annual Japanese National Conference at the Kyoto Gospel Church and a reunion with their good friends the Fujibayashis; Brother Fujibayashi had resigned from his position as superintendent due to ill health.

Brother Shalm traveled with the Dennises back to Okinawa so he could meet with the Townsleys who had been approved for another year as AIMers.

"Brother Shalm, what would you like for breakfast?" his blue ribbon hostess asked.

Their Canadian RFS chuckled. "I'd like hot porridge."

Ohio-born Shirley raised her eyebrows, as she thought of the three bears. "I'm not sure I know how to make porridge," she admitted.

"No problem. I prefer to fix my own breakfast, if you will let me in your kitchen."

The next morning Brother Shalm cooked enough porridge, which was made from raw oats, for the whole family. He taught

Shirley his special technique, and porridge was added to the Dennises' breakfast menu.

Paul clicked off the radio and went to call Paula. "Have you heard the news? Typhoon Nelson is headed our way. It's time for a lock-in.

On the other end Paula squealed, "We'll tie things down around here and tape the windows. Then we'll be over tonight. Do I need to bring anything?"

"Just your board games," Paul answered. "Oh, yes, if you have any extra flashlight batteries, bring them."

Typhoon lock-ins were as much fun as the snow days in Hokkaido. True, typhoons were noisier than snow, but being locked in with family was a treat, despite the imminent danger. They prayed for safety; then trusted God and had fun.

After the storm, Paula devoted her time to planning a secret reception for her parents' twenty-fifth wedding anniversary. She reserved a whole section at Sam's by the Sea restaurant. Shirley's cup overflowed that evening when the Fujibayashis from Kyoto walked in.

Then came Christmas. Paul and Shirley were at the dinner table surrounded by their military family, when the phone rang. Paul went to answer it and came back grinning. "Sea Condition Red."

Big smiles spread around the table. Everyone recognized the code name; it was time to head for the East China Sea for a baptism, where the blood of Jesus would wash away sins.

Paul continued, "That was Brother Terry Plumer. One of their Christmas guests just received the Holy Ghost and wants to be baptized."

Order My Steps

Shirley pushed back from the table. "Let's go. We can have dessert when we get back."

A week later the watch-night service ended with another "Sea Condition Red." Three more were baptized in the lovely name of Jesus.

A few days later Paul called Keith, "Do you know Aiko Sprinkel?"

"Isn't she the lady that Shirley Ann has been teaching Search for Truth?"

Paul nodded. "She wants to be baptized and receive the Holy Ghost. Would you like to do the honors and baptize her?"

"Absolutely," Keith responded.

Had he known that Keith was suffering from a migraine, he would not have asked him; and that would have been a mistake.

As Keith and Aiko stood in the East China Sea, Keith asked God to take away the pain she suffered from rheumatoid arthritis. He also asked God to heal his headache. God answered that prayer, and they received a triple-header miracle. One miracle of remission of sins and two miracles of healing.

In April 1986 Paul and Shirley were again at the Naha International Airport. The Townsleys were headed back to the States to meet the foreign missions board, seeking a full-time appointment as missionaries to Okinawa, Japan, and the Asia Military District. This parting was much easier than previous ones because it was overshadowed by hope.

Paula and Keith turned at the entrance to the jetway and waved. Paul turned to Shirley and grinned. "They shall return."

From Hot to Cold

Two words describe Okinawa any time of the year—hot and humid. Two words describe Seoul, Korea, in the winter—cold and colder.

One missions project of the military church in Okinawa was to purchase pews for the church in Inchon, Korea. When the building was completed, Paul and Shirley were invited to the dedication in January 1986.

When they left Okinawa, the temperature was in the 70s; but that combined with high humidity spelled "h-o-t." In two hours they went from the tropical climate of the island to the frigid mountainous zone of the Korean peninsula. When they arrived in Seoul, Korea, the temperature was sub-zero.

Missionary Elizabeth Turner and her son Nate met them at the airport to take them to the dedication. At the church they were surprised to discover that everyone wore coats, hats, gloves, and boots. Were they late? Was church over? No, there was no heat.

The clapping was a bit muffled. Every praise ushered a glory cloud of breath into the room. Foot stomping and hand clapping accompanied every "amen" and kept the blood flowing.

After the service the Dennises went home with the Turner family, which, in addition to Elizabeth and Nate, included dad William and daughter Becky. The Turners lived in the second-floor apartment at the Korean Bible School in Kwang Myung City. Paul and Shirley were adopted aunt and uncle to Nate and Becky. Time together was like a family reunion.

When the Turners (or anyone else) visited in the Dennises' home, they were treated to Shirley's hospitality supreme. This included room service each morning—a tray

Order My Steps

with coffee in elegant demitasse cups (uniquely different each time) and a flower. That was the first treat of the day. All day Shirley's hospitality surrounded her guests.

But each missionary wife adjusts to the conditions of the host country. Life in Korea was a world apart from life in Okinawa, even though they were in the same region of the world.

The freezing wind seeped through the window frames of the Turners' apartment, billowing the curtains. Their little oil furnace huffed and puffed, but did not faze the plummeting temperatures outside and in. The Turners were pretty well acclimated to the conditions, thanks to sweaters and long underwear, but the Dennises were not prepared.

Over and over Elizabeth apologized, as she pulled out their extra blanket and handed it to Shirley. She directed them to Becky's bedroom.

"Don't fret. We'll be fine," Shirley assured her.

Shivering, Shirley, fully clothed, and Paul crawled under the covers and huddled together. About the time one would get warm, the other one would move; and the shakes would return.

Finally, Shirley crawled out of bed, put on her coat, scarf, and gloves. "There, that's better," she told Paul, as she crawled back under the covers.

The next morning the Turners and Dennises laughed, as they recounted the wonderful hazards of missionary life.

After that the Dennises managed to visit Korea in the summer, a wise decision. But even then life was not always comfortable and things were not always convenient. One summer the water in Kwang Myung City was off for two weeks. When Paul and Shirley arrived for a military retreat, the Turners reserved them a room at a hotel. Again Shirley's hospitality came through. She invited the Turners to their room every day for showers.

Paul A. Dennis

Paul and Shirley's trip to Taiwan to attend the Chinese camp meeting reminded them that in many parts of the world traffic can be hazardous to your health.

When they landed at Chiang Kai-Shek Airport, Garry and Sandy Edmonds, fellow Ohioans, were there to convey them on the last leg of their trip to Mount Lebanon, Kaohsiung, site of the camp meeting.

"It's a seven- to eight-hour drive," Garry informed them, as they loaded their luggage into the car.

Sandy laughed, "Barring any unforeseen problems."

In Taipei it was bumper-to-bumper traffic. No big deal; after all, Paul and Shirley had driven all over the States on deputation. Rush hour in Dallas, L.A., Cincinnati—bumper to bumper they understood.

But when they reached the four-lane expressway on the outskirts of the city, bumper to bumper took on a new meaning. The four-lane expressway became eight and nine lanes, if motorcycles count. Apparently, motorcycles served as "family cars," transporting four and five people at a time. Other cycles doubled as family pickups and delivery vans with boxes stacked five and six feet high.

For the first few hours the Dennises tensed and cringed every time Garry hit the brakes or didn't hit the brakes. They soon lost count of the accidents, fender benders, and overturned trucks they encountered. Eventually, the Edmondses' business-as-usual attitude helped them relax. The SFC car arrived at Mount Lebanon without a dent or scratch. Paul and Shirley had a few more gray hairs and wrinkles, but they chalked it up to life on the mission field.

Missionaries Tom and Sandy Bracken and Leonard and Ping Richardson welcomed them and helped them get settled in their quarters. After a good night's sleep, everyone was up early. Breakfast was delicious, hot, soupy rice with peanuts. Sandy

Bracken with her Mr. Coffee saved the camp; well, at least, she saved the missionaries. God saved the sinners.

The services were glorious, as the Spirit of God swept through the congregation. Many received the Holy Ghost and were baptized in the tank set up outside the meeting hall. These courageous souls went down in the freezing water and came up blue, but cleansed and forgiven!

After the last night's service the missionaries headed back to Taipei. To keep the driver awake, they talked and laughed all the way. The lack of motorcycle traffic in the middle of the night was a big relief to Paul and Shirley.

The next day the Edmondses took their guests shopping, and that night they hit the famous Taipei night market where they purchased gifts and computer software.

A shopping expedition with fellow missionaries provides more than gifts and souvenirs; it nourishes their fellowship-starved spirits. The trinkets are soon forgotten, but the memories live on.

Cockroaches and Customs

Paul read the letter from George Shalm, regional field supervisor for Asia, nodded, and went to find Shirley. She was at the kitchen table writing to Paula.

"Brother Shalm wants me to go with him to help teach, minister, and carry materials and clothing into Burma and Dhaka, Bangladesh, with a stop first in Thailand. If I can, he'll arrange to stop here; we can connect and travel together."

"That's a wonderful opportunity for you. You have never been to Bangladesh," Shirley said. "When are you going?"

Paul checked the calendar. How could it be January 1987 already? "February and March."

"How long will you be gone?"

Paul checked the letter. "Three weeks."

Paul did a countdown. Finally, D-day came and off they went. The visit to Thailand went well; then they flew on to Burma.

They stayed at the old, but famous, five-story Inya Hotel built by the Russians. Only the first two floors were occupied. The top three looked like they had been caught in the middle of a fight between the weather and a fire. Paul expected the upper floors to collapse onto the lower ones at any moment.

Rates were $10–12 a day, including breakfast, hot showers, and daily room cleaning. This sounded like a bargain deluxe until Paul found out that the water ran in a trickle and the rooms were cleaned with brooms that merely repositioned the dust. He carried a pair of hospital scrubs to sleep in, for obvious reasons.

As they walked down the corridor to their room followed by the bellboy toting their luggage, the world's largest cockroach, so

Order My Steps

Paul thought, scuttled across the floor. This hairy creature was at least 4–5 inches long and 1–2 inches wide.

Brother Shalm pinned it against the wall with his foot. Motioning to the bellboy, he challenged, "What are you going to do about this?"

The boy's eyes widened. He ooohed. With a big smile, he rushed over, grabbed the cockroach, and deposited it in his pocket. "These are very good fried."

In one class Brother Shalm taught on not eating blood and things strangled. At the end of the lesson, one man raised his hand. "Brother Shalm, I am from the northern country. We are hunters and farmers. We trap much of our food in the forest. When rats run into our traps, they are caught by the neck and have been dead for hours when we return. They are strangled, but you say we cannot eat things strangled. What shall we do?"

Paul grimaced. This question was for Solomon.

George Shalm smiled and said firmly, "You will have to learn a new way to catch your rats."

Paul decided to carefully study the menu at the hotel restaurant. He had no intention of eating rats or cockroaches, strangled or fried.

Time to move on to Dhaka, Bangladesh. Usually, customs and arrival cards are given out on the plane to save time when checking into the country. This time they were not given these cards until they were standing in line in the airport. Paul knew that in many third world countries a visitor had to be careful what he put on his card as his occupation. Anti-Christianity sentiments are high.

He was behind Brother Shalm in the line, which was jump-starting and stopping like a cranky motor. Each time the line stopped, Paul filled out a line or two.

By the time he reached the customs check-in desk, his RFS had finished checking in and was ready to get his luggage. He glanced over his shoulder at the card in Paul's hand. When he saw that Paul had written "minister" in the occupation line, a big grin split his face. "You're going to have fun with that one," he said, as he left his traveling buddy standing there looking bewildered.

The clerk read Paul's card and scrutinized him. He called for reinforcements. The second man gave Paul and his card a thorough inspection. Then he called for more reinforcements. The third man repeated the action. Paul felt like an ant under a microscope.

Then the questions came from three directions. "Where do you live in the United States?" "Where is your family?" "What is your work?"

Paul had no idea what was going on until one of the inquisitors asked, "In what office are you a minister?"

The light bulb in Paul's head flashed. No wonder that ornery George Shalm was grinning. Paul stammered, "I-I-I am a Minister of Family Living in the United States."

That was sufficient. The customs clerk stamped Paul's card and waved him through.

Brother Shalm later enlightened Paul. In Bangladesh all ministers work in a government office and wear government-issued white shirts and trousers. Paul was wearing plain dark trousers and a short-sleeved shirt.

After the guys collected their luggage, they stepped out into a heat wave that scorched their lungs. Surrounding them were men grabbing for their bags, wanting a tip from the rich Americans. Paul and George tightened their hold on their bags, while trying to protect their pockets, and pushed their way through the mob to their taxi.

Their travel arrangements had been made by Biaky, their only contact in Bangladesh, who was not allowed in the airport area because she was a refugee from Northeast India.

They stayed in first-class rooms at the Sheridan Hotel for $24 a night. Brother Shalm called Biaky, and she told him it would be two days before she could get to Dhaka to act as their guide.

So the men went sightseeing and shopping. Paul purchased a throw rug made from pure jute, which he hand carried back to Okinawa.

This was George Shalm's last trip to Asia. He was admitted to the hospital in May with a brain tumor. He took his final trip on February 17, 1988, destination Glory, where he had no problem getting through customs.

Homeless

Shirley walked into Paul's office opening a business envelope. She pulled out an official-looking document. As she read, a curtain of unbelief dropped over her face. "We're homeless, Paul."

"Homeless?" Paul's eyebrows jumped up and down.

"Read this." Shirley handed the letter across the desk to him.

Paul read silently for a few seconds; then he exploded. "Denied. Request denied! Our request for visas to South Korea has been denied?"

Shirley nodded.

"B-b-but everything's p-p-packed or stored or sold to cut down on the cost of moving to Korea," the bewildered missionary said. Shirley knew that and God knew that, but Paul needed to verbalize it to absorb the shock.

Shirley chuckled. "Wonder what this is all about. Remember what Paula says, 'The Lord moves in mischievous ways.'"

Paul was not amused. He leaned forward, palms flat on his desk. "But the headquarters for the Asia Military District is supposed to be in Seoul, Korea. That's what the board ruled."

Shirley's chuckle grew into a laugh. "Apparently God and Korea have different plans."

Paul leaned his head on the back of his chair and twiddled his thumbs. Shirley sat down across from his desk and waited.

Paul reviewed the last two years. May '87 he had been officially appointed as director of the Asia Military District, giving him the oversight of all military works in Asia. Keith and Paula had returned in November. January '88 Paul and Shirley had started their third deputation, leaving the Townsleys as their

Order My Steps

furlough replacements. Various meetings at headquarters had been squeezed into their deputation schedule, and that summer they had returned to Korea for the AMD retreat. Garry Tracy had been appointed regional field supervisor for Asia, and—

Shirley had waited long enough; she interrupted Paul's mental review, "At least we won't have to leave baby Barak."

Paul snorted, "We may have to move in with baby Barak."

"Paul, where is your faith?" Shirley reprimanded gently. "Hasn't God always provided a home for us?"

Paul, feeling duly chastised, returned to memory lane.

In December '88 their grandson, John Barak Townsley, "made in Japan," had been born. Becoming a grandparent was right up there with becoming a missionary. They returned to the island for the baby's dedication and installed Keith as the pastor of the First United Pentecostal Church of Okinawa, turning their living quarters and SFC car over to the Townsleys. Then back to the States to finish deputation, and in March '89 home again to Okinawa.

Home? Where was home? Paul felt as adrift as Shirley must have felt the first years of their marriage.

Not only were the Dennises homeless, they were carless.

OK, God, what's the next step? It's Your call.

Paul relaxed. He stood up and grinned at his wife. "Mrs. Dennis, may I take you to lunch?"

Word of the Dennises' plight sped through the church grapevine. At the next service a military couple approached Paul. "Brother Dennis, we are going home to the States for an extended vacation. We would love for you and Sister Dennis to stay in our house."

Settled.

God, You came through right on time again. We have a home, although a temporary one.

Paul, aren't all homes temporary?

End of discussion.

They reapplied for visas.

In May Paul received a letter from Tim Thomas, pastor of the military work in Misawa, the last stop on the island of Honshu before crossing over into Hokkaido. He was having church problems and needed help. That fell under Paul's new job description as director of the Asia Military District.

Paul flew to Misawa and met with Pastor Thomas. After several days of discussion, the problem remained. Paul decided to pastor the church for whatever time it took to work through the issues.

The military couple returned from their vacation. The Dennises moved to Misawa into a rented Japanese-style apartment (which means petite), temporarily furnished. Paul figured they would be there a couple of months.

Second request for visas denied.

They reapplied through AMD. The answer was fast forwarded that time. No! What part of "no" do you missionaries not understand?

A foreign resident of a country cannot simply move from city to city without a lot of red tape. Changing their residence from Okinawa to Misawa required a trip to the government office in Hachinoe. Paul and Shirley lost count of how many times they made the trip—thirty minutes by train or two hours by car. But they persevered. Missionaries are known for that quality.

They reapplied for visas to Korea.

The climate in Misawa was similar to Ohio with four seasons, except, like in Hokkaido, snow was measured in feet. In summer, to Shirley's delight, Misawa was a farmer's market wonderland.

But the island had its dangers. Often they were awakened by tremors. They would run to the stairwell for refuge until the earth stopped quaking and they stopped shaking.

They flew to Korea to attend an Asia Military District retreat. There they were with RFS Garry Tracy and their son-in-law Keith. After the retreat they flew to Okinawa to be with the Tracys and Townsleys in special services.

While there, they received another solid "no" from the Korean government. RFS Garry Tracy recommended that the Dennises stay in Misawa and Paul work out of there as the Asia Military District Coordinator.

Back to Misawa to look for a house. Shirley was a pro at this.

The church's landlord had a two-bedroom American-style (not petite) apartment with a living room, kitchen, and bath. It was only a hundred or so steps from the church—48-6 Minamiyama W-314-D. Very convenient, especially since Paul and Shirley still did not have a car.

Months flew by as they worked to stabilize the saints and reach the lost, while learning their way around another part of Japan. Squeezed into Paul's schedule were trips to various military works in Asia.

On October 9 he was returning from the Philippines when his back started hurting. "I drank too much Coke," he muttered

Paul A. Dennis

to himself. The flight was long, and the layover in Taiwan longer.

When he finally arrived home, Shirley could tell he was in pain. "Take a hot shower and go to bed," she said. "You can tell me about your trip tomorrow."

But before dawn Paul was in extreme pain, passing blood, and in an emergency clinic. After running a few tests, the doctor said in broken English, "Bad. I not help you. You go to hospital."

Paul was in such torment that he did not argue. He went to the hospital. More tests. After a few more hours the diagnosis was made: a severe case of kidney infection. The doctor gave him some medicine and told him that he should be better within a week. It was a long week.

A few days later missionary Richard Lucas and his AIMer Richard Kepler from Tokyo brought Paul his SFC car, as the Lucases were leaving for deputation.

After the men left, Paul and Shirley cuddled on the couch in their cozy, comfortable home. Shirley's eyes twinkled. "All is well, PD. I have a home and you have a car. Isn't God wonderful?"

Paul tightened his arm around her shoulders. "Yes, God is wonderful, and so is my wife."

Needed TLC

"How long will you be gone this time?" Shirley sat on the couch, munching popcorn. Paul was at his desk working on lessons for a seminar in Thailand that he and Frank Poling were scheduled to teach.

He handed her his bowl for a popcorn refill. "About a month. We leave September 28. Thailand has a special place in my heart. Billy Cole was telling about the revival in Thailand when I first heard God speak to me about missions."

"Remember the first time we were in Thailand?" Shirley's eyes took on a far-away look. Before Paul could answer, she continued, "It was the Asia Regional Retreat in Bangkok, September '86, almost four years ago. George and Margaret Shalm put it together. What a wonderful time we had with all the missionaries from Asia and some of the native preachers."

Paul looked at the antique blue-and-white pedestal dish reigning over his desk. "Remember when Thailand's superintendent Wat-what-tanachant—"

Shirley giggled as Paul stumbled over the name. "Wattanachant Chaiyong," she pronounced. "Asian people have such aristocratic names. I don't think I'll ever get used to Jones and Smith and—"

"And Dennis." Paul's turn to interrupt. "You'd better never get tired of that name because it's yours for life."

Shirley's smile turned upside down. "Oh, Paul, will you be gone for our thirtieth anniversary?" Tears pooled in her eyes.

Paul stared at the calendar on his desk. October 15 was circled in red. He exhaled softly. "'Fraid so, Charlie Brown." He moved to the couch and put his arm around her. "Tell you what, I'll take you to the farmer's market when I get home."

"Oh you!" Shirley poked him in the ribs with her elbow.

Paul A. Dennis

Paul grunted. "Now what were we talking about? Oh, yes, when Brother skip-the-first-name Chaiyong gave me that antique dish. Remember that lovely Thai dinner his wife fixed for us?"

"Yes, and how Sister Elly Hansen stood at the door to greet us with a traditional welcome of Thai flower bracelets. I don't usually wear bracelets, but I was honored to wear that one."

"That was my second trip to Thailand," Paul remembered. "The first trip I went with Brother Cook to the Thai camp meeting. Sister Elly translated for me when I preached.

"The camp meeting was at an old campground on the beach by the Siam Sea. It was absolutely gorgeous—the white beach, emerald sea, and swaying palm trees." Paul shut his eyes and pictured the scene. "The service was held under a bamboo-thatched roof over a wooden floor. I sat in awe, enthralled by the divine worship: the drums and a handmade marimba, the Thai dance, the presence of the Lord. I have never been in any service to compare with it."

"I'm glad you get to go, even if I will be alone on our anniversary." Shirley couldn't keep from piling on a little guilt.

Little did she know what awaited her globe-trotting husband in Thailand; it was a trip he would never forget.

Paul and Frank Poling had been in Thailand about two weeks and were teaching in Kamphangphet, eight hours north of Bangkok, when dysentery struck Paul with a vengeance. Each day he got weaker and more dehydrated. He was seriously considering changing his flight and going home. However, getting there would be a challenge in his condition.

Paul was so sick he hardly realized when their thirtieth anniversary came and went, but at home in Misawa, Shirley knew.

Finally, desperate for help, Paul missed a class to go into a small country town in search of a pharmacy. After about thirty

Order My Steps

minutes he found one. Then came the missionaries' plague—the pharmacist could not speak English.

After some unusual sign language, the guy got the message and gave Paul four tiny white pills, imported from England. The directions on the package were written in Thai and English.

Within a very short time Paul had taken all four and was feeling much better. He decided to stay, but Brother Poling assured him that he could finish the classes. No problem. It did not take much persuading to convince Paul that he should go home.

While waiting at the hotel for a driver to pick him up, Superintendent Chaiyong asked, "How many of those pills did you take?"

"All four."

A shocked look crossed the Thai's face. "Oh, Brother Dennis, that was too much too fast."

The instructions on the package directing that the pills were to be spaced out every four hours were written only in Thai, which, of course, Paul could not read.

By the time he arrived in Bangkok nine hours later, he was feeling fine. But he could not get a flight out for three days. His ticket was unchangeable, non-refundable, and could not be endorsed by another airline. So much for cheap tickets!

He checked into the cheapest room he could get in the Airport Hotel—$125 a night plus tax.

A few hours later stomach cramps twisted his innards and pain stabbed his lower back. Brother Chaiyong was right. Next came a kidney and bladder infection, which spiked a fever. He took the antibiotic he had brought with him, and that helped some.

He did not feel like leaving his room, and he had crackers, so he munched on them.

Paul A. Dennis

On a trip to the bathroom, he looked in the mirror. A front tooth was missing from his partial. He had eaten his tooth and not known it.

He sat in the bathroom, a lonely, miserable missionary—stuck in Bangkok, sick all over, a big gap in his smile (or was that his grimace?), a three-day's growth of beard, and needing a shower. He could feel his fever shooting up. He felt as though he were surrounded by fire. Then he realized, the water tank on the commode was a heated water tank. The seat was heated. Flush! A gush of hot air.

Shirley, your globe-trotting husband needs some TLC. He's coming home.

Preachers' Wives

Shirley pulled a king's robe out of the church's costume closet. "Looks like this needs some minor repairs." She placed it in the pile on the table and pulled out another robe for inspection. "The holidays were wonderful in Misawa, but now that we are back in Okinawa, I am excited to be directing another Christmas play. I will miss Paula though. She did an awesome job every year."

In May Keith and Paula had moved to Tulsa, Oklahoma, to pastor Life Tabernacle, Keith's home church. His parents, Johnny and Bonnie, lived in Tulsa.

Paul and Shirley had moved back to Okinawa to pastor again the First United Pentecostal Church. The headquarters of the Asia Military District had moved with the coordinator. Robert Courtright, Paul's right-hand man, had stepped into place as the pastor of the church in Misawa.

As Grandpa Dennis watched Grandma sort costumes for the Christmas play, his eyes misted. "I'm going to miss Barak. He'll be three next month."

Shirley exhaled, determined to dry up the moisture accumulating behind her eyelids. She added a shepherd's costume to the repair pile on the table. "Three is such a fun age. It's been six months since we've seen him. I wish we could be together for Christmas. We had so much fun last year. It will be Barak's first Christmas in the States. He'll have so much fun with Keith's family, he won't even miss us."

"Now, Shirley, let's don't even go there. Next thing you know you'll be crying."

"No, I won't," Shirley declared. "I am thankful that our grandson has another set of grandparents who love him. I am thankful that we have our church family here in Okinawa. I am

Paul A. Dennis

thankful that you and I will be together this Christmas season. We can Christmas shop and—"

Paul cleared his throat. Shirley turned and waited. Apparently her husband had something to tell her.

"Brother Tracy has invited me to join him on the last leg of his tour of the region."

Shirley felt as if the wind had been knocked out of her. Paul cleared his throat again. His Adam's apple bobbed like a cork on a fishing line. "It's just a short trip—Taiwan, Hong Kong, China, Thailand—"

"Thailand? Paul, remember how sick you got last year when you went there?"

"I know, but I won't get sick again. I promise."

Shirley snorted. "Paul Dennis, you can't promise that!"

He grinned, "I know, but you can pray, and I'll be fine."

Shirley's eyes locked with his. Paul was the first to look away. "I'll be back in time for the Christmas drama."

Shirley dug deep inside her and pulled up a cup of courage. It was all she could manage, but it was enough. She gave him her gentle smile. "Thank God for sending the Elmores and the Grahams."

Paul nodded. "Yes, I believe they are answers to the petitions I've been sending heavenward."

The Elmores and the Grahams had arrived the month before on the same flight, although neither knew the other had been assigned to Okinawa. They had met while stationed in Germany. Marvin Elmore was in the army and Dennis Graham was in the air force. Both families had blended into the church and blessed the Dennises with their willingness to work.

The last year had been a busy one for them, as were all years. Between his travels to the Philippines to take care of business for the military district and the world conference in Amsterdam, Paul had sandwiched in conferences and retreats in Japan and Korea. In addition, he pastored the Okinawa congregation and taught ministerial training classes to sixteen young ministers.

Shirley taught Sunday school and Bible studies, directed the music and church programs, entertained a constant stream of officials coming and going on business in Asia and missionaries coming to Okinawa for R&R (often at the Dennises' insistence and expense), plus a dozen other things that pastors' wives do behind the scenes.

Paul put his arm around his wife's shoulders. "Do you know what Brother Elmore said about you the other day?"

Shirley rolled her eyes. "I have no idea."

Paul chuckled. "He said you are the only person he knows who can make serving international coffee a dining extravaganza."

Shirley laughed and swatted at Paul with the angel's halo she had retrieved from the closet. "Go on and get ready for your trip. And this time you had better not get sick, or your nurse is going on strike."

Paul and Regional Field Supervisor Tracy traveled dressed like tourists, no suits or ties. Many third world Asian countries are not open to ministers or missionaries, either as residents or guests. Anti-Christian feelings build spiritual walls around their borders. Missionaries who are allowed to reside in these countries are under hair-raising surveillance; they are expected to teach when, where, and what the government approves.

When George Shalm was Regional Field Supervisor of Asia, he had made contact with a preacher in Vietnam. After Garry Tracy was appointed to fill Brother Shalm's position, he found the name and address of this man, although he had no idea where the address was located.

Paul A. Dennis

Brother Tracy had received word that the contact had been arrested for preaching and given a nine-year sentence, after already serving an eleven-year term.

The missionaries-turned-tourists arrived in Vietnam at midday and checked into a hotel. The next day they checked out and moved to another hotel for security reasons.

The third day they called a taxi and gave him the address of their contact. He smiled and nodded. The men were totally at the mercy of the driver, hoping he knew what he said he knew. He did.

The taxi stopped. A woman came out and talked to Garry. He got back in the taxi and they returned to the hotel.

In their room he explained to Paul, "The woman was the wife of our contact. She could not talk to me or be seen with a foreigner because she and her home are under surveillance by the government."

The men rented a room in a third hotel and waited for the church members to contact them.

In the meeting they learned that the preacher had been sentenced to nine years of hard labor. The wife had no support for herself or her two children. Yet she and her husband's followers were faithfully committed to propagating the gospel, even though they were under close observation. Like the apostles in Acts 5, there was no question in their mind whether they would obey God or man.

The wife told Garry and Paul that anyone the police suspected of being a Christian was followed constantly by undercover officers. At times the police forced their way into homes, searching for Bibles, tracts, or any written material that would connect them to Christianity. Before the men left, they took the ladies to dinner and gave them funds for a month's provision.

Paul was overwhelmed by an unfathomable appreciation for these ladies and all Christians who are living under government suppression.

Order My Steps

He returned home healthy and grateful, in time for Shirley's Christmas program, "Christmas Glory." After the play three ladies and one man were baptized in the lovely name of Jesus in the East China Sea.

As they gathered around the table with their military church family that holiday, Paul gave special thanks for his wife, the preacher's wife in Vietnam, and others like them around the world. Their sacrifices were different, but their commitment was the same—take the gospel to the lost.

Peace! Be Still!

The typhoon was bearing down on Okinawa. The FEN (Far East Network) was warning all military personnel to prepare for the typhoon. "If you are off base, return to base. . . ."

But they were having church. Who can leave a powerful move of God's Spirit to run from a little old typhoon?

Marine Juan Garcia and his hippie wife Louise were on their knees in the altar, crying out in desperation. The saints were travailing for their deliverance. Divorce and disgrace lurked outside the Garcias' door. Juan was a backslider. His wife knew nothing about Pentecost. In his wallet was a razor blade. Prayer was his last hope, his final effort at fixing his life. If something didn't change this night, he planned to slash his wrists.

Outside and inside the storm raged until the Master of the wind stepped into the room. "Peace! Be still!"

Juan and Louise, hands raised, tears flowing, broke through speaking in a heavenly language. Joy flooded the room. Streaks of tears diluted with black mascara formed muddy trails down Louise's glowing face.

When she stopped praying, she placed her palms on the chair where she had been praying and pushed to her feet. As she tugged unconsciously at her black mini-skirt, she turned to Paul. "Pastor Dennis, I have to be baptized."

"Wonderful," Paul responded. "We can take you to the East China Sea after the typhoon—"

"Pastor, I have to be baptized now—tonight," she insisted.

As Paul looked into the face of the repentant soul, he visualized the raging sea. He turned and spoke into the microphone, his voice rising above the rejoicing of the saints, "Sea Condition Red."

Order My Steps

The praising and shouting concluded with a loud "hallelujah." A few brave souls piled into the church van. Off they went to the East China Sea. The wind and rain pounded the van; the driver could faintly make out the white center line. But the saints were not to be deterred.

At the shore they tumbled out of the van. Holding hands, they turned into the wind and stumbled toward the sea. The waves were crashing over the barrier. Paul stared unflinchingly at the violent tempest reaching out to grasp them.

He and Dennis Graham, whom Paul had delegated to baptize Louise, stepped into the water. The Master of the wind spoke. "Peace. Be still." The winds ceased; the water calmed. An aura of peace hovered over them.

Louise walked into the sea and stood between Pastor Dennis and Brother Graham. Brother Graham spoke, "Louise Garcia, upon your confession and repentance and the Lord having filled you with the Holy Ghost, I baptize you in the name of our Lord Jesus Christ for the remission of your sins." Then he immersed her in the serene sea, repeating, "In the name of the Lord Jesus Christ."

As soon as they came out of the water, the storm returned with renewed fury—crashing, swirling, reaching over the wall as if to pull those who had dared to defy it back within its grasp. The storm lost the battle. The saints prevailed. Hallelujah!

Not all storms were outward. With sixteen preachers-in-training in one small building, it was inevitable that sooner or later a storm of dissension would arise. It was enough to challenge the apostle Paul; missionary Paul was challenged, but not threatened.

Paul and Shirley Dennis were ministry makers; it was their calling. On an island in the sea, far from the Bible schools of

Paul A. Dennis

North America, they trained preachers who would take the gospel to the four corners of the earth.

Young men who perceived that they were better, more zealous preachers than their leader did not intimidate Paul Dennis. He encouraged them to develop their calling and to allow the gifts of the Spirit to work through them. He trained, encouraged, and made room for each one. He rejoiced with those who succeeded; he wept with those who failed, then lifted them up and told them to try again.

So when the winds of jealousy blew into the congregation and waves of tension crashed, he prayed. Then he got up and took action, calling for a foot-washing service for the ministers. As these men knelt and washed their brothers' feet, spirits of pride and envy were broken. Again the Master of the wind spoke, "Peace. Be still."

The storm passed and peace prevailed.

ASAP

Rinnnngggg! Keith left the dinner table to answer the phone. He returned promptly, "PD, it's for you. Doctor Peter Aran."

Fear crossed Shirley's face. She intertwined her fingers and pushed her linked fists against her lips. Paul shoved back from the table, placed his napkin beside his plate, and patted Shirley's shoulder. "It's OK; he's probably just calling to tell me everything is fine."

Shirley nodded, but her expression did not change. As Paul went to the phone, he realized the hollowness of his statement. *Since when does a gastroenterologist call a patient at home to tell him everything is fine?*

The Dennises had arrived in the U.S. on September 17, the day before Paul's fifty-seventh birthday, leaving the church under the leadership of the assistant pastor, Marvin Elmore, and his wife. Paul and Shirley had spent a couple of days in St. Louis taking care of business; then they headed ASAP straight down I-44 for Tulsa. Papa and DarDar Dennis had already missed too many days with three-year-old Barak.

In Tulsa, on September 29, they had undergone complete physicals, as all missionaries do after a tour of duty on the field.

One day later Paul picked up the phone and said, "*Moshi moshi.*" Oops! Wrong country. "Hello. Paul Dennis speaking."

"Reverend Dennis, Doctor Aran here."

As if Paul didn't know. *Get to the point, doctor.*

"Could you come into my office first thing in the morning?"

"Well . . ." Paul hesitated, thinking of all they had planned.

"It is important," the doctor insisted.

"We'll be there," Paul said. The doctor hung up.

Before they went to bed, Paul's family, including little Barak, gathered around him and prayed. Hearing his grandson's earnest prayer caused Paul to smile and cry.

Paul A. Dennis

"Let's trust God and get some sleep," Paul told his family, as he hugged his grandson good night. They tried, but no one under the Townsley's roof got much sleep that night.

Paul and Shirley were at the doctor's office when it opened. When Paul's name was called, they were led into a small consultation room. Doctor Aran did not keep them waiting. Paul's and Shirley's hearts dropped. When a doctor does not keep a patient waiting, it is not good news.

After the briefest of greetings, the specialist said, "There are eleven polyps in your lower colon." He clipped an X-ray to a fluorescent light screen and pointed. "Four of these do not look good. We need to operate ASAP."

"But I feel fine," Paul argued as he stared at the X-ray, which meant nothing to him.

Doctor Aran sat down on a stool and rolled over until he was knee to knee with Paul. He looked him straight in the eye. "Mr. Dennis, this is urgent. The polyps that are malignant are at the stage where they could spread. If they do, you will not live a year."

Shirley gasped as tears pooled in her eyes. Paul's last argument evaporated.

On October 13, Paul checked into the hospital. Doctor Rodger Siemans, head surgeon at St. Francis Hospital, had rearranged his schedule so he could do Paul's surgery. As Paul lay in the sterile hospital bed waiting for the men in blue scrubs to roll him into the brilliantly lit freezer called an operating room, he struggled to brush thoughts of Brother Fujibayashi out of his mind.

Seven months earlier, while in Tokyo, Paul had received a call from Shirley telling him that the former superintendent of the United Pentecostal Church of Japan and his best friend had gone to Glory. Brother Fujibayashi and Paul, "David and Jonathan," were the same age.

The men in the blue scrubs arrived. As Shirley bent to kiss Paul, she whispered, "Don't worry. Barak is praying for you."

Order My Steps

Hours later Paul was back in his room with Shirley hovering over him. There was a light tap on the door and Doctor Siemans walked in smiling.

He greeted Shirley and turned to Paul. "Reverend Dennis, Someone greater than we doctors is looking out for you. The fact that you're here in the U.S. at this time and that we found these polyps at this stage tells me Someone has His hand in this matter."

With his eyes Paul sent his wife a silent message. *God is ordering our steps.* Shirley nodded.

Two days later the Dennises celebrated their thirty-second wedding anniversary in the hospital, giving thanks to the Giver of life for a good report. By the end of the month, Paul went to Life Tabernacle to hear his son-in-law preach. Soon afterward, he and Shirley traveled to Carlinville, Illinois, where they attended the UPCI School of Missions. Paul wasn't doing pushups or running races, but he was grateful to be present.

Because their budget was in excellent shape, the Dennises did not have to do any deputation. Every penny (or was it yen?) they pinched in Japan testified to their conservative management. What a blessing to relax and recover, rather than trudge the deputation trail.

"Happy birthday to you, dear Barak; happy birthday to you." As Barak blew out four candles, Papa and DarDar glowed.

Then came the holidays with their families in Oklahoma and Ohio. During the Thanksgiving and Christmas dinners, they felt twinges of homesickness. Their military family was celebrating without them. It seemed that no matter where they were, they missed someone.

Paul replaced his date book with a new one—1993. Time to go home to Okinawa and play catch-up ASAP.

Ditched!

"I'm gonna get you, Pastor," teenage Marvin Elmore II ran toward Paul with a cup of ice water from the picnic cooler.

Sputtt! Right in the face!

Paul jumped up and took off after the rascal. The running squad of two sped across glistening White Sands Beach. Picnic sounds surrounded them: squealing children, laughing adults, splashing water. Saliva-starting smells teased them: grilled hamburgers and hot dogs. It was a glorious day for the annual church picnic.

As Paul raced, he thought, *That kid does not know that I was one of the starters on the McLuney baseball, basketball, and track teams. He should have thought twice before he threw that cold water in my face. Just because I'm almost fifty-eight, doesn't m-m-mean . . . that . . . I c-a-an't catch that kkkkid.*

Huff-puff! The panting pastor was gaining on his tormentor, when he tripped over his shoestrings. Hadn't his mother always warned, "Tie your shoes, Pauly, or you're going to trip and break your neck"?

Through the air sailed the IFO—Identified Flying Object. Crash! Down came the pastor in a drainage ditch lined with coral. Splash! Silence!

Screams! Sirens!

But Paul did not hear them. When he came to, he was strapped to a gurney and being loaded into an ambulance by military medics. Shirley was squeezing his hand, crying, "Paul! Paul! Are you OK?" Church folks were standing some distance away praying for their ditched pastor.

The driver turned on the siren and away they went. Destination: the base hospital. For the next six or seven hours Paul

Order My Steps

lay immobile, waiting for the medical personnel to decide whether or not he had broken his neck.

He tried to look at the clock. How long had he been strapped down? He wanted to look at his wife and see if she was suffering as much as he was. Instead, he stared at the ceiling, counting the tiles. His elbow throbbed; his face burned; his dentures . . .

"Where are my dentures?"

"You broke them when you fell," Shirley told him.

Paul moaned, "I hurt all over."

"Just be thankful you do," Shirley countered. "You could be singing with Brother Fujibayashi and the angels. Whatever possessed you to act like a teenager?"

Just when I need sympathy, I get a lecture. "I feel like the apostle Paul in stocks," he growled.

Shirley turned her head and grinned. Then she remembered she didn't need to turn her head. Paul was counting the ceiling tiles. "Maybe you should sing."

A man wearing a military face and blue scrubs entered Paul's prison. "Mr. Dennis, your neck is not broken." He loosed Paul from his bondage, put a temporary splint on his elbow, and vicious medicine on his scratched face. "You can go home. The doctor wants you to come back Monday morning so he can set your elbow."

The next morning no one had to tell Paul to stay in bed. It wasn't worth the effort to try to get up, even if it was Sunday. He listened as Shirley and their guests, missionaries Richard and Jean Lucas, got ready for church. Laughing and joking, talking about how much fun they had at the picnic. Laughing about the IFO, no doubt.

Paul moaned as he turned over. Then his short-term memory kicked in. He remembered the cold water in his face and his run across the squishy sands; then suddenly he was airborne. He chuckled. What a sight that must have been, all 180 pounds of him flipping through the air like a killer whale. Too bad he didn't get to see it. He laughed aloud; then moaned. Even laughing hurt!

With everyone gone to church, it was too quiet, so Paul reached over with his good arm and flipped on the radio. "Typhoon condition 1." Oh, no! What next?

That afternoon the Lucases changed their flight and returned to Tokyo while they could still get out. Paul managed to get to church that evening, although he did not clap his hands or preach.

As they were getting ready for bed, Paul said, "We were having such a good time. The Lucases were right on target as they ministered in the special services this weekend. Then I had to get hurt and now a typhoon."

As Shirley gently helped her disabled husband unbutton his shirt, she comforted, "It could have been worse. I'm just glad you are not paralyzed. Next time, Paul, tie your shoes before you run a race. OK?"

On Monday, Shirley drove Paul back to the hospital so they could set his elbow. He was not looking forward to the experience.

"Sorry, Mr. Dennis, we are not authorized to treat you because you are a civilian," the military doctor said.

"But you treated me Saturday," Paul protested.

"That's because you were hurt on military property."

"If I was hurt on military property, I should be taken care of by the military. You need to do something about this elbow," Paul reasoned.

The doctor twisted his lips and scratched his nose. "Well," he hesitated, "well, I'll put a temporary cast on that elbow. Then you need to make arrangements to see a civilian doctor."

Paul called headquarters and got permission to take an emergency medical leave to have his elbow and other major conditions treated. Within days they were on their way back to Oklahoma to see an orthopedic surgeon.

"One good thing has come out of this," Paul told his wife as he settled into the narrow, rutted airplane seat. "We get to see Barak."

Shirley glared at him. "You didn't plan this so you could see your grandson, did you?"

Paul grimaced. "Not hardly. It would have been easier and probably cheaper just to send them tickets to come here."

In Tulsa, after a thorough examination, the surgeon said, "I'm going to have to do surgery on that elbow to remove bone fragments before I set it. Your left wrist is injured too. What in the world did you do to yourself?"

Paul didn't want to tell him, but he did.

After his bones were set, he went to see Doctor Aran. "Sorry, Paul, more polyps. You have to have another colonoscopy."

Thank God, this time the polyps were benign.

The Dennises' medical leave lasted for three and one-half months. On October 15, their thirty-third anniversary, they shared a hot dog in the airport restaurant and then celebrated 34,000 feet above the Pacific on their way back to work.

Section IV
Regional Field Supervisor
Paul A. Dennis

November 2006 - Paul with Victor Hobday, superintendent in Madras, India

Church dedication in Madras, India, 1996

Billy Cole meeting with Pakistan Minister of Religious Affairs Jehangir Badar and Paul Dennis

Burma Bible School graduation

*Paul and Gracie
at Adur Compound*

*Paul and his footsteps—
in the background
is the Mediterranean Sea*

Ministers' ordination in Pakistan

Paul on Mars Hill

*Members of the
Pakistan Crusade Team—
Billy Cole, Paul Dennis,
Douglas Klinedinst, Allan Shalm*

Paul and Garry Tracy at the Chu Chi Tunnels

Paul and Shirley at the Temple of Apollo in Greece

Paul receiving shawl at installation as Regional Field Supervisor in Thailand - Paul and Shirley are with Reverend Lerthainsung and wife

Paul and his memory maple tree

Paul goes back to #8 Hollow

Fitting into New Shoes

When Paul answered the phone, he heard the cheery voice of Harry Scism, foreign missions director of the UPCI. "Praise the Lord, Brother Dennis. I trust you are well, and how is your lovely wife?"

Polite greetings. Necessary etiquette. Paul replied just as courteously, while inside he was begging, *Please get to the point.* Calls from headquarters put him on edge. The FMD did not call to discuss the weather, unless a major typhoon was threatening. It was September 24, but no typhoons were in the forecast, meteorological ones anyway.

"Your exciting reports of revival in the Asia Military District make our day here in the office."

Paul relaxed somewhat and waited for the message.

"Brother Dennis, I am calling to ask if you will accept the position of regional field supervisor for Asia? The foreign missions board is in session at this minute. We are waiting for your answer."

Paul was stunned. He sat in silence.

For almost five months he had known this was a probability, ever since RFS Garry Tracy had called in May. "Brother Dennis, I am accepting the position of director of education and associates in missions. That leaves the position of RFS for Asia open, and your name has been mentioned as my replacement. I wanted to let you know so you could fast and pray about this."

Paul remembered how seventeen years ago God had brought his petite family of three to Okinawa, directing their steps all the way. Since then the military church of ten or eleven saints who were meeting in homes had grown into a strong, autonomous work.

Hardened soldiers repented of their sins, were baptized, and filled with the Holy Ghost. Young airmen and marines came in off the streets and gave their lives to Christ. They traded in their blue jeans for their first suits; they became ushers, sound technicians, and ministers.

The Dennises and the saints cheered and cried as the military sent these new sons and daughters out on assignments around the world. They rejoiced to know that the gospel was spreading everywhere that God sent these new ambassadors.

They witnessed the birth of the Japanese church on the island. Precious Asians, who had never heard the name of Jesus Christ, received the truth and obeyed Acts 2:38. Backsliders returned to God and went out preaching the Word with signs following. The church saw revival, tasted it, participated in it, and lived it.

Since the first of the year the building had been renovated to make room for the growing congregation. They were in continuous revival, focusing on the theme, "Restore in '94."

The Asia Military District was expanding. Young men with great potential like David Doan, Calvin Cooper, and Robert Courtright had been licensed.

The Military United Pentecostal Church of Japan was blossoming.

As pastor of the First United Pentecostal Church of Okinawa, coordinator of the Asia Military District, and first-term superintendent of the United Pentecostal Church of Japan, Paul's plate was filled with appealing projects. He was satisfied right where he was, doing what he was doing; and he had told God that numerous times.

He thought about the trips he had taken with his former supervisors, Paul Cook, George Shalm, and Garry Tracy, traveling to most missionary countries of the Asian region. He had

Order My Steps

witnessed firsthand the heavy burdens the regional field supervisors carried and the wear and tear on their bodies. For that reason he and Shirley had made Okinawa an oasis where these men and their wives retreated for downtime before returning to the United States. Paul was satisfied hosting these men and occasionally assisting on their missions. *Do I even want to step into the regional field supervisor's shoes? Will they fit me?*

He prayed earnestly and often for the next RFS. But the harder he prayed, the more he heard a voice in his inner ear. "Your name has come up."

The possibility overshadowed him. It drained him. He spent hours talking to God.

One day kneeling in prayer in his office, Paul surrendered. "God, I am happy being pastor. I am happy being the Asia Military Coordinator. I am happy being the superintendent of the UPCJ. If You want me to choose one of these, I would be happy to do just one." Then he drew a deep breath and exhaled. "If You want me to fill the RFS's shoes, I will do it. I only ask for two things: one, I would like for us to keep our residence in Okinawa; and two, I want a unanimous vote. Order my steps according to Your Word."

Paul got to his feet. The shadow disappeared. The load lifted. It had all been a bad dream. He settled into the work at hand.

"Brother Dennis? Did you hear me?" Brother Scism asked.

Paul swallowed. "Yes, sir, I heard you. Before I answer, could I ask you a couple of questions?"

"Certainly."

Paul's toes curled in his shoes as he phrased his question. "May we remain living on the field?"

"Certainly. The policy states that the RFS can live wherever he wants."

Paul did not know if that answer pleased or frightened him. Only one more question stood between him and the biggest step of his missionary life.

"Can you tell me what the vote was?"

"The board voted unanimously for you to fill this position."

He had his answer. "Then I will be honored to accept the position."

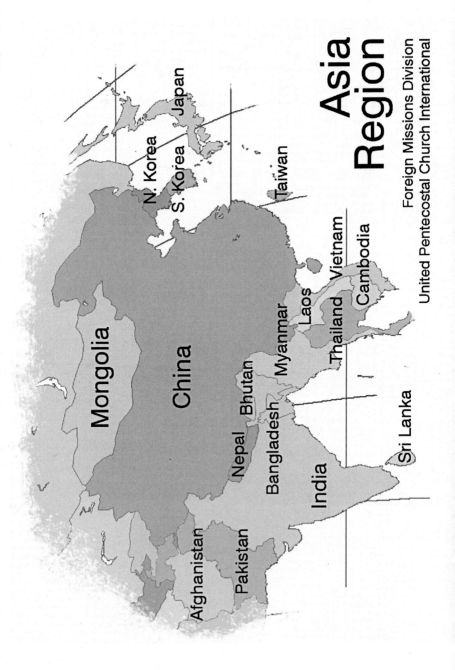

Missionaries to Asia Region 1994-2002

BANGLADESH
James and Elizabeth Corbin

CHINA/HONG KONG
Robert and Dorothy Arthur
Tom and Sandy Bracken
Jerry and Fayetta Holt
Steve and Lynette O'Donnell

INDIA
General Overseer: Stanley Scism
Northeast: Nat. Supt. Singson
 (Paul) Chunga
South: Nat. Supt. Victor Hobday

JAPAN
Richard and Jean Lucas

KOREA
David and Jean Banta
Ey Ja Kim
William and Elizabeth Turner

MYANMAR (Burma)
Nat. Supt. J. Raul Buai

OKINAWA
David and Angela Doan
Rufus and Pam Parker
Edward and Naomi Hosmer

PAKISTAN
Everett and Lois Corcoran
Allen and Georgene Shalm
Lynden and Kathy Shalm

SRI LANKA
J. Prince and Suzana Mathiasz

TAIWAN
Tom and Sandy Bracken
Leonard and Pin–Lan
 Richardson
Kevin and Lolita Vacca
Vic and Diana Votaw

THAILAND
Nat. Supt. Chaiyong
 Wattanachant
Jack and Michiko Coolbaugh
Robert and Gayle Frizzell

VIETNAM, LAOS, CAMBODIA
Robert and Gayle Frizzell

In Their Steps

Paul hung up the phone and fell to his knees. The weight of the responsibility he had accepted pushed his face to the floor.

He could not face the future until he looked back. The memory film rolled.

Rub, battered lunch bucket in hand, yelling, "Tell Paul if those weeds in that backyard ain't cut when I get home tonight, he'll answer to me." The order that sent him running out of #8 Hollow.

An air force attorney barking, "You are under arrest." The $2 mistake that changed his life.

A sergeant flipping a coin. "Get packed, Dennis. You're going to Japan." The gamble that wasn't a gamble at all.

The fiery evangelist from Bulgaria delivering a message from God. "You cigarette sucker, booze drinker, woman chaser, and fornicator, if you don't change your ways, you're going to end up in the pit of Hell."

God had ordered his steps, one by one, from McLuney, Ohio, to Okinawa, Japan, and He would direct his steps across the vast continent of Asia.

Asia—the least missionary populated region in the world with the largest number of souls (over 3.2 billion), 50 percent of the world's population.

Paul's travels with the former RFSs had acquainted him with some of the challenges faced by missionaries in Asia—challenges as disagreeable as the governments, as diverse as the weather, and as difficult as the languages. He had seen enough to know that each nation was multicultural, populated by sundry tribes, ethnic groups, and religions.

In many places the transportation was archaic, the food contaminated, and the accommodations filthy. Travel was unpredictable and dangerous.

In each nation where he had traveled he had heard mother languages split into an unbelievable number of dialects. In India alone there were over 1600 dialects with approximately 850 used daily.

He closed his eyes and visualized the faces of missionaries in Japan, Korea, Taiwan, Hong Kong, Sri Lanka, South India, Thailand, Pakistan, and Bangladesh. Each had the heart of a child and the hide of a hippopotamus, the flexibility of a straw and the stability of a rock, the brain of a genius and the grit of a bulldog. They were in Asia for the long haul, for the Asian culture was not synchronized to the American clock. How he respected these men and women of God.

To his prayer list he added the names of national leaders overseeing the works in Thailand, Cambodia, Vietnam, Laos, China, Northeast India, Burma, Bhutan, and Nepal.

Living conditions in the third world countries were primitive. How glad he was that the Foreign Missions Division of the United Pentecostal Church insisted that their missionaries find the best location for a base and rent as modern a home as possible. Missionaries travel into dangerous areas, unsanitary villages, and poverty-stricken regions. Their home is their oasis, where they recharge, refill, and replace the nutrients in their minds, bodies, and spirits. Missionaries who lack this refuge quickly burn out emotionally and physically.

He thought about those who had walked the way before them—Telie Dover, Ellis and Marjorie Scism, Elly Hansen, Billy and Shirley Cole, Harry and Audrene Scism, Frances Foster, George and Margaret Shalm, Elton and Loretta Bernard. He breathed a prayer of gratitude for the paths they had hacked

Order My Steps

through the jungles of witchcraft, traditions, and false religions. Each step these men and women of God had taken enabled those following them to take two steps.

All of this, and so much more, passed through Paul's mind as he lay on the floor gaining strength for the journey. Then he stood to his feet, straightened his shoulders, and went to tell Shirley.

After the shock wore off, Shirley smiled, "You can do it, Paul."

He put his arm around her shoulders. "With God's help, we can do it, Shirley." Together they would follow in the steps of those who had blazed the trail before them.

Follow the Leader

Destination: United States of America.

Getting orders, giving orders, creating order. Paul was listening for and giving orders. Shirley was endeavoring to create order out of chaos.

"This reminds me of deputation," Shirley laughed, as she looked at her husband's calendar. "Keeping it straight where you are to be, when, and with whom, is a challenge."

Thank You, Jesus, for my efficient secretary, Paul repeated this prayer multiple times after he was appointed regional field supervisor for Asia. *And thank You, Jesus, for wheels on luggage.*

Once Paul stepped into the RFS's shoes, he was on the go most of the time. His schedule included visiting each of the missionaries in Asia once a year. In the months of January, February, May, August, September, and October, he attended board meetings, Planning for Progress meetings, interviews for missionaries, and special meetings.

The first month after Paul was appointed RFS, he and Shirley spent in the States—at general conference in Milwaukee, board and committee meetings in St. Louis, and visiting with family in Ohio and Oklahoma.

Destination: Bangkok, Thailand

The first week of November 1994, they flew to the Asia Regional Retreat for Paul's official installation as RFS for Asia. During the ceremony, the Northeast India delegation presented him with a handmade shawl of many colors.

"Only the chief of the tribe wears these colors," Paul was told. "When the chief wears these colors in battle or in any march, the tribe follows." The missionaries and native preachers

Order My Steps

of Asia pledged to follow their leader, Paul A. Dennis. As these men of God from all over Asia laid hands on Paul, the sweet presence of the Lord filled the room, strengthening the new RFS for the journey.

Clips from Paul's days in the military reeled through his memory: old loudmouth shouting orders, learning to pay attention, marching in sync, racing into the inferno. Looking over his shoulder, he realized how God had orchestrated his steps, even before he surrendered to God's service. Only after he learned to follow orders was he authorized to give orders. Even Rub was part of God's plan for Paul.

Run, Paul, run. Running from God, running to God, and running with God.

After the installation Paul and Shirley returned to Okinawa, where major changes faced them.

Turning the First United Pentecostal Church Military District over to another pastor was a bittersweet experience. Since Marvin and Lucy Elmore had arrived in 1991, they had filled many positions, including assistant pastor. When Paul traveled for the Asia Military District, the Elmores took care of the church. They loved the saints and in turn were loved and respected by the saints. They also had a passion for reaching the lost. Paul could see how God had prepared, not only him and Shirley for the transition, but He had prepared the church and the Elmores.

Between trips Paul and Shirley taught the new pastor and his wife the business side of operating the church: the banking, taxes, utilities, insurance, advertising, and other matters relating to working in the Japanese culture and with the Japanese government.

Paul's new appointment left the Asia Military District in need of a coordinator. God had that under control too.

Paul's memory film rolled.

Paul A. Dennis

On July 4, 1993, Rufus and Pam Parker were welcomed to Okinawa by the army commander that Rufus would be working with. While they were sitting in the airport lounge getting acquainted, the door opened and in walked a jovial group from the First United Pentecostal Church. They too had come to welcome the Parkers. The commander and his wife were taken by surprise.

"I didn't know that you knew this many people on the island," he said.

"We don't," Rufus replied. "They are from the church we will be attending, but we have never met them."

The officer raised his eyebrows. What a welcome. He was impressed.

The Parkers had not been on the island forty-eight hours when Rufus had to go on temporary duty (TDY) to mainland Japan, his new headquarters. He had to meet the new command group and receive a mission briefing. Pam and their daughter Martha were left in temporary lodging without transportation. Their new church family stepped up to the plate—provided transportation, helped them find housing, and met various needs. By the time Rufus returned, his family was settled into a house.

When Rufus attended his first service, Paul met him at the door and introduced him to the other ministers and ministers-in-training. Later Rufus told Paul, "You made me feel a part of the team from the first moment I entered the building. The 'newcomer's brief' to the First United Pentecostal Church of Okinawa and the loving welcome we received made our transition so smooth."

Rufus and Pam yoked up with the Dennises and started pulling. They often responded to the "Sea Condition Red" code and showed up at the East China Sea to witness another baptism.

Order My Steps

So God had a man in place for the Asia Military District Coordinator position. (Later in July 1996 when Marvin Elmore was PCSed, Rufus Parker also became pastor of the church.)

Paul remained superintendent of the UPCJ until the winter board meeting in 1996. At Paul's recommendation, Richard Lucas was appointed to fill that position.

Paul was free to devote his full attention to the mission field of Asia.

Destination: Asia

After the plane taxied up to the gate, Paul always had miles to travel by taxi, bus, train, van, boat, motorcycle, tractor, or even by foot. He was either headed to or in the middle of continuous adventure. Learning the manners and ethics of the church and culture, what to do and what not to do, stretched his brain. One day he would travel with royalty and the next day he would sit on the ground with the peasants.

The training the Dennises had received on deputation was expanded. "When in Rome do as the Romans do," was not too hard to adhere to in the States. In Asia, it flexed their mental muscles.

On the field working hand in hand, shoulder to shoulder with the missionaries and the people, the adrenalin pulsated through every vein in their bodies. There was no blockage. As they witnessed the dedication and sacrifices of God's people, the RFS and his wife poured themselves into helping others reach their goals. They were at the summit of excitement and fulfillment, walking in the steps ordered by the Lord, following their Leader.

India—Rags to Riches

Destination: New Delhi, India. Reservation: International Hotel.

"This is your captain. Crew, prepare for landing."

Passengers all over the plane jumped up and shoved their way up and down the aisle, pulling their carry-on luggage down from the racks.

"Please remain seated until the captain has turned off the Fasten Your Seat Belt sign. Please remain seated—" The flight attendant's pleas were ignored.

People lined up to be the first off the plane. Paul and Shirley rolled their eyes. Shirley leaned over and yelled in Paul's ear, "What in the world?"

Paul raised his voice several decibels. "Reminds me of a cattle stampede at the rodeo." Luckily no one heard him but his wife.

"We are about to land. Please return to your seats or you could get hurt," the flight attendant shouted over the PA.

Surprisingly, the stampede calmed into controlled confusion as passengers returned to their seats. As soon as the tires bounced and squealed on the runway, the stampede was on again.

Shirley shook her head in amazement. Paul's eyes were glued on the unruly line forming in front of the closed door. When the exit door opened, the stampede resumed. Who could be the first to get on the bus taking them to the customs terminal?

As the passengers piled onto the bus, they hovered around the door. By the time the Dennises deplaned, they had to shove their way through the me-first crowd huddled at the door. For some reason, no one wanted to sit down. Eventually, the driver convinced them that the bus would not roll until the seats were filled.

At the terminal, Paul and Shirley waited until the passengers had piled out of the bus. Then, locking their carry-ons in a death grip, they dove into the chaos.

As soon as they walked into the terminal, the smells of India assaulted them—sweat, alcohol, cigarette smoke, curry, garlic, and a few other smells better unnamed. Shirley pulled a perfumed handkerchief from her pocket and pretended to be catching dribbles from her nose. The handkerchief covered her lips, but Paul saw the smile in her eyes as she said, "Come on, PD. When in Rome do as the Romans do." It was the only way to get through customs.

Then came the mad dash for the baggage area. It was rush, push, shove, give looks to stop the clock. The noise smothered the warning bell, but the blinking light got everyone's attention. The conveyer belt growled and began spitting out suitcases—a humongous number of huge suitcases. Every one of the 250 or so passengers had at least three or four giant bags. Their smallest bags were the size of the Dennises' largest ones.

Paul grabbed Shirley's arm and steered her to the back of the line, the place no one else wanted to be. There they waited.

Finally, the crowd dispersed and they were next in line. They removed their bags from the belt.

"One is missing, Paul," Shirley said.

Paul groaned and headed for the agent's desk.

"Your bag will be on the next flight, and we will deliver it to your hotel," the agent promised him.

By the time they checked into their room, it was after midnight. They ordered sandwiches and waited for sleep to come. As they were checking the bed sheets searching for bugs, the room phone rang.

"Mr. Dennis," a male voice said in broken English, "the airline has found your bag. We will bring it up."

Paul A. Dennis

Before Paul could answer, the voice asked, "How much would you charge to let us have your wife for the night?"

Instant rage gripped Paul. "Do not bring the suitcase to the room," he shouted. "I will come down and get it!"

Paul instructed Shirley on how to secure the door; then he went down to get their bag. The only person in the lobby was the desk clerk.

When he returned to the room, he told Shirley about the phone call.

"We've got to leave here right now," she demanded. "We've got to go to another hotel."

"Shirley, it's 2:00 in the morning. We can't be on the street," Paul reasoned. "We would be in more danger there than here."

They stuck knives and forks around the door casing to secure the lock. Then they lay down on the bed fully clothed. The next morning they checked out and went to another hotel. It could have been worse.

Location: Mizoram, Northeast India

From his vantage point on the platform, Paul's memory snapped the scene before him for future study. It was more than he could absorb at the moment. Dim flickering lights outlined the vast congregation spread out before him. Hundreds of saints were lost in fervent worship, oblivious to the bugs dive-bombing them.

Paul knew that most of these people survived on one small bowl of rice, a piece of bread, or a banana a day. Their clothes were clean, but ragged. Their homes were hovels. Their hollow eye sockets and skinny bodies exposed their hunger. But their radiant faces revealed their communion with the Spirit of God. They were far richer than many Paul knew who lived in mansions and fared sumptuously.

Order My Steps

The men in one circle and the women in another, they danced before the Lord in tempo with the drums. As they sang and worshiped in spirit and in truth, their language changed. Paul stood breathless as the congregation of several hundred praised God in the same heavenly tongue.

Could this be a little taste of what Heaven will be? he wondered. *Perfect unity.*

Many who had not received the baptism of the Holy Ghost did so as their natural language melted away and was replaced by a heavenly one. At the same time others were healed. It was a divine work of the Spirit; no flesh could glory in what God did in that service.

Location: Calcutta.

Paul and Shirley walked through the hotel lobby, smiled at the desk clerk, and went out the door. They were headed for the market to purchase a few keepsakes and gifts for the folks back home. Every block or two the environment and caste system swung from rags to riches. The extremes were mind boggling and heartbreaking.

After a few blocks Shirley grabbed Paul's arm. "Paul, I cannot do this." Tears pooled in her eyes. "Let's go back to the hotel."

"Let's try another street," Paul suggested.

They did, but the scene did not get any better. At one place there was literally no way around the street people. They were forced to step over and between the people lying on the sidewalk. They grimaced, shut down their emotions, and determined to do what they had to do to get back to the hotel until . . . they had to step over a dead baby. The begging mother had placed it in their way to draw attention to her plight.

Paul A. Dennis

Back in the hotel, Shirley shuddered. The thought of what those people had to do to survive tormented her. It could not have been worse. It was her last trip to Calcutta.

Location: South India.

Paul sat down and drew a deep breath. The election of officers at the South India conference that he had chaired was over; they had voted only sixteen times before electing a superintendent. It could have been worse.

After the conference he and Shirley were scheduled to speak at a couple of local churches. Getting to the first church was not a problem. The trip to the second church made lasting memories.

Mode of transportation: a worse-for-the-wear van. Paul, as the head honcho, was given the seat of honor in the front next to the driver. Shirley and the others, including missionary Stanley Scism, occupied the second and third rows.

Paul wrinkled his nose and blinked. Where were those fumes coming from? He looked down and saw the ground. Jagged holes disfigured the floorboard.

The sun bid them good night while they were some distance from the church, so the driver turned on the headlights, which created ribbons of light at least three feet long. The lights were not for the driver; he knew where he was going. They were to alert oncoming traffic.

In the distant past the road had been blacktopped. Currently, it was broken slabs of asphalt, stone, and dirt. They bumped and twisted down a hill and had traveled another half-mile when the driver pulled the van onto the side of the road and stopped. The excited, chattering passengers piled out.

Surely this is not a rest stop, Paul thought. "What are you doing?" he asked.

Order My Steps

"We are looking for the van key," the driver said. "It fell out of the switch on this bumpy road."

They searched the van thoroughly. No key.

It must have fallen out one of the holes in the floorboard. The road was too narrow to turn the van around, so using the headlights for the search was not an option. The men started walking back up the road, searching for the key in the dark.

Paul pulled his emergency light, a small pen flashlight, from his Bible bag. Seven men lined up behind him and the search was on. They were successful, so successful that they found a dozen keys.

The driver looked at the keys, then randomly picked one and said, "Any one of these will do." He inserted it in the ignition and off they went.

Paul never did figure that one out.

They drove to the end of the road, then walked about fifty yards into the middle of a rubber tree plantation. The saints greeted them with flowers and good wishes. Small electric bulbs swayed over the congregation. The brightest lights were over the five chairs behind the small pulpit.

The service began and slowly progressed—introductions, songs, more introductions, more songs, testimonies, then a couple of special songs. *They like singing as much as the folks did in Crooksville,* Paul thought.

The longer the service went, the more the bugs congregated. Big black bugs gathered around the lights directly over their heads.

Paul glanced at Stan Scism, lifetime missionary to India. He was tucking his trouser legs into his socks, locking the bugs out. He leaned over and whispered to Paul, "They won't hurt you. They are rubber bugs and attracted to the light." Paul nodded. That was good news, he guessed.

He looked at his wife sitting on the chair beside him and mouthed, "Look at the back of your chair."

Paul A. Dennis

Turning as little as possible, Shirley used her peripheral vision to pinpoint the pests. It was a mistake. He should have not alerted her.

Shirley tensed; Paul waited for her to jump and run. Instead, she took a deep breath and raised her elbow, knocking the marching intruders off her chair. They were replaced by their cousins.

Paul, following Stan's example, bent over and tucked his trouser legs into his socks. When he looked up, Shirley had put on her headscarf. She looked like she was preparing to walk into a blizzard. The little boys sitting on the floor in front of Paul were laughing and enjoying the show. One flicked a bug off his hand onto Paul, so Paul flicked it back. The game continued until Paul remembered his age and position.

For several days after that when Shirley shivered, Paul knew memories were bugging her. He grinned and said, "It could have been worse, Charlie Brown. They could have been hungry."

Location: Adur, India.

Conference time. Guest preachers Paul Dennis and Lynden Shalm checked into the seven-star hotel, the Adur Compound House.

"Seven-star hotel? I have never heard of a seven-star hotel."

Paul explained, "At night I saw seven stars through the cracks in the roof, and I was lulled to sleep by the pitter-patter of flying squirrels running across the rafters."

The ancient house, the former home of the late Ellis and Marjorie Scism, was used for guest lodging during special events and conferences. A hall bookmarked the length of the building separating right and left. A quick inventory showed three bedrooms, two baths, a large living room, a dining area,

Order My Steps

a workroom (for ironing and similar tasks), a maid's small room, and the kitchen.

Each bedroom had double doors on opposite walls. The doors were divided in the middle horizontally, so either the top or the bottom could be opened to increase air flow. For privacy, curtains hung over each door. Each room had a fan, but no air conditioning. The beds, thin mattresses on board bases, were canopied with mosquito netting.

Not elegant or even comfortable by American standards, the Adur Compound House was adequate. Superseding the temporal amenities or lack of them, an aura of glory hovered over it; the atmosphere was saturated with the vibration of past prayers.

The star of the compound was Gracie, the cook, whom the late Sister Scism had trained.

"This is some of the best fried chicken I have ever eaten," Paul complimented Gracie every day, because chicken was on the menu every day.

The clerk at the market knew when guests were at the compound because a conference called for many chickens and several dozens of eggs.

Paul and the other guests chipped in and gave Gracie money to buy the groceries. The breakfast menu was eggs, porridge, toast, coffee, and occasionally juice. Lunch menu consisted of fried chicken, mashed potatoes, gravy, carrots, or cauliflower. Dinner was a repeat of lunch; sometimes they had mixed veggies (carrots and cauliflower, as in leftovers). They consumed cases of bottled water.

Each night the guests sat around in the living area unwinding from a power-packed Pentecostal service, eating and talking, much like Apostolics do around the world.

Paul A. Dennis

The first day of the conference the temperature soared. Paul, ministering on God's care for His people, took his text from Matthew 9, the story of the woman who touched the hem of Jesus' garment. As he preached, he used a hand towel to wipe his sweat-soaked forehead.

Walking down the center aisle, he held the towel first in one hand and then the other, saying, "This is the hem of Jesus' garment. Do you want to touch the hem of His garment?"

He had gone about six rows deep into the congregation when a woman in the middle of one row jumped up and forced her way across six or seven other women. She stretched out her hand and touched the towel. A current of God's power shot from the towel in the preacher's hand to her. Instantly, she broke into praise. Paul released the towel. An awesome move of God's Spirit swept through the congregation, as worship ascended into the heavenlies.

After the service Sister Alexander and her husband, a board member, told Paul her story. For two years she had suffered severe pain from a swelling in her abdomen. The moment she touched the towel, the growth deflated, like air out of a balloon. The pain vanished.

She offered to return the towel, but Paul told her to keep it. Three years later that towel was still on the wall in her home as a reminder of God's power.

In another service as the ladies sat cross-legged on the floor clapping and swaying, totally lost in worship, their bodies slowly lifted off the floor and floated in the air. The glory of God covered the congregation. The awesome presence of God flowed through Paul like liquid fire, humbling and emboldening him at the same time.

Most of the people had no transportation and no money for medical care. But they had great faith in God. So when a healing line was announced, they lined up. Many brought their

Order My Steps

children, asking the ministers to pray for protection and good health for their little ones.

Paul carried individually wrapped candies in his pockets because he knew that wherever he went, the children would surround him during prayer time and after the service. Some simply wanted to touch him. Others were looking for an opportunity to show off the little English they knew. "Hello." "How are you?" "What's your name?"

When Paul returned to one village where he had passed out candy, the children went wild. They waved and clapped, shouting, "Here comes the candy man." Paul loved it. It was one of the rewards for hours of sitting on hard, rutted airplane seats.

Cambodia—Step by Step

Location: Phnom Penh, Cambodia.

Dressed in rags and lying on a bed of wooden slats, the frail boy who looked about eight years old did not move when Paul and missionaries Robert Frizzell and John Wolfram approached. They were in a village on the outskirts of Phnom Penh, the capital of Cambodia. Robert had introduced Paul and John to the village leaders whom he had met when making arrangements for a service. The men were walking around the village when they spotted the boy.

As Paul gazed at the lad, the Lord spoke to him, "Anoint this boy with oil and pray for him. He will be healed."

Paul pulled a vial of oil from his pocket. "Robert, John, pray with me for this lad. The Lord will heal him."

"This boy has not walked in many years," one of the city leaders told them. "Day after day he lies on his bed and does nothing."

The trio of missionaries gathered around the lethargic boy. It was enough—three in His name. After a simple but powerful prayer in the name of Jesus, the men waited.

The boy started wiggling. He scooted on the wooden slats, tossed his legs over the edge, and stood up. All eyes were glued on him. One step, then another, a little wobbly at first, but step by step, he kept walking.

In the villages medical care is nonexistent: no hospitals, no doctors, no medicine. The sick are treated with old home remedies. What better home remedy than an old-fashioned prayer in the name of Jesus?

Location: Neah Leung, Cambodia

Order My Steps

Robert had arranged for a service at the village Neah Leung, located along the famous Mekong River. During the Vietnam War, someone from Neah Leung had lifted a homing device from Ho Chi Minh City and hidden it in his home. When a U.S. B-52 approached, it locked in on the device, and dropped its load on the village.

When Paul learned that John could not conduct the service as planned, he volunteered to do it. What Paul did not know . . . oh, the things that missionaries do not know until too late . . . was that his mode of transportation to the village was a small motorcycle, with Paul riding as the hitchhiker. Neither did he know that it would take three hours to get there. Paul arrived with TB—a tired backside.

The cycle driver was Paul Ba, their main contact in Cambodia, who also served as Paul's interpreter. After Paul taught on the name of Jesus and the power of the Holy Ghost, the congregation moved twenty yards to the Mekong River.

The rushing, gushing, filthy river was at high tide. Ba went out onto a makeshift platform and clutching the edge with one hand, eased into the muddy water. He lowered his legs until his feet touched the bottom, and he got a solid foothold in the mud.

Three sin-laded men followed him into the thick brown water. They were immersed in the name of Jesus and came up washed as white as snow. The river that had brought death to so many during the war brought life to these men. The name of Jesus made all the difference.

Paul turned from the river rejoicing; then he remembered the motorcycle. He had a three-hour ride ahead of him. Never mind, he sighed. He would gladly do it again to see men baptized in the name of Jesus, but he did wish the ride was over. Oh well, he had learned something on the trip to Neah Leung. He had a plan.

Paul A. Dennis

On the return trip they stopped often to see this-and-that, to buy a Coke, and for any other reason Paul could invent to save wear and tear on his TB.

Location: Tonle Bassac, Cambodia.

"We'll take a taxi most of the way," Robert told Paul. "Then because of the water, we'll have to take a walkway fifty- to seventy-five-yards to the building where we will have the Bible study." It was the monsoon season.

"No problem," Paul replied. His confidence evaporated when he saw the walkway: a 2" x 6" board fastened to a post in the water and tied to stakes on each side every ten- to fifteen-feet. The only consolation was that the water was only three- to four-feet deep.

Step by step, they crossed, no slips, no dips. The building was a long-legged hut standing some ten feet above the water.

Paul was so engrossed in the Bible study that he did not notice when the sun slipped into bed. As they climbed down the ladder, darkness enveloped them. Robert, the veteran missionary of the area, pulled a tiny penlight from his pocket. It cut through the inky curtain about twelve inches.

Step by step they crossed the walkway with Paul praying earnestly for their equilibrium as his hand clutched Robert's belt. Again, no slips, no dips.

Location: Cambodia Killing Fields.

Paul and Robert had a couple of days off from preaching and teaching in the villages.

"Would you like to do a little sightseeing?" Robert asked.

"Absolutely." Most of Paul's time was consumed in meetings, services, and traveling. He seldom had time to visit the landmarks. He was ready to relax.

Order My Steps

Robert took him to Choeung Ek Killing Field, the place where over 200,000 people were killed under the reign of Pol Pot and the Khmer Rouge government. The victims were buried in mass graves; later, they were exhumed.

Paul and Robert silently gazed into the opened graves, each lost in his own thoughts. Then they softly walked into the *stupa,* a four-story building filled with skulls. Each room was about 40' x 40' x 12'. The skulls bore the marks of blunt trauma deaths. The soldiers had been ordered to save their bullets for the battlefield. They used hammers, ax handles, shovels, and even steel rods rammed through skulls to kill the civilians. These people were from all strata of life, from highly educated to peasants.

Near a large tree they viewed the bones of children. About shoulder height on the tree trunk was a large dark black spot. A Khmer Rouge soldier would hold a child by his feet and ankles, and then bash his head against the tree and toss him into a mass grave. This heinous act was repeated thousands of times.

The last place they visited was a torture camp, Tuol Sleng, where 20,000 people were tortured until they gave false confessions. The Khmer Rouge had converted a school into a jail. How like the enemy to convert a school, which had offered enlightenment, into a prison of darkness.

Remembering his days in the United States Air Force, Paul praised God for the privilege he had to serve his country. Realizing his position in the kingdom of God, he prayed for wisdom to fill the RFS's shoes.

It was not a relaxing sightseeing tour. What a responsibility they had to bring the gospel to this hurting nation. It could only be done village by village, step by step.

Sri Lanka—Checkpoints and Coconut Water

Location: Colombo, Sri Lanka.

As soon as Paul walked into the terminal, the hair on the back of his neck stood up. Tension tightened his nerves. The Tamil Tigers had attacked the international airport, bombed religious buildings, burned homes, and killed several thousand people. Missionaries and ministers were not welcome; so on his customs check card, he listed his reason for being in Sri Lanka "to visit friends."

At the customs check in, he answered multiple questions before he was allowed to go to the baggage claim. After collecting his bags, he went through more checkpoints.

On the outside of the terminal Prince Mathiasz, a native of Sri Lanka, was also undergoing hard scrutiny—a car search, a body check, and inspection of personal identification. Getting in and out of the airport was not for wimps.

As Paul walked down the concourse to meet Prince, he remembered his first trip to this dazzling island, "the teardrop of the Indian Ocean." He had been with his RFS Paul Cook. They had stayed in the Mathiasz's home for three days, just long enough for Paul to get addicted to *flan,* a delightful syrupy pudding, and to fall in love with "Paradise Island."

If only the political scene was as tranquil as the scenery, it would be a paradise, Paul thought. But that day in 1995 the streets of Colombo portrayed a shell-shocked state, not a peaceful island.

Prince greeted Paul with a wide grin and firm handshake. He loaded Paul's luggage; then as he climbed into the driver's seat and turned to his passenger, his grin faded, "Welcome to our war-torn world."

Order My Steps

Between the airport and the Mathiasz's home, they went through numerous checkpoints. Paul's heart grieved as they passed the burned and bombed shells of homes, churches, and businesses. Carnage was everywhere. Anti-government posters spouted vile slogans, incinerating anger and violence.

To lighten the atmosphere in the car, the men reached back in their memories.

"Remember when we first met?" Paul asked.

"I sure do," Prince replied. "It was in Winnipeg, Manitoba, Canada, at Bethel Tabernacle with Pastor Kiefling."

"We enjoyed the international dinner after the service. We were on our first deputation," Paul scratched his chin. "It must have been in . . . '76."

"Right," Prince said. "Suzana was expecting Natasha."

"Shirley and Suzana sure hit it off. I remember that was the night we saw our first Muslim baptized in the name of Jesus. And you told me about your burden to return to Sri Lanka to share the gospel with your family and countrymen."

Prince looked out the window at the ravages of war. "Oh, how my countrymen need Jesus. I am so thankful God has allowed me to be here at such a time as this." He smiled at his passenger, "And I am thankful to be working with you, my field supervisor."

Another year. Another trip. After Paul and Shirley deplaned, they were directed straight to passport and customs check. When they were cleared, Paul asked, "Where do we pick up our luggage?"

A guard pointed them toward the exit. "It will be waiting for you at the exit."

Down one corridor, past soldiers carrying AK-47 rifles and shotguns. Down another corridor, past soldiers carrying AK-47 rifles and shotguns. Down another corridor, past soldiers carrying AK-47 rifles and shotguns.

Paul A. Dennis

Shirley clutched Paul's arm. "I don't know whether to feel safe or threatened," she said.

"Might as well go for 'safe,'" Paul chuckled.

At the end of the third corridor, several people were lined up. Paul and Shirley fell in at the back of the line. "Baggage claim," Paul told his wife.

They produced their luggage claim tickets and followed as their bags were loaded on a waiting bus, not knowing where the bus was going.

Paul stood aside and waited for his wife to get on. As she stepped into the bus, she looked over her shoulder. "Full up. Looks like Japan. We stand."

The door closed. The motor roared and they were on their way through a well-lit area of the city. Then they turned down a dark narrow road. When that road ended, the bus kept going through a field.

Shirley grabbed Paul's arm. "PD, are they taking us all out to this field to kill us?"

Paul forced the corners of his lips up, but he didn't fool his wife. He was concerned too. Outside people were lined up on both sides of the bus.

Then the bus pulled up to an area lit by lights on poles where a crowd had gathered to await the arrival of the passengers. "And there's Prince Mathiasz! Oh, thank God, they are not going to kill us."

Another year. Another trip. Paul struggled through customs and retrieved his luggage. Prince was waiting for him.

Prince rushed to him and took his bags. "Brother Dennis, you look awful. Are you sick? Do you have a fever?"

Paul nodded and climbed into the passenger seat. "Could you take me to the hospital, please?"

Order My Steps

"Of course. But first I will pray for you." After a brief but sincere prayer, Prince started the car and turned toward the hospital. "Tell me what is wrong."

Paul leaned his head back against the seat, closed his eyes, and reviewed the last few weeks of his extended tour.

"This has been a hard trip with back-to-back conferences in Northeast India, South India, and Burma. In Calcutta I was on a confidential assignment and stayed in a one-star hotel for security reasons. I sent my clothes to the laundry. My whites came back gray, but that was the least of my worries."

He cringed, "I went on to the conference in Burma where I was scheduled as the daytime Bible teacher. About that time I started having bladder and kidney problems. I've had enough urinary infections to recognize it. My back was killing me. I had a fever. I was in sheer misery.

"I told Brother Buai that I needed to see a doctor and why. He didn't know of an English or American doctor in the area, but he offered to take me to a doctor who had treated his wife. I was desperate so I said, 'Let's go.'

"The doctor's office was a shack off of slum row. We walked into the first room. Empty. A sheet hung over the doorway to another room. We pushed it aside and went in. The doctor looked like a man of the street. His office was furnished with a chair and a table; the table was a half-sheet of plywood lying across two sawhorses.

"The doctor and Buai talked; I have no idea what they said. Then Buai told me to lie back on the table. I did. The doctor proceeded to examine me. He said, 'This man has very, very bad kidney infection and needs a hospital.'

"*So what else is new?* I thought, but didn't say anything.

"Then the doctor said, 'But there is no hospital in this city.'

"That wasn't news either. I was in such anguish that I didn't feel like being tactful."

Prince moaned, "It has not been a good time, I can see."

Paul shook his head but didn't open his eyes. "The next day I left for Thailand, where I had a day and night layover, enough time to go to the emergency room at the Christian Hospital, an excellent facility."

"Good! Very good," Prince said.

Paul exhaled. "Not really. I got a lady doctor. What an embarrassing situation. Long story short, she gave me a prescription for two weeks of penicillin. She said it was a very strong prescription, and I should take three pills a day and not stop until they were gone. I started taking them before I left the hospital." Paul stopped.

Prince waited a minute before prompting, "Then?"

"I have taken two days' worth of pills, and I am sicker and hurting more than ever. I think the penicillin is too strong, and I am having a reaction."

"Not good," Prince sympathized, as he turned into the hospital parking lot. "We are here, my friend."

They checked in. Paul was taken to a cubicle and Prince was told to wait for him. After a few minutes, a nurse came in. "Mr. Dennis, the doctor has gone and cannot see you until tomorrow. But he has left instructions for me to run some tests."

Paul cringed in embarrassment as not one female nurse, but two, worked on him. One female nurse could not be in the room alone with a male patient. One examined him and the other drew blood.

Prince took Paul to his house where they prayed again. Then Paul took a shower, more penicillin, and went to bed.

First thing the next morning they went back to the hospital. The doctor started explaining the results of the tests to Prince. Both men looked like they had eaten lemons. Paul was sure he had contacted a deadly disease that after intense suffering would end his life.

Then Prince remembered that Paul could not understand the doctor, so he translated. "You have many different germs

Order My Steps

in your kidneys. Infection is running through your body. Stop taking the penicillin immediately."

So we know the problem and we know what not to take, Paul thought. *But what do we do?*

Prince was talking. Paul pulled his mind back into focus. ". . . what he tells you, you will be completely healed and clear in twenty days. And you should have relief from the burning and pain within a couple of days. Buy a large amount of king coconuts and drink the water in them three times a day."

Paul wanted to laugh, but he didn't. He mulled over the instructions. Coconut water certainly wasn't going to hurt him, and it might help. It was a sure thing that penicillin wasn't helping.

"The water in the king coconut is so pure that we use it for IVs in the hospital," the doctor said.

As they got in the car, Prince said, "That is very good advice. King coconuts do not produce meat, just water. Everyone in Sri Lanka drinks this water, and we do not have kidney infections."

They stopped on the way home and purchased a stock of king coconuts. Paul was in Sri Lanka for twenty-two days for conferences and services. Just as the doctor said, in two days the burning and fever left.

Checkpoints aside and coconut water inside, Sri Lanka is one of Paul's favorite islands. And his favorite memory? Praying with the Mathiasz's daughter, Natasha, when she received the baptism of the Holy Ghost. The turmoil of the political scene and the tranquility of the scenery blend to make Sri Lanka a fertile field for Holy Ghost revival.

Bangladesh—the Right Door

Destination: Biaky Island.

At Dhaka airport Paul and Northeast India Superintendent Singleton "Paul" Chunga took a two-hour flight to Chittagong. As they settled in for the flight, Paul turned to the native preacher. "Brother Chunga, I am depending on you to translate exactly what I say in English to Biaky in Mizo, and I am asking you to translate what she says in Mizo to me in English truly. Exactly—no twisting of the words or the meaning. You represent the United Pentecostal Church International. Do you understand?"

Brother Chunga assured Paul that he understood and could be trusted.

They were on their way to meet with Biaky, the FMD's one and only contact in Bangladesh. A freedom fighter against the Northeast India military government, she had fled to Bangladesh for refuge. She was in exile and banned from her native country. She lived on a small island, called Biaky Island, where she had built a house.

Missionaries Everett and Lois Corcoran had made trips to Bangladesh to hold doctrinal seminars. Senior missionary to India Stanley Scism had also made trips into Bangladesh, as time and finance allowed. RFSs Cook, Shalm, and Tracy had contacted Biaky, depending on her to establish a cell group of Christians as a UPCI outreach. Funds and materials had been sent to her for this purpose.

Previously, Paul had met with Biaky to try to determine the extent of her outreach. Although she spoke broken English, each time he asked about the size and progress of the cell group, she responded that she did not understand. So this trip he brought a translator and intended to get some answers.

Order My Steps

After landing in Chittagong, the men took a taxi to a small boat dock, where they boarded a makeshift boat taxi—destination: Biaky Island.

It was not a friendly visit. Paul hated confrontation, but he was not one to run from it either. This time he had no choice. The situation had to be resolved. He felt like an attorney cross examining a witness.

"When and where does your home Bible study group meet?"

I do not understand.

"Oh, yes, you do. Brother Chunga is translating it into your native language. Is anyone coming to your home regularly to study the Bible?"

I am busy. I have not been able to start the group.

So the grilling went. Bottom line: Biaky had no intention of starting a Christian cell group. She had been using the funds to pay for household help.

As Paul and Chunga boarded the taxi-boat for the trip back to Chittagong, Paul thought about Jesus' words to the seventy. "And whosoever shall not receive you, nor hear your words, when ye depart out of that house or city, shake off the dust of your feet" (Matthew 10:14).

He chuckled as he pictured himself shaking dust off his feet as they chugged across the Bay of Bengal. *I could wash my hands though,* he thought. But a quick examination of the tottery rail changed his mind. No leaning over *that* to wash his hands.

Chunga sent him a questioning look. Paul shrugged. "When God closes one door, He opens another. Maybe we've been knocking on the wrong door." He closed his eyes and prayed. *Now where, Lord? Show me the right door. Order my steps according to Your Word.*

By the time they arrived back in Dhaka, Paul's shoulders had sagged and his spirits flatlined. He needed spiritual nourishment, fellowship with fellow missionaries. So he called James Corbin, an independent Apostolic Pentecostal missionary, whom he had met on a previous trip. "I'm in Bangladesh and would like to visit with you and your family, if you are available."

"Wonderful!" James responded. "Tell me where you are staying, and I'll come pick you up. We'd love for you to have dinner with us in our home." Paul wasn't the only one hungry for fellowship.

When Paul entered the Corbins' home, he realized that many comforts were missing. "It's feast or famine around here," James admitted. "Our only income is what our friends and family send. They do their best, but it is sporadic."

The Corbins were teaching Bible studies in their home, but without consistent support, they struggled to survive.

After a delicious meal and refreshing visit, James returned Paul to the hotel. They agreed to keep in touch.

On Paul's next trip to Dhaka, James offered to pick him up at the airport and invited him to stay in their home. When Paul arrived, a *hartal* (transportation strike) was in progress. Travel was dangerous; Paul was grateful for a safe haven from the political storm.

During that visit, Paul extended to the Corbins an invitation to join the UPCI. They replied that they would pray about it. Four months later they accepted. Applications were filled out; they met the foreign missions board and were approved as UPCI missionaries to Bangladesh. Paul assisted them in writing a simple constitution and bylaws to solidify the UPCI with the Bangladesh government.

The group of about twenty-five people multiplied rapidly until ten years later it consisted of 107 churches and preaching points, and over 13,000 members.

And the end is not yet. Doors are still opening.

Pakistan—Signs and Wonders

Location: Lahore.

"Bulletin: Due to an uprising in the government, all city functions scheduled for this evening have been cancelled. Everyone is urged to stay inside."

Paul and the other members of the Billy Cole crusade team froze in their tracks. It was October 24, 1996, the first night of the crusade. For two years missionary Allan Shalm had prepared for this crusade. He had contacted all the necessary government offices, rented the cricket field and stadium (capacity 50,000 to 60,000), scheduled the advertising and transportation, as well as instructed the national team on their duties.

The crusade team had arrived: Billy Cole, Douglas Klinedinst, Jerry Burns, Allan Shalm, Lynden Shalm, and RFS Paul Dennis.

The cricket field was ready. Large tarps tied together formed a temporary ceiling 100' x 60'. The rest of the field was open. The only seating under the covering was on the platform. Those attending would sit on bamboo mats, blankets, or the ground. Surrounding the field were 1,300 to 1,400 plastic chairs.

Brother Shalm had rented fifteen buses that would go to designated locations to pick up people. After the service the buses would take them back to the same spots, all according to government regulations. Billboards, posters, and flyers blanketed the city, announcing the crusade.

"This is an attack from the enemy," the team determined, as they gathered for prayer. "We will pray and go forward. If only the church folks come, we will have church!"

The buses rolled. The team boarded rented vans. Destination: the crusade site. As the van pulled into the parking lot, praises erupted. Over 10,000 people were gathered under the covering. The Spirit of the Lord hovered over the field as the word of faith moved among the crowd. They had church.

The next evening over 25,000 people crowded under the tarps, ready to receive their miracles. Muslims, Christians, rich, poor, young, old—people from all walks of life reached out in faith to the one true God, the Lord Jesus Christ.

Brother Cole was giving the charge of faith when an uproar drew everyone's attention to the back, some fifty to sixty yards from the makeshift platform.

Paul held his breath. *Was someone trying to start a riot?*

Suddenly a man came running, pushing through the crowd. He jumped four feet up onto the platform and wrapped his arms around Brother Cole. Together they jumped up and down. The platform creaked and cracked.

Someone handed the man a microphone and he testified, "I came to this crusade on a stretcher. I had not walked for years. When I heard the word of faith, I believed. I got up and started walking. Now I am running!"

The crowd went wild, yet totally controlled by the Spirit.

A man placed his little daughter on the platform. "My daughter cannot hear. She has not heard for years." Paul and the other members of the team gathered around to pray for her. While they were praying, the little girl slapped her hands over her ears. The noise was almost deafening after years of silence.

A father brought his little boy to the front. Paul's heart broke. The child's eyeballs were solid white. "He has been blind from birth," the father said. As the men of God prayed, dark irises formed in the child's white eyeballs. An act of creation occurred before their eyes.

Another man brought his deaf-mute son to the platform for prayer. In the midst of the excitement, no one paid much attention to the child until he started to walk away. Then a national pastor, who was holding a microphone, noticed. Not

Order My Steps

knowing that the child was deaf, the pastor asked, "Son, did you want something?"

The little boy stopped, looked back, and nodded his head. When he opened his mouth to tell the pastor what he wanted, a loud "Hallelujah" burst from him. It was the first word he had spoken in nine years! *Hallelujahs* exploded from the crusade team.

Paul felt the floor shiver. The team jumped off as the platform started to collapse. Brother Cole stepped in front of a woman with stiff arthritic arms and hands who was crying out to God. He reached out and touched her "in Jesus' name." Instantly her hands opened and her arms shot up in praise.

At the last service over 40,000 people crowded under the covering and spilled into the chairs surrounding the field. The fifteen buses, the tops filled with people, parked around the fence area. From his vantage point on the platform, Paul watched as a wave of praise started on the left side and swept across the congregation and then back; thousands of people worshiping in perfect praise.

Over 10,000 miracles and healings were reported; 3,000 to 4,000 received the Holy Ghost baptism. It was the Book of Acts repeated—signs and wonders in the name of Jesus.

Vietnam—White Shirts and Orange Soda

Location: Saigon.

"In thirty minutes be on the street corner on the north side of your hotel. I will come by on my motorcycle. Hop on," the voice on the other end of the line instructed.

Paul hung up the phone and looked out the hotel window. The rain had slowed to a drizzle, and the sun was pushing away the clouds.

Dressed in his tourist's garb, Paul felt like an undercover agent for the kingdom. Vietnam was not friendly to missionaries. He was in Saigon, formerly Ho Chi Minh City, to meet with fourteen pastors who had requested to be ordained as ministers of the UPCI FMD. These men, who had been baptized in the name of Jesus and received the Holy Ghost, pastored congregations ranging from 200 to 5,000. Had Paul's mission been discovered, he could have been expelled from the country . . . or worse.

Thirty minutes later he stood on the street corner, staying out of reach of the dirty water splashing onto the sidewalk. A motorcycle pulled up. Paul recognized his contact and jumped on the cycle behind the driver. Varooom. Off they went. Down one small street, then another and another, turning, twisting, thumping. Forty-five minutes later, Paul's head was spinning. He was completely confused. He could never find his way back to the hotel. He had trusted the contact man with his life.

They parked in front of a small, decrepit building struggling to stand. Puddles of chocolate-colored water reminded Paul of the pigpen in #8 Hollow. As he sloshed toward the building, the dirty water spilled over his shoe tops.

Order My Steps

Inside fourteen pastors waited patiently. Paul was introduced to each man, forgetting one name as quickly as he heard the next.

When the men lined up for ordination, the first two were the only ones wearing ties and what used to be white shirts. Paul briefly instructed the pastors and read a Scripture. Then he gave the charge to the first man and ordained him. As he moved to the second man, the first man removed his shirt and tie and handed them to the third man. After the second man was ordained, he removed his shirt and tie and handed them to the fourth man. So it went until fourteen men were ordained, wearing two shirts and ties. These poor men were rich in respect for the Word of God and the position to which they were ordained. Mentally, Paul saluted them.

"Brother Dennis, I will take you to my house for dinner. The other men will meet us there."

So they climbed back on the motorcycle and away they went, turning, twisting, thumping.

Dinner in the humble, but clean, home was soup, rice with meat, and tea. Paul avoided a few objects in the soup. The meat with rice was tasty.

"What kind of meat is this? Beef?" As soon as he asked, he knew he had made a mistake.

"Oh, no, Brother Dennis. It is rat." His stomach tightened and threatened to expel the rodent. But mind over matter prevailed. He did not embarrass himself and his host.

Lesson learned: don't ask; don't tell.

Location: Northwest of Saigon.

Missionary Robert Frizzell and Paul stood on the edge of a crater large enough to hold a house. "Five- and seven-hundred-pound bombs were dropped from our B-52 bombers," Robert, a Vietnam veteran, told Paul. Another ground zero.

Paul A. Dennis

Paul's stomach knotted as he viewed the remains of U.S. tanks and helicopters. In his firefighter crash rescuer's mind, he saw American soldiers trapped in burning aircraft and tanks.

"People of both sides are still searching for human remains," Robert's voice broke, as memories overtook him.

Location: Cu Chi City

Garry Tracy and Paul had met with the leaders of several large Christian groups to discuss them coming under the UPCI banner. Their business was wrapped up sooner than expected, so they had a couple of days before their flight.

"Let's drive up to Cu Chi City," Garry suggested. "Some fierce underground fighting took place there."

At the site a tour guide led them around the battlefield. He pointed out various weapons: tanks, cannons, landmines, rifles, pistols, hand grenades, and bamboo stakes that had been sharpened to a needlepoint.

He explained how the Viet Cong dug miles of underground trenches and tunnels from South Vietnam to North. They stopped in a wooded area and the guide asked, "Do you see a trapdoor?"

The missionaries peered through the brush. They crinkled their foreheads and looked again, then shook their heads. No trapdoors.

The guide moved Paul to one side and brushed away leaves, twigs, and dirt. Lo and behold, a camouflaged trapdoor. He then explained that Vietnamese soldiers would pop up from these doors, throw hand grenades, and duck back into the tunnel.

"Would you like to go into the tunnel?" he asked.

Paul bit his lips and looked at Garry. Garry shrugged. The guide raised the trapdoor.

Order My Steps

Following the guide, they squeezed through the opening sized to fit a Vietnamese man and dropped into a small dugout. On each end was an exit barely large enough for a small man to stick out his head, arms, and a rifle.

Carefully, tourists Paul and Garry dropped into another tunnel leading to another room about thirty yards away. Both men were several inches under six feet, yet in many places they had to duck and crawl. Post-war electricity and ventilation lessened the oppression but did not totally eliminate it.

Their guide identified the purpose of each room: sleeping, treating the wounded, and storage of food, weapons, and explosives. Some of the tunnels came up under houses with trapdoors inside. Dead-end tunnels led to "Punji stake traps." On the surface holes were camouflaged. When an enemy fell through, he landed on bamboo stakes whose sharp points impaled him like a piece of steak on a skewer.

After ducking, crawling, and creeping fifty to sixty yards, Paul's knees felt as if they had gone a mile. They were back to "start."

Location: Vang Tau City

A communist country. A Catholic church. Three Pentecostal preachers. It was an explosive mix with endless possibilities.

John, David, and Paul were in Vietnam to meet with leaders from other churches interested in connecting with the UPCI. Following the directions of their contact Trung, they chartered a large tour bus to take them from Saigon to Vang Tau City, where it was safe to preach the gospel . . . if they were careful.

The bus delivered them to the government lodging. They checked in and rented two motorcycles. They were *persona non grata* and under close surveillance by the communist govern-

Paul A. Dennis

ment, so they came and went via circuitous routes and at confusing times.

One of the leaders of the Vietnamese group had a connection with a leader of the local Catholic church. He obtained permission for them to hold their meeting in one of the upper rooms, provided they (1) kept this information to themselves, and (2) did not become too boisterous with their singing, praying, and teaching. Government men patrolled the area regularly. It was not exactly a welcome-we're-glad-you're-here setting.

For three days the missionaries conducted Bible studies with about forty leaders from all areas of Vietnam. By the end of the third day, every one of them requested to be baptized in the name of the Lord Jesus Christ. As they prayed for those who had not received the Holy Ghost, several received their Pentecostal experience.

"Before we baptize these, let's take communion," Paul suggested. He handed some *dong* (Vietnamese money) to one man and asked him to purchase grape juice and crackers.

An hour passed before the guy returned with crackers and orange soda. "There is no grape juice or even grape soda," he reported.

Jesus turned water into wine. Could He turn orange soda into grape juice? If He chose. If not, orange soda was acceptable. In the upper room of a Catholic church in a communist country, three Pentecostal missionaries and forty Vietnamese leaders partook of orange soda and crackers in remembrance of their Savior's death. It was one of the most moving communion services Paul had ever conducted.

Next step: a baptismal service. But where? There was not a baptismal tank in the Catholic church, and the missionaries were not interested in sprinkling their converts. The solution: the Vang Tau beach on the South China Sea about two or three miles away where tourists from around the world were gathered. Where better to hide from government spies than in plain sight?

Sunbathers splotched the beach. The Americans rented chairs and large umbrellas; then attempted to blend in with the bikini crowd. The leader of the Vietnamese group stripped to his T-shirt and boxer shorts. Then he swam out a good distance and waited.

One by one the fully clothed candidates for baptism swam out to meet him. The twenty-third and last person was a small woman with a clubfoot; one leg was much shorter than the other. Just as she was about to reach the baptizer, a powerful wave knocked her back. She got up and started again. Whap! It happened again and again, but she was determined. Eventually, she reached the baptizer, and like those before her was baptized in the name of the Lord Jesus Christ for the remission of her sins.

The sunbathers on the shore had not a clue that twenty-three people had been baptized contrary to the laws of the communist government and in obedience to the Word of God.

Tulsa—Home

Paula watched her parents as with misty eyes they stared at the new brick house in front of them. It was their dream come true. Tears glistened in Shirley's eyes as her smile grew. "Oh, Paula, it's beautiful. And look, PD, at the gorgeous hibiscus at the front entrance."

Their daughter had chosen the perfect house-warming gift—the national flower of Okinawa. With that one act of love she had bound their worlds together.

Shirley turned to Paul, "The promise God gave you when He called you to missions has become a reality. 'And every one that hath forsaken houses, or brethren, or sisters, or father, or mother, or wife, or children, or lands, for my name's sake, shall receive an hundredfold, and shall inherit everlasting life' (Matthew 19:29)."

In 1995, the global economy had dropped until it was no longer feasible for the Dennises to base in Okinawa. Once again they started packing. Since Paul was in Asia for months at a time, Shirley needed to be close to family. They had to decide where to live: (1) Ohio, near Paul's remaining family and Shirley's two sisters and her aging mother; (2) St. Louis, the foreign missions headquarters; or (3) Tulsa, Oklahoma, where their only child, Paula, along with her husband Keith and son Barak pastored Life Tabernacle. Tulsa won.

When Paula Ann learned of their decision, she smiled through her tears. "Mom, I feel such peace and happiness knowing that you and Dad will be so close. I will be able to come home whenever I want. After all these years, we can be together again."

Order My Steps

After looking at countless houses on the Tulsa market, Paul and Shirley realized they could build for a fraction more than it would cost to buy a house and make needed repairs. They bought a lot, picked out a blueprint, hired a contractor, and promptly boarded a plane for Asia, leaving Paula and Keith to oversee the construction. When they returned three months later, their dream house stood on the once wooded, rocky lot.

As they gazed in wonder at their new home, Paul's memory film rolled . . . back to his first home at #8 Hollow and his mother.

"Paul! Paul!"

Paul tuned out his mother's voice as he dribbled a basketball on the hard-packed ground and threw it at the hoop fastened to the magnificent maple in their front yard. The tree was his age, but it had long ago outgrown him.

"Paul Allen Dennis! Get in here and take your bath. And bring a bucket of coal as you come."

Saturday night bath time in the #10 bathtub in front of the kitchen cookstove was not his favorite time of the week. He preferred to play basketball, or jump in the hayloft, or be with his cousins Clifford and Billy watching baseball on their dad's snowy black-and-white TV. But Mom was a stickler for cleanliness.

When Paul came in from school, the first thing he had to do was change from school clothes to play clothes. And every night before he went to bed he had to double-wash his feet.

Mary washed clothes on a rubboard before she got the gasoline-powered wringer washing machine. Paul loved to crank the engine for her, but that's where his interest in washday ended.

His memory film fast-forwarded as he thought about another washing machine.

Paul A. Dennis

He and Shirley were in Burma (Myanmar) in the home of Superintendent Buai. In the small, humble kitchen, Sister Buai had prepared dinner for them. She gave them her best—a few small shrimp, chicken wing tips, rice, and boiled potatoes.

As they ate, the conversation turned to home appliances. When the Dennises realized that Sister Buai had washed her family's clothes on a rubboard or a rock for twenty-four years, their hearts melted.

That night Paul and Shirley talked about it. Shirley said, "I have saved $1,000 for a new washer and dryer for when we move back to the States, but I would like to buy Sister Buai a washer. God will replenish my *hesokuri* (secret money)." Adding money to her stocking fund was one of Shirley's favorite diversions.

The next morning they went to town; and using the money that Shirley had saved, they bought a new washer for Sister Buai. They gave her their best.

The sound of a passing car brought Paul back to the present. He squeezed Shirley's hand. "I am thinking about Sister Buai and her washing machine," he said.

Without taking her eyes off the house, Shirley answered, "Oh, Paul, God is so good to us. We gave Sister Buai our best, and now God has given us this. Everything we have given away has been returned to us many times over. I am so thankful."

Paul looked at his wife; she was even lovelier than the day they married. "We've lived a lot of places, Charlie Brown—#8 Hollow, apartments, rental houses, parsonages, mission quarters—"

"Remember our little house in Lima? It was the only house we ever owned," she laughed. "Well, we didn't really own it. The bank did, but the deed did have our name on it. When we sold it, I didn't know if we would ever own another house."

Order My Steps

"But now we do," Paul swept his hand toward the brick house in front of them. "From #8 Hollow to Japan to Okinawa to Asia to Tulsa, God has ordered our steps. He has taken all the negatives, hardships, and wrongs and made a walkway of blessings for us, just as He promised."

"Just like you told the foreign missions board that He would do. And, Paul, the best is yet to come," Shirley added. "But why are we standing here? Let's go in."

Hand in hand, step by step they went up the sidewalk and into their new home.

Epilogue

Fourteen years have passed since the Dennises moved into their new home in Tulsa. Standing like a sentinel in the front yard of their home is an October Glory maple, a symbol of his and Shirley's wedding anniversary, as well as a constant reminder of Paul's roots in Ohio's mining country and his parents, Dorsey and Mary Dennis.

On September 8, 1998, Paul and Shirley had just arrived at their hotel in France for a Missions Global Outreach meeting when Audrey called to tell Paul that his mother had moved to Glory. They had found her sitting in her wheelchair, looking as if she were asleep. Immediately, the Dennises closed their unpacked suitcases, rescheduled their flight, and flew to Ohio.

As a boy Paul had not appreciated the sacrifices his mother made to meet his needs. As a rebel he had given little thought to her prayers. But as a missionary he realized that all of his life his mother had worked with God ordering his steps.

Paul served as RFS for Asia until 2002. Shirley accompanied him on his tours in Asia and to board meetings in St. Louis, when possible. After resigning as RFS, Paul worked with the UPCI FMD International Ministries, ministering and teaching in Asia. He and Shirley also served as furlough replacements, returning to Okinawa to minister when the Rufus Parkers were on deputation. Paul retired from foreign missions in 2007.

Life Tabernacle continues to reap the fruit of the Dennises' work in Asia. The mission field has come to them.

In March 1995, Paul and Shirley were in Burma for the national conference. They opted to stay over for two days to help

Order My Steps

with the Burma Bible School graduation. As they handed a diploma to each graduate, a photographer took a picture.

On that trip the Dennises met graduates Awn Pau and his wife Man Niang. This couple had made great sacrifices to attend Bible school, commuting from their home, working, caring for their daughter, Nam, and their home. They also met Kam Kap, who graduated the next year.

In 1999, Kam Kap came to Tulsa; his goal was to attend a Bible school, but he lacked the funds. Kam worked long hours at his cousin's sushi shop; but he didn't have to work on Sundays, so he looked up Life Tabernacle and the Dennises.

In 2001, Kam was accepted at Oral Roberts University to study for his master's degree. In 2004, he graduated.

While in college, Kam Kap married Nam, the daughter of Awn Pau and Man Niang, and they had two sons. In 2007 they moved to Nashville, Tennessee, to direct the Burmese outreach for Pastor Ron Becton. This outreach grew into a church, which Kam now pastors.

Kam referred his Burmese friends and family in Tulsa to Life Tabernacle. He told them, "Brother and Sister Dennis, along with Pastor Townsley and his wife, were missionaries. They understand our culture and care about us."

As a result, a number of Burmese faithfully attend Life Tabernacle. Shirley and Paula go to their apartment complex weekly to teach them English and the American way of life.

The Dennises continue to serve God as they assist their son-in-law at Life Tabernacle where Paul preaches and teaches as needed. He ministers in other churches by invitation. He is on the church board of directors, directs the ushers, and ministers to drug and alcohol addicts through the ACTS program, going to the jail regularly to conduct classes. He maintains their lawn and enjoys taking care of his 5' x 4' garden. Getting his hands in the soil keeps his country culture alive.

Paul A. Dennis

Shirley is the church secretary, pianist, and a substitute Sunday school teacher, along with teaching the Burmese.

Paul enjoys the freedom of coming and going as he wants or needs. Shirley loves being a homemaker and hostess, as friends from around the world drop by for some of her hospitality extraordinaire.

"The steps of a good man are ordered by the LORD: and he delighteth in his way" (Psalm 37:23).

Before Paul Dennis was a "good man," when he was a rebellious teen and an immoral airman, God was ordering his steps. When he was rushing into the fire-drill pit without a thought of eternity, God was preparing him for the day he would rescue men from the pit of Hell.

By God's grace and power an abused and defiant teen running from orders was transformed into a man of God obeying orders and eventually, a leader giving orders. From #8 Hollow to the United States Air Force, New York, Washington, D.C., Kyoto, Hokkaido, Okinawa, Asia, and Tulsa, Paul's steps were ordered by the Lord.

In his office hangs a Japanese scroll that reads, "*Senri no michi mo ippo kara*" ("A thousand miles begins from the first step.") Little did Paul know that day when he took his first step toward the altar in Crooksville Apostolic Gospel Church that he was starting a journey that would take him halfway around the world.

The journey is not over yet. Paul and Shirley Dennis wait for their next orders. Whether to step out in faith or move up to Glory, they are ready.

Order My Steps

"A thousand-mile journey begins with the first step."